RELIGION
under
SOCIALISM
in CHINA

中
CHINESE
STUDIES
▪ ON ▪
C H I N A

RELIGION under SOCIALISM in CHINA

Luo Zhufeng, Editor

Translated by
Donald E. MacInnis and Zheng Xi'an,
with an introduction by
Donald E. MacInnis
With a foreword by
Bishop K. H. Ting

M.E. Sharpe, Inc.
Armonk, New York   London, England

Library of Congress Cataloging-in-Publication Data

Chung-kuo she hui chu i shih ch' i ti tsung chiao wen t' i. English.
    Religion under socialism in China / Luo Zhufeng, editor : Donald
MacInnis and Zheng Xi'an, translators.
       p.   cm.—(Chinese studies on China)
    Translation of: Chung-kuo she hui chu i shih ch' i ti tsung chiao wen t' i.
    ISBN 0-87332-609-1
    1. China—Religion—20th century. 2. Communism and religion.
I. Lo, Chu-feng. II. Title. III. Series.
BL1802.C59413   1990
291′.0951′09045—dc20
                                         90-33534
                                            CIP

Printed in the United States of America

BB   10 9 8 7 6 5 4 3 2 1

Contents

7

K. H. TING

Foreword

IN RECENT years there has been a brisk growth in social science research, including research on religion. With the objective of seeking truth from facts, new ideas and viewpoints have arisen on all sides, along with very animated discussion, much livelier than our own theological discussions. Fortunately, we Christians have also been a part of this.

We should not regard the research on religion in the social sciences to be as unyielding as a piece of iron. Because of lively thinking, a healthy variety of ideas at various levels has appeared. For example, there clearly are two different approaches among those doing research on religion. One is only willing to see the generalities of religious phenomena, always drawing a line between religion and nonreligion, and taking religion as nothing but religion, like a piece of iron; it is singular, unitary, with little or nothing in common with nonreligion. This approach, which makes no careful distinctions, in the end sets the tone, saying that "all religions are opiates," and thus preventing the discussion from going any deeper.

Other researchers have discovered that one cannot treat different religious phenomena in the same way; although all of them are religious phenomena, their social, historical, and political functions are quite different, so these researchers will not jump to conclusions about religion, feeling that specific analysis of concrete religious phenomena is essential.

Some writers ignore the differences between national cultures and historical periods, and the unique characteristics of each religion; they talk about religion in a general and abstract way, as if their theories can be the standard for understanding religion in any nation and any period of time. The present book edited

---

Bishop K. H. Ting, principal of the Nanjing Theological Seminary, president of the China Christian Council, and chairperson of the Protestant Three-Self Patriotic Movement, delivered this foreword as an address to the students of the seminary. It is published here with his kind permission. Translated by Donald MacInnis.

by the well-known scholar Luo Zhufeng does not approach religion in this way. The title of the book is worthy of our attention. It doesn't discuss religion in a general way; rather, it approaches the subject of religion in China. Nor does it discuss the topic of religious issues in China in a general way; it deals with religious issues in the socialist period in China. This book follows the best Marxist traditions, approaching religion not from a definition or concept, but from the real situation of religion in China today. Therefore, religious leaders will not feel as if the book is "scratching the boot while the foot continues to itch," nor will they feel wronged or misunderstood. This book gives a clear, theoretical presentation of the origin and purpose of the religious policy of the Chinese Communist Party in a very convincing way, a policy that is scientific rather than expedient.

Chairman Mao was strongly opposed to dogmatism, but as far as research on religion is concerned, it seems extremely difficult to get rid of dogmatism. The reason may be that many religious researchers don't know even one religious believer, to say nothing of having friends among them, so how can they be sensitive to their thoughts and feelings? They build the cart behind a closed door, making contact only with books instead of religion. Since they have been told since childhood that religion is opium, and since they are quite familiar with China's disastrous experience with the Opium War, they find religion so abhorrent that they unconsciously substitute emotion for science. Another reason is that "leftists" in religious work have not been systematically criticized since rectification was begun. Even so, since the Third Plenum of the Eleventh Party Congress, the situation has changed. Many thought-provoking articles in the field of social science research have been published, most of them in scholarly journals devoted to philosophy and the social sciences published by colleges and universities. This book is a significant contribution to this research.

The book makes the following points:

1. It approaches religion as a social entity with various elements at different levels, instead of limiting it to religious dogmas only.

Religious doctrines are important for believers, since no church or member can speak or behave contrary to those doctrines. But this does not mean that religious believers can only do what is stipulated in those doctrines and are prohibited from doing anything not stipulated. There are many new ideas and new things in the world that religious believers can accept and support without violating religious doctrines. This shows that there is a breadth of freedom for religious believers; but some religious researchers take it for granted that God and religion are completely authoritarian, and that religious believers can only do what religious doctrines say; so, thinking that believers are oppressed by these doctrines, they are determined to liberate them from the prison of religious dogma. They regard themselves as critics of religious dogma. For them, religious research means research and criticism of religious dogma and propagation of atheism in order to "liberate" religious believers. This is a great misunderstanding.

Several years ago someone wrote an article expressing the opinion that a religious believer will become an "idealist," therefore religious belief will make one become an "eccentric." Such a person, he said, becomes muddle-headed, taking the "physical body as the grave of the soul," and regarding the "improving of one's reasonable, material needs as the source of sin for the soul," even to the point of "closing the eyes to the colors of the world" and "closing the ears to the sounds of the world," and "if it is not written in the scriptures one should not think about it," and so on. They describe believers in these simplistic terms in order to spread a fear for the dangers of religion, with the result that religious believers feel wronged and upset. The reason for this is that religious research scholars have no acquaintances among religious believers. This reminds me of what Lenin said: "It is the usual practice of a not very bright person to impose obviously foolish ideas on his enemies and then criticize them."

So let us put aside the issue of religious doctrines and ask this question: Even if there are errors in religious doctrine, would that cause believers to be always in error, looking ridiculous, accomplishing nothing, and, whatever they do, ending up in trouble? I believe Lenin would say no. Lenin knew that Leo Tolstoy was a devoted Christian and a landlord; despite his rather fanatical religious beliefs, Lenin regarded him as a "talented artist," noting that he "thoroughly criticized capitalist exploitation," "was a most sober-minded realist" who "tore off the masks of hypocrisy," and "created literary works in the top rank of world literature." Although Lenin did not believe in God, he shared a good deal of common language with the theist Tolstoy. He did not ignore Tolstoy's contributions to literature and social struggle, or the fact that he was a talented artist, because he was a committed religious believer. This kind of broad-mindedness is praiseworthy. Religious policies based on the principles of the united front contain the same idea: a religious believer can at the same time be a patriotic socialist and member of the united front, and his religious beliefs should be respected and protected. This kind of broad-mindedness is also admirable.

The influence of religious doctrines on people's minds and behavior is after all, limited. Many scientists in ancient and modern times have been religious believers. Their religious beliefs did not prevent them from accomplishing scientific achievements; in fact, some scientists relate their scientific achievements to religious inspiration.

Religion under Socialism in China does not ignore the differences between the teachings of various religions, nor does it ignore the specific positions of religious doctrine in each religion; but the writers of this book do not get mired down in religious doctrine. They treat each religion as a social entity, with its doctrines, believers, sects, administrative system, principles and regulations, literature and arts, theology and history, ethics subgroups and organizations, and opinions on contemporary social issues—and the ways in which it either contributes to or harms society. Scientific research on religion should take all these into consideration with equal emphasis.

2. This book gives a balanced critique of the aphorism that religion is the opiate of the people.

Some writers who only know some of the sayings of Marx but do not understand the spirit of Marxism are very likely to approach religious issues by identifying religion with opium, believing that as long as they stick to this formula all religious questions can be easily explained. They take this saying as originating with Marx, as the marrow of the Marxist viewpoint on religion, and as the succinct expression of the essential nature of religion. It seems strange, if opium is to Marx the essence of religion, how he could mention this so lightly, with no amplification. How could Marx's creative writings on religious issues consist only of this single phrase, one which was used by others both inside and outside the church before his time? Does this raise or lower Marx? Fortunately, among the social scientists doing research on religion, few are still using the theme of "religion as an opiate."

Regrettably, we cannot say that religion never functions as an opiate. As Christians, we should ask ourselves whether or not we allow religion to function as an opiate in ourselves. We remember that when some compassionate persons offered Jesus wine mixed with gall to numb his feeling of pain while he suffered on the cross, he refused it after tasting it.

Religion functions in many ways in society; religion can even mobilize and unify people for revolutionary struggle. This was confirmed by Engels in "The Peasant War in Germany." Only one of the functions of religion is that of an opiate or anesthetic; that is not the only function, nor is it the main function under all circumstances. Therefore, it is quite inadequate to define religion as an opiate.

Dom Helder Camera, the retired Catholic archbishop of Recife, Brazil, once said, "When I give bread to the poor, I am called a saint; but when I ask the poor why they can't have bread, I am called a Communist." Such preaching is very effective in exposing the darkness of society and awakening people's conscience. Is not this function, which arouses people, the opposite of opium, which puts them to sleep? His words, which "raise a reasonable demand for improving the material life of people," certainly do not "treat the reasonable need to improve material life as the source of sin for the soul." Can the religion that raises serious questions, as Camera's does, such as, "Why can't the poor have bread?" and "What kind of party is the Communist Party?" and "Why do people oppose the Communist Party?" be identified with a religion that functions as an opiate, demanding that the people submit to oppression and willingly accept the blows and kicks of their enemies?

Our people's liberation movement, socialist construction movement, and Protestant Three-Self Movement, and the work of Dom Helder Camera all have the same goal, which is human justice. We should oppose the narcotic function of religion and educate religious believers to be clear-minded.

As for the concept that religion is an opiate, I do not think it is a significant theoretical breakthrough, though somewhat suggestive; which is to say, it does not provide a breakthrough for resolving theoretical questions. One can say that it is also "a flower which bears no fruit."

Religion under Socialism in China does not bog down in a discussion of religion as an opiate. The editors raise three points on this question in the closing chapter of the book: (1) "Opium" is a metaphor for the negative function of religion in the particular context of a class society. (2) The historical function of religion differs in different times and social contexts, and cannot be indiscriminately defined as "opium." (3) Even less can the function of religion under socialism be described as "opium."

I think that these three points are scientific, fair, and quite acceptable to us Christians.

3. This book acknowledges the ethical content of religion and has a positive attitude, affirming the function of religious ethics for the majority of religious believers under socialism.

All religions "admonish people to be good"—this is the most universal view of religion. It is reported by many local officials [in China] today that there is little crime in places with numerous religious believers. Religion has the function of guiding and disciplining people's behavior. But there was a time [in China], under the negative influence of leftism, when some research scholars of religion divorced religious ethics from religious dogma in order to defame religion, claiming that religious ethics are a reflection of the people's customary behavior norms, and have nothing to do with religion; religion is only concerned with the divine-human relationship, they said, but not human relationships. One person even claims that the last six of the [Judeo-]Christian Ten Commandments deal only with ethics, and thus do not belong to religion as such. By including these six commandments, he says, religion is intruding upon ethics. Fortunately, religious teachings are not determined by this scholar, otherwise we would be left with only four commandments. It is worth reminding this writer: Isn't it true that, according to historical materialism, religion itself is also the product of social productive relations?

Religion under Socialism in China contains absolutely no Quixotic attacks like this. It maintains that different roads can lead to the same destination: "Both religious doctrine and religious ethics admonish religious believers to be good instead of bad. If they work for the good of the nation and the people, whoever they are and whatever their motivation, the results benefit socialist modernization. Religion can be in harmony with socialist society when seen from this viewpoint."

This is also an important reminder for us Christians. Christianity is a religion which lays emphasis on ethics. The Bible distinguishes between right and wrong, goodness and evil, and good and bad behavior; much of it is about how society and political life should be. But some Christians only pay attention to salvation of the individual, accusing the Christians who are also concerned with ethical behavior of having impure faith, and also saying that those who do not distinguish between right and wrong and who don't believe in Christ in a certain way are bad. I would like to point out to them that, as Christians, they have gone to be part and parcel of those outside the church who hold leftist views.

4. This book deals theoretically with the subject of harmonizing relationships between socialism and religion.

During the time of leftist domination, any Marxist who spoke of harmonizing socialism with religion would have been considered guilty of [political] apostasy, while religious believers who did the same thing would have been called opportunists.

It has been more than thirty years since Liberation, and leaders of all religions in China are supporters of socialism. As for religious believers, the majority of them are working every day in socialist production. We have been informed that the proportion of Christians selected as model workers in many places is higher than those in the general population. All the religions in China have undergone many reforms, and, compared with the past, they have made great progress toward socialism; this is obvious to everyone. This is from the side of religion.

From the side of the nation, although the ruling party advocates atheism and openly expresses its nonbelief in religion, it acknowledges the rationality and legality of religion and its right to exist, and opposes any act to destroy or discriminate against religion; it only attacks counterrevolutionary sabotage and criminal activities which hide under the guise of religion, as well as all superstitious activities that do not fall within the parameters of religion and are harmful to the interests of the nation and the lives and property of the people.

How should we deal with this, since it is not a matter of who extirpates whom? We can only ask that both sides work together so that some kind of mutual accommodation can be achieved.

To put forward this task of mutual accommodation requires, on the one hand, that all religions, insofar as their own beliefs permit, step up their efforts to eliminate those things which are not compatible with socialism and to carry forward those things that are compatible with socialism; on the other hand, it requires that nonbelievers resolutely get rid of leftist influences, clean out remnant old ideas of wiping out religion, and enforce the policy to provide the essentials needed for all religions to carry on their religious affairs better.

In recent years, as we Protestant Christians have emphasized the three-self principle in order to run our churches well, we have given first priority to seeing to the spiritual needs of our members, providing what they love and giving support to our church; at the same time we have run the church in a way that is compatible with socialism so that the people [masses] will have affection for it. We know that if we only emphasize accommodation to socialism, the church will gradually give up its particularity as a church, and will be in danger of losing unity with the believers. But if it has only one goal, to run the church well, while ignoring the three-self patriotic principle and the need for compatibility with socialism, the church will inevitably be spurned by the people, and perceptive church members will stay away as well.

There is a new spirit abroad in the world—to replace mutual extirpation with mutual accommodation. This offers great potential for theological students to devote themselves to running the affairs of the church well, and this is a very welcome development.

5. This book does not exclude religious believers, but welcomes them to join in research on religion, and expresses appreciation for the contributions of religious believers to this research.

I mentioned earlier that some scholars who carry on research in religion do not know even one religious believer. Worse than that, some people think that research on religion can only be carried out in the absence of religious belief; they are opposed to religious believers taking part in research on religion.

Lenin said that Marxism is able to "win universal historical significance because it does not throw away the most valuable achievements of the bourgeois period; on the contrary, it absorbs all things of value accumulated throughout the development of human ideas and culture for over two thousand years."

Before and after Marx, religious believers among natural and social scientists, as well as religious scholars, have made great contributions in the sciences. At present, those doing serious-minded research in the sciences need every valuable legacy from the past. To cut off cooperation with religious believers because of their religious faith can only be called sectarianism. We say that the kind of religious research that rejects the results of research by non-Marxist scholars, while allowing self-proclaimed Marxists to "set up a new shop," will inevitably bear no fruit.

As a matter of fact, when I read the works of our Marxist scholars on religion, I find that they quote the works of many scholars from both the East and West; some are recognized authorities; moreover, often they are religious believers. As a result, these Marxist scholars put themselves in a ridiculous position: religious researchers can cooperate with religious believers abroad, but not in China!

Most of the contributors to this book are nonbelievers, but some are persons with religious faith who use scientific methods of research, treating religion as a social and historical phenomenon; they neither advocate nor oppose religion. From the perspective of Christian faith, we feel that this book is inadequate, especially in dealing with the reasons for the persistence of religion over time. But we have no reason to expect this to be a book for the church. Compared to other works of research on religion [published in contemporary China], I think this book is the least dogmatic, the most perceptive in its explanation of the party's policy on religion, and the most convincing in its arguments. I would like our students to know that this book deserves our serious attention.

DONALD E. MACINNIS

Translator's Introduction

THIS IS an important book, the only study of religion in contemporary China based on field research by Chinese social scientists. While other works on the history and present situation of religion in China are in preparation at both national and provincial levels, this is the first one to be published.

Written by a group of scholars at the Institute for Research on Religion of the Shanghai Academy of Social Sciences and first published by the academy in 1987, this work is a response to the designation of religion as one of twelve "key topics" for special study in the Sixth Five-Year Plan for Economic and Social Development of the People's Republic of China—an astonishing turnabout from the days of the Cultural Revolution, when nothing was published on religion for a dozen years, all public religious practice was suppressed, religious clergy and believers were persecuted, and the Leftists then in power sought to eliminate religion completely and forever.

We decided not to use a literal translation of the title ("Religious Questions during the Socialist Period in China") because it does not accurately describe the contents of this book. Neither of the two parts deals in depth with the difficult questions about religious policy and practice that face policy makers among government, party, and religious leaders in China today.

The first part comprises seven chapters, which include a historical overview of the five officially recognized religions in China, the changes that have taken place inside those religions and their relationships with the state and society at large since 1949, analysis of the reasons why religion has not died out under socialism, the basic policy on religion, and a refutation of the Marxist dictum that religion is a spiritual opiate. The second part (the appendix) consists of nine reports written by Chinese social scientists based on field studies carried out in a variety of urban and rural communities in China in the 1980s. In contrast to the first seven chapters, these reports are remarkably free of ideological bias and rhetoric, which suggests that they were written by a different group of scholars.

Since the Third Plenum of the Eleventh Central Committee of the Chinese Communist Party in late 1978 reinstated the policy of freedom of religious belief, later articulated in Article 36 of the 1982 revision of the national constitution, all of China's five officially recognized religions have renovated and rebuilt damaged churches, temples, and mosques; revived local religious activities; reopened clergy training schools and institutes; and reorganized long-defunct religious organizations at national and local levels. The nine reports in the appendix use case studies to document the extent of and reasons for revival since 1979 of the five religions: Buddhism, Islam, Daoism, and Catholic and Protestant Christianity. (While passing mention is made of folk religions and superstitious practices, these are not protected by the constitutional guarantee of freedom of religious belief and so are not included in this research volume.)

The Reasons for This Book

Five questions to be answered in this work are set down in the opening chapter:

1. Why do religious beliefs and practice continue in China now that the bases for social classes have been destroyed?

2. Why have the number of religious believers in some areas increased in recent years?

3. What influence does religion have on social life and discipline, and on building the four modernizations?

4. How can religion exist in harmony with socialist society?

5. What is the proper way for the party, government, and society to deal with religious believers?

"Document 19," in twelve sections, is the most definitive statement on religion and religious policy ever issued by the party or government. It was circulated internally through party channels throughout China in 1982.[1] Called "The Basic Viewpoint and Policy on the Religious Question during the Socialist Period in China," this party directive sets forth the rationale and guidelines for the party's policy on religion, based on the "five characteristics" of religion: Religion is complex, mass-based, long-lasting, with implications for relations with both ethnic nationalities in China and the nations of the world, particularly those with strong religious traditions. For these reasons, it is incorrect to try to suppress religion by force or administrative decree.

Why would the top leadership of the Chinese Communist Party, by definition atheists, officially sanction "freedom of religious belief"? One purpose of the work by the Shanghai social scientists presented in the first seven chapters of the book is to answer that question, using "Document 19," and particularly the "five characteristics of religion," as their hermeneutical

---

[1]See D. MacInnis, *Religion in China Today: Policy and Practice* (Maryknoll, NY: Orbis, 1989), pp. 8–25.

framework, and basing their conclusions on both classical Marxist analysis of religion and the results of field studies of actual religious practice among the five recognized religions in various parts of China.

Why Do People in a Socialist Society Turn to Religion?

A second purpose is to search out explanations for the continuing existence and, in some places, explosive growth of religion in a socialist society. "We are faced with a historically unprecedented new situation and new problem: Why does religion continue to exist in a socialist society where the exploiting classes have been eliminated?" Their explanations are both theoretical and empirical, based, first, on standard Marxist theory and, second, on their own field research. While the writers are identified by name only, and not by academic discipline, their field studies are limited to social science methodology that leaves their published reports narrowly focused on sociological phenomena. One yearns for a broader understanding of the meaning and content of religious faith in the minds and hearts of believers.

While the writers would describe their method of presentation as dialectical, it is, in fact, beset with contradictions. Marxist theory tells them that religious belief will wither away when the inequalities and "crushing system of exploitation" of feudalism and capitalism are eliminated. Under those systems, "the suffering of religion is, in reality, a manifestation of real suffering, and is a sigh of protest against that suffering." But now, as their own field research demonstrates, religion not only survives, despite the elimination of former class inequities, but thrives under socialism. Even more puzzling, the religion that seems to be growing the fastest, Protestant Christianity (from 700,000 members in 1949 to an estimated 5 million in 1989), is still viewed by many as a "foreign religion" (yang-jiao), although the achievement of the "Three-Self" autonomy movement (self-support, self-government, self-propagation) has done much to alleviate that stigma.

In chapter 4, the writers sum up the reasons for religious belief under two headings: objective (social and economic) reasons, and subjective (mental, emotional, or psychological) reasons. Of the two, objective social existence plays the decisive role, they say. Included under the social sources of religion are the persistence, under socialism, of poverty and backwardness, inferior education, and poor medical care; a low level of cultural and recreational activities, especially in the rural areas, leading to boredom among young people and depression among middle-aged and older women; backward ideas and customs left over from the old society, such as the inequality of women, and corruption and bureaucratism leading to disillusionment among young people; and emotional suffering and despair due to Leftist errors, false accusations, persecution, and factional struggles. (The writers report that over half of the eight hundred Buddhist monks and nuns in one county in Fujian Province converted to religion as a result of disillusionment and world-weariness brought on by the Cultural Revolution.)

How should persons who turn to religion because of personal problems, ill health, emotional depression, and so on be dealt with? "Since food and clothing alone do not provide a satisfying life, we must intensify the building of a spiritual civilization at the same time as we build a socialist material civilization. The diverse needs of the people can only be satisfied with a rich spiritual life." "Socialist spiritual civilization" and "rich spiritual life" exclude, however, any religious or transcendent dimension. In the report of field research on the growth of Christianity in Anhui Province, the writers draw this conclusion:

> All people are pragmatic, and peasants even more so. Peasants can begin to abandon religion only when the pace of socialist modernization has greatly quickened, when their material and cultural life has risen to a sufficient level, when the knowledge of science has become universal, and when they can easily free themselves from the ills and pains of their real lives. Only when their spirit is fulfilled can they consciously place their hope in socialism.

Religion and Socialist Nation Building

There is another, utilitarian reason for this research project: "The results of our research will help to carry out China's religious policy and unite the tens of millions of religious believers. It will also help in dealing with religious matters and will promote the building of a socialist material and spiritual civilization." This reason is particularly emphasized in dealing with the fifty-five ethnic minorities, many of them living in strategically sensitive areas along the Sino-Soviet border. Ten of those nationalities are Islamic in faith, whose traditional relationships with Islamic countries have significant implications for China's international relations. The field research report "Adapting Islam to Chinese Socialist Practice in Xinjiang" describes how Kazakh and Uyghur villagers, all devout Muslims, have adapted religious traditions and practice to socialism in Xinjiang Province.

No Transcendent Dimension

Although the writers are historical materialists, they do not hold rigidly to the narrow Marxist view that religion is the result only of historical and economic forces—"the outside forces that control the daily lives of people." While "the main reasons for religious belief" are poverty, ignorance, deprivation, social inequities, and so on, they acknowledge that there are also basic questions of life, death, sickness, and old age "which lead people to look for a life hereafter." But they avoid any reference to a transcendent source or supramundane dimension for the faith experience of believers—the *mysterium tremendum et fascinosum* (what Paul Tillich called "the experience of 'the ultimate' in the double sense of that which is the abyss and that which is the ground of man's being").[2] While

---

[2]"We are grasped, in the experience of faith, by the unapproachably holy which is the ground of our being and breaks into our existence and which judges us and heals us." Carl J. Armbruster, *The Vision of Paul Tillich* (New York: Sheed & Ward, 1967), p. 67.

they acknowledge the need for developing both a spiritual and material civilization under socialism, "spiritual" is shorn of any religious connotation: "Only . . . when humanity completely frees itself from all poverty, ignorance, and spiritual emptiness, when a highly developed material and spiritual civilization has been built, and when people can consciously deal with life and the world scientifically with no need to seek sustenance from the illusory world of God, will the religious reflections of the real world finally fade away."

Here is a fundamental contradiction in their overall analysis. They point to the social, psychological, and emotional factors, the religious ideologies, ethics, arts, culture, and philosophies that contribute to religious feelings and beliefs; time and again they praise the *results* of religious experience, which earn the respect of their nonreligious neighbors—the transformed temperament, improved family relations, and moral discipline of religious converts—but, as materialists and atheists, they avoid any reference to the spiritual or "holy" nature of that experience and the possibility that a transcendent, infinite "ground of all being" is both the subject and object of those transformed lives.

In dealing with the role of foreign missions, particularly the Roman Catholic church, the writers present a partial and one-sided picture as well. From their point of view, the role of the church and its hierarchy in the early 1950s was implacably hostile and destructive to the cause of China and the Chinese people; the church's point of view is not presented. In similar fashion, their description of the personal theology of the Catholic fishing people of Qingpu County is distorted; the fishermen, they say, were taught to endure the sufferings of this world as God's punishment for their sins, but to do nothing to change their world for the better, for God and the Blessed Mother of Jesus would give them a happy life in Heaven. No mention is made of the schools, hospitals, orphanages, rural improvement projects, and other institutions of social change and welfare organized by the church.

An Empirical Research Methodology

The writers claim to use both a scientific world view and the methods of Marxism and dialectical materialism as "guiding principles and methodology" for their work. They follow these guidelines:

—Adhere to basic Marxist principles.

—Seek truth from facts.

—Follow the principle that "everything proceeds from [material] reality."

—Never mechanically copy out of context the opinions of revolutionary veterans about religion.

—Never substitute historical experiences for actual research on religion in the socialist period in China.

They take issue with those Chinese ideologues and theoreticians who have published countless articles on religion based purely on Marxist theory. "It is not enough to rely only on philosophical debate and logical inferences for research on religion. Philosophers should come down from their lofty abstract stratosphere and get close to their research subjects in order to understand the thoughts and feelings of religious believers and the . . . function of religion in society." The philosophical and ideological approach to religious studies is too limited. "We must engage in comprehensive, multidisciplinary studies of this multifaceted religious phenomenon . . . [including] sociology, psychology, ethics, ethnology, folklore, and so on."

Even so, for their basic theoretical analysis the writers depend heavily on Marx, Engels, and Lenin. But, they say, the religious theories of Marx and Engels were based on their observation of Christianity in a particular time and place—Europe in the mid-nineteenth century—while the situation of religion in contemporary China is quite different. In the immediate years after Liberation, religion, as a tool of the former feudal overlords and imperialists, was viewed as an "antagonistic contradiction" (a contradiction between the people and the enemy), while today it is merely a "nonantagonistic contradiction" (among the people), one that can be worked out peacefully over time as religion accommodates to socialism. "The main question now is how to deal properly with religion, unite the large numbers of religious believers [with all the people for socialist nation building], and vigorously promote the progress of China." Chapter 5 examines ways in which religion can and does live in harmony with socialist society.

Field Research: Religious Practice in China Today

The second part of this work, the nine field studies, consists of social science data and analysis virtually free of ideological rhetoric. Based on extensive investigations of religious belief and practice in cities, towns, and villages of twelve provinces and municipalities, the reports offer heretofore unpublished insights into the actual state of religious revival since 1979 in all five religions (excluding folk religions and what are defined in China as superstitions). Five of these nine reports focus on Christianity—Protestant and Roman Catholic—since, among the dozen or more centers for research on religion in China today, the Institute for Research on Religion of the Shanghai Academy of Social Sciences specializes in research on Christianity.

Based on interviews and field studies, these reports search for answers to the question of why religious faith and practice have revived with such vigor after total repression for over twelve years. They describe the social and economic progress in the rural areas, contrasting that with the lingering problems of illiteracy, poor schools and medical care, and other social sources of religion. "In short . . . religion may be taken as a mirror of society. In a complex way, it reflects the problems of building material and spiritual civilization in the villages [and cities] today. If we overlook this fact and think we can handle religious questions by arbitrary measures, that is not realistic." The only way to solve the religious question is "by a great leap forward of socialist material and spiritual civilization" (quoted from *Selected Writings on the United Front in the New Period*).

Two reports, "Why Some Young People Become Buddhists" and "A Survey of Christian Retired Workers in a Shanghai District," find different reasons (none of them the classical experience of the numinous) for religious conversion among different age and religious groups. Some young Buddhist monks and nuns came from Buddhist families, but most, it seems, were fleeing worldly problems: failure in love, disappointment in prospects for higher education or employment, health, and other emotional reasons. Some, with little education, were influenced by "fatalism and superstition," while others were bored with village life and wanted to travel, some even aspiring to an assignment in a temple or monastery abroad.

The retired workers in Shanghai, in contrast, are looking for spiritual tranquility in the final years of life and a "final home" after death. Others are led to Christianity by devout neighbors, or by the yearning for companionship to combat loneliness. Some are still struggling with emotional trauma resulting from the political chaos of the Cultural Revolution, while ill health and family troubles (often mentioned in these reports) are common reasons given for religious conversion.

The writers conclude that "it is both possible and necessary to carry out correctly the policy of freedom of religious belief, 'giving glory to God while helping other people.' This will lead these elderly Christians to love both Christianity and the motherland, and make their contributions to the building of the two civilizations."

In addition to the five essays on Christian faith and practice, two discuss Buddhism, one Islamic life and practice, and one Daoism. While Buddhism and Daoism lack the hierarchical and grass-roots organization, evangelistic zeal, and parish and neighborhood-group identity of Christians, Islam in China is passed on within the families from generation to generation and, in many areas, forms entire well-organized communities combining ethnic with religious identity. According to many reports, Islamic religious organization and practice recovered quickly from the period of repression during the Cultural Revolution. Daoists, with virtually no hierarchy or local organization, are much harder to locate and identify, which may account for the lack of substantial information in this report.

Christianity, in particular Protestant Christianity, has rebounded from the years of repression with surprising vigor. In some cases, as with certain tribal groups in the Southwest and the Korean Christians in the northeastern provinces, the Christians are linked by ethnic as well as religious ties. But in most cases Christians are Han Chinese, distinguished only by their religious faith and lifestyle. The report on Pi County says that Christian lifestyle has a strong social influence. "Many cadres and others say that Christians do not fight or swear, nor do they smoke and drink; they seldom have disputes with their neighbors or within their families. Because they are honest and do not steal, production team

xxii RELIGION UNDER SOCIALISM IN CHINA

leaders usually ask them to watch the fields prior to harvest, and put them in charge of the grain barns.''

The Korean Christians in the Northeast are also known for their moral standards, which attract new believers. Examples are cited of a once hard-drinking, abusive husband and two young hoodlums whose lives were transformed after conversion.

The lengthy report on Catholic fishing people in Qingpu County includes a history of these Catholic communities tracing back many generations, ways in which the faith was passed on during times of repression, the spiritual formation and nurturing of Catholic children, and the ''gratitude'' of these one-time ''fishing beggars'' to both God and the party for the good life they now enjoy. According to this report, religion and socialism exist comfortably together here. One man is reported as saying, ''The party and government have reopened the church and my soul has found peace. Since Liberation I have earned a happy life, I have a television set and a sofa at home. Hereafter, God will take care of my soul and the people's government will take care of my body.''

The writers conclude that ''It is important for us to carry out diligently the policy of religious freedom, to be completely forthright with religious believers, to do a good job in [politically] educating and uniting with them, and to make them feel that they can be both 'good for the body' and 'good for the soul' in their daily lives, and thus, loving both their country and their religion, contribute to socialist construction.''

Despite the contradictions between fact and theory and its underlying ideological bias, this research volume makes a unique and valuable contribution to our understanding of religious policy and practice in China today. On the one hand, the Chinese Marxist theory of religion and its implications for religious policy are clearly presented; on the other hand, examples and statistics drawn from field research provide a clear and objective picture of religious faith and life in specific religions and places in China today. The reader may object to the theoretical dogmatism and ideological rhetoric, or differ from the writers in how to interpret this information, but their generally scholarly approach in the nine field studies, their rejection of the ''religion as a spiritual opiate'' dictum, and their attitude of respect for religious belief and practice promise a new era in Chinese research on and analysis of religion.

Glossary

Weights and Measures

1 mu—1/15 hectare or 1/6 acre
1 jin (catty)—1/2 kilogram or 1.1 pounds
1 li—1/3 mile
1 yuan—U.S. $ .27 (1988)
1 fen—1/100 yuan

Administrative Units

cun—hamlet
xiang—village
zhen—market town
xiang—county
qu—district
sheng—province

Terms and Abbreviations

ahong, imam—Muslim clergyman
CBA—Chinese Buddhist Association
CCP—Chinese Communist Party
CCPA—Chinese Catholic Patriotic Association
CDA—Chinese Daoist Association
CIA—Chinese Islamic Association
CPPCC—Chinese People's Political Consultative Conference
CYL—Chinese Youth League
Four Modernizations—modernization of agriculture, indsutry, national defense, science and technology
PLA—People's Liberation Army
PRC—People's Republic of China
TSPM—Three-Self Protestant Movement

RELIGION
under
SOCIALISM
in CHINA

LUO ZHUFENG

Preface

WHEN PEOPLE address themselves to a topic or question but do not start from reality, only drawing inferences from abstract and generalized concepts, one suspects that they "can't touch the real point." It is like this with religion.

Marx said that his contribution was not the discovery of the existence of classes in society, or of class struggle, but that his new contribution was to demonstrate that the class struggle would of necessity lead to the dictatorship of the proletariat. Marx's starting point for his discussion of religion was the situation in Germany and Europe of that time, where Christianity was in a dominant position; but what is more important is that Marx particularly emphasized that the proletariat must closely organize themselves and strive for the improvement of their lot here on earth, and that the conflict with religious belief was of minor importance. Lenin proposed that religious belief should be considered a private matter of each citizen; by this he meant that religion should be separate from government authority, and that to believe or not to believe in religion was a matter of personal choice. He also based his comments on conditions in Russia.

Everything should trace back to its original aspects, and religion is no exception. The complex phenomenon of religious belief cannot be completely explained by the "cultural theory" that maintains that raising the scientific and cultural level of the people will make it possible to eliminate religious belief. The "class theory" that maintains that religion will automatically wither away with the elimination of [social] classes still doesn't cover everything, because even in the socialist society, after the basic elimination of the exploiting classes, there are still religious believers.

Mankind has entered the space age, but some American astronauts while in space still felt the awesome creative power of God and believed even more deeply. Although science has already refuted the "fairy tale" that God created the earth, why is it that some scientists still believe that man and all things are created by God? It is easy for man when impoverished or in danger to draw close

3

to religion, but aren't even the wealthy "big bellies" still praying to Buddha, not only enjoying this world, but also praying that they may continue to enjoy life after death in the Western Paradise?

Religion is a complex historical and social phenomenon, which must be examined from its many entities and related conditions. For example, when looking at religion from the class viewpoint of the people, their thought patterns, psychological characteristics, social relations, and so forth, we can draw fairly clear and demonstrable conclusions. For example, it would be useless to search for a pharmacy speaking in vague, general terms only, without being specific about the time, place, and conditions. In a class society, class oppression is the soil in which religion exists and grows. Lenin used the example of an "earthquake" to describe the disaster resulting from class oppression.

But now, placed right in front of us, is a historically unprecedented situation and problem: Why does religion continue to exist in a socialist society where the exploiting classes are basically eliminated? The reasons, of course, are complex. In our country, particularly when the level of development of the means of production is still not high, poverty, suffering, backwardness, sickness, and so forth are the main reasons for religious belief. Also, the questions of "life, old age, illness, and death," as some say, are long-lasting and perplexing questions. When there are no reasonable answers, then hope has to be entrusted to the "life hereafter." With this in view, the question of religion in the socialist period must become an important topic for exploration in the field of religious studies.

Following the Marxist viewpoint, position, and method, and guided by the ideological line set by the Third Plenum of the party's Eleventh Central Committee, the Institute for Research on Religion of the Shanghai Academy of Social Sciences immersed itself in the actual religious situation of our country, conducting extensive field research. After summing up, analyzing, studying, and reflecting on large quantities of primary materials, it produced several drafts and this final work, "Religious Questions during the Socialist Period in China." [Religion] is included in the key topics of the Sixth Five-Year Plan designated for social and philosophical studies nationwide. This book has seven chapters and nine appended reports based on field research, altogether 200,000 words. The main writers included Ruan Renzi and Xiao Zitian, especially the latter, who did most of the work.

In the process, we combined field investigation and theoretical research, going deeply into twelve provinces, municipalities, and autonomous districts, and numerous towns, villages, and cities. Contacts were made with religious believers among the masses, the clergy, and various levels of party and government cadres as well as nonbelievers among the masses, stressing the history, present situation, and changes in each religion; the reasons for religious belief among the masses; and the relationship between religion and socialist life. We collected and organized over 40,000 words about the historical and present situation of each religion since the founding of our country, and we solicited the ideas of sociological research organizations, higher education institutions, cultural affairs units, party and state organs, and persons who pursue religious studies, in order to produce a high-level study.

This is a specialized work that attempts to make a theoretical breakthrough in the exploration and research of the following questions:

1. The relationship between religion and culture in China: on the one hand, there is the deep rooting of Confucian ideology for thousands of years, especially its ethics and theory of "entering into the world," in the ideology of the masses; on the other hand, there is the [Confucian] assumption that religious authority must be obedient to the supreme authority of the emperor; therefore, in the lands of the Han race there has never been a "state religion," and religious wars could never occur, as they did in the West. Not many of our people believed in formal religion; rather, they believed in gods and ghosts and followed popular customs and habits of worship.

2. Analysis of the situation of each religion since the founding of our nation. The profound changes brought about by the establishment of socialism in every area have naturally affected religion. Protestant and Catholic Christianity, Buddhism, Daoism, and Islam in particular experienced changes in their politics, economics, administration, and doctrine, especially after control by imperialism and the feudal ruling classes was cast off. Religions became enterprises run by the Chinese believers themselves, and religious belief became a truly personal matter for each citizen, not as it had been for thousands of years in a class society. The reasons for the existence of religion in the time of socialism, its social status, social function, and its laws of evolution all require our understanding.

3. Religion as a social and historical phenomenon will not immediately perish with the elimination of the sources of social classes. Religion has its own innate laws and functions. To not understand fully this point and to try to use administrative authority to wipe out religion is to follow the [erroneous] understanding of "Leftist" administrative policies, with the result precisely contrary to what was intended. Nearly forty years of actual experience since the founding of our nation proves this point, with many lessons worth learning. Religion has its mass nature, its long-term nature, its complex nature, its [ethnic] nationalities nature, and its international nature; all must be conscientiously, seriously, and correctly dealt with. We certainly cannot subjectively and arbitrarily do something that should not be done.

4. Having demonstrated that religion has an objective existence, we maintain that all genuine religious believers in socialist new China, each one at his own job, can join in striving for a happy life on this earth, based on love for one's country and seeking the common ground while preserving differences, and uniting with the broad masses of nonbelievers working together for the Four Modernizations of our country. As religious believers will affirm, almost all of the laws and ethics of religion serve the function of avoiding evil and doing good. No matter who, all should do that which benefits the country and the masses, no matter what the source or motive; all basically are beneficial for socialist modernization. Speaking from this angle, religion can be in harmony with society under socialism.

5. Harmony, or coordination, has two sides. The government, of course, follows a firm and stable policy of freedom of religious belief, making no differentiation between belief in this religion or that religion, and treating religious believers and nonbelievers alike, without discrimination. From time to time religious believers are reminded to be on guard, to cherish the unity of the Chinese people, a unity that did not come easily. Religious believers should be law-abiding, love their country and their religion, enthusiastically carry on the tasks that benefit society, and prevent any foreign influence from interfering with or manipulating the religious affairs of our country.

No one inside our country has systematically investigated the topic of religion in China under socialism. This specialized work is the result of exploratory research only. Since subjective ideas are often far removed from objective facts, errors are unavoidable. We sincerely hope that specialists in religious research will give us their critical suggestions.

January 15, 1987

1 | Introduction

RELIGION is both an ideology and a complex social historical phenomenon. The field of religious research is vast. In China, religious studies is a subject just beginning to open up, while the question of religion under socialism is a completely new topic for study.

People are faced with many questions in actual life. In China, now that the bases for social classes are virtually destroyed, why does religion continue to exist? Why have the number of believers in some religions increased in some districts in recent years? What influence does religion have on social life and the building of the Four Modernizations? How can religion be in harmony with socialist society, and what are the effects to be expected? How should the party, government, and the rest of society properly deal with religious questions? These are all questions of general concern for specialists in research on religious theory, as well as for government and party cadres, for members of religious circles, and for the broad masses of the people.

The Sixth Five-Year Plan for Economic and Social Development of the People's Republic of China included this recommendation in the section on philosophy and social sciences: "that research on theoretical and practical questions regarding the establishment of socialist modernization in China should be particularly strengthened." Research on religion was placed first in a list of twelve key topics. This book is a response to that call, an initial exploration of this current and significant subject—questions about religion in China during the socialist period.

I

Religion as an ideology that believes in and worships supernatural gods is a reflection of man's illusory understanding of the powers of nature and of society. Religion is the product of social development up to a certain point. The earliest religions reflected the extremely low-level productivity and sense of fear felt by primitive peoples who had no way of combating the forces of nature.

After the beginning of class societies, the main source for the persistence and growth of religion was the inability of the people to escape from the alien social forces that controlled them, and the suffering, fear, and despair of the workers under the crushing system of exploitation that was erected. The suffering of religion is, in fact, a manifestation of real suffering and a sigh of protest against that suffering.

Marx said: "Religion is indeed man's self-consciousness and self-awareness so long as he has not found himself or has lost himself again. But man is not an abstract being, squatting outside the world. Man is the human world, the state, society" ("Contribution to the Critique of Hegel's *Philosophy of Right,*" introduction, in *Selected Works of Marx and Engels*). Engels said: "All religions are merely the illusory reflections in the human brain of outside forces that control man's daily life, and in such reflections human power adopts the form of superhuman power" ("Anti-Dühring," in *Selected Works of Marx and Engels*, 3:354).

The writings of Marx and Engels reveal, both objectively and subjectively, the ideological nature of religion. In the mid-nineteenth century, German philosophers discussed the question of the nature of religion. The "young Hegel school" said that religion was a product of the human spirit. In his book, *The Nature of Christianity*, Feuerbach denounced this as, in essence, idealism. He said, "God did not make man in his image, but man made God according to his own image; the concept of God is really the concept of man; to know God is to really know man himself."

But the "man" that Feuerbach speaks of is an abstract man far removed from real life. Critically taking over the materialist basis of Feuerbach, Marx moved a step forward, saying, "Man is the human world, the state, society." Religion is man's consciousness of self, his perception of self; this self-consciousness and self-perception are not cut off from society, but are contained in all of man's social relationships. This self-consciousness and self-perception comes from feeling that one has no control over one's destiny when living under certain natural and social conditions.

In his review of the illusory content and basis for religion, Engels said, "The outside forces which control the daily lives of people" include both natural and social forces. The writings of Marx and Engels point out the objective sources of religion and analyze the subjective reasons why people believe in religion. They review the common nature of the various kinds of religious consciousness that prevail in different societies. Their writings also guide us in making the connection with Chinese reality, providing a compass for our research on religious questions under socialism.

Marx pointed out that "Religion is the general theory of this world, its encyclopedic compendium, its logic in popular form, its spiritual *point d'honneur*, its enthusiasm, its moral sanction, its solemn complement, its general basis of consolation and justification" ("Contribution to the Critique of Hegel's *Philosophy of Right,*" introduction, in *Selected Works of Marx and Engels*, 1:1).

Although this refers to conditions in nineteenth-century Europe, it is not difficult to see here that religion is not only a question of world outlook, it also includes many ideological and theoretical questions about one's view of life, one's ideas, values, and morality. Therefore, if we wish to research the realities of religion, we cannot limit ourselves to philosophical thought only. As Marx said, "If I only hear about religious philosophy, etc., as the true reality of religion, then I regard religious philosophers as the only true religious believers, thereby denying the reality of religious believers and actual religious belief" ("Economic and Philosophic Manuscripts," *Complete Works of Marx and Engels*, 42:173).

The substance of actual religion is complex. It is usually said that all religions have a concrete, synthesized system, at least some form of organization, ideological elements such as a religious philosophy or doctrine, religious rules and morality, and both clergy (religious professionals) and the mass of religious believers. The important factors that constitute religious life are the interacting elements of psychological and religious feelings, rites, organizations, structures, and so forth. These elements are certainly interrelated. It can be seen that religion is not only an ideology but also a complex social phenomenon, one kind of social reality, and an organized part of social life that cannot be ignored.

As a social ideology, religion is not linked, in its origins, only to an economic basis; to restrict [analysis] to an economic basis in fact generates a countereffect; religion also has parallel links with other ideologies, political viewpoints, laws, philosophies, ethics, and arts in society. In differing degrees, all these affect the genesis of religion, while the influence that religion has in each of these fields, especially in regions where all of the people are religious believers, or where religion is quite widespread, cannot be underestimated. By ignoring religion, precise explanations of social ideology, moral norms, folk customs, literature, and arts are not possible.

In addition to the effects of religious ideology on society, there is an intimate relationship between the existence, growth, and change of religious institutions, religious believers, and religious activities and the growth and change of politics, economics, and so on in society. Religion is certainly not fixed and unchanging; on the contrary, it is constantly undergoing growth and change. Therefore, it is not enough to rely on philosophical debate and logical inference for research on religion. Philosophers should come down from their lofty abstract stratosphere and get close to their research subjects in order to understand the thoughts and feelings of religious believers and the position and function of religion in society. Marx investigated nineteenth-century German religion; Engels investigated early Protestant Christian movements and the era of religious revolution under the capitalist class; Lenin investigated religion in Russia. All paid close attention to the unity of religion and society and theorized about the existence of religion, its evolution, and its social effects from the angle of society itself. They did not look at religion in different times and different societies as if they were all the same, nor did they draw inferences from generalizations.

II

To conduct research on questions about religion in the socialist period in China, the topic must be placed in a specific and coherent frame of reference. Enormous changes have occurred in human history and in society under socialism, changes that are bound to affect religion carried over from the old society; these, in turn, bring about various changes in religion and related factors, with the result that society is further affected by religion.

Of course, all factors bringing change to religion are interrelated, but they are not of equal relevance. To research the conditions, trends, and laws of change that affect religion, one must approach it from every side, and only after grasping the overall reality of religion, the complex relationship of religion and society, can we thoroughly understand the special characteristics of religion under socialism.

In the early years of national construction, Zhou Enlai, Li Weihan, and others suggested the "five natures" of religion: its mass nature, long-lasting nature, international nature, complex nature, and [minority] nationalities nature. These are of primary importance for guiding people to understand and to deal with religious questions. It seems that religion in any social system has these five natures. In fact, these five natures have been, from the Marxist point of view, a part of the reality of China since Liberation. When summed up scientifically, these religious characteristics have special implications.

China is a nation with many religions. The three great world religions, our own Daoism, and the various religions of the national minorities all have their believers, a total of over one hundred million. This many religious believers among the masses unquestionably poses a mass question. There are middle-aged and elderly people, workers, peasants, and intellectuals among them. Some of the people who could not stand the suffering caused by the oppression of the exploiting classes in the old society sought comfort in religion, showing little interest in social revolution.

Under socialism, however, religious believers among the masses actively take part in socialist construction, benefiting both politically and economically. But they still hold their religious beliefs, take part in religious activities, and have special needs for places of worship, religious scriptures, publications, and so forth. For these hundreds of millions of religious believers to take part in the great enterprise of the Four Modernizations, we must not fail to understand their religious feelings or to show concern for their special needs.

There are fifty-five national minorities in China, 6 percent of our population, but living on about 60 percent of the land area of China. A significant number of them live in the regions of the high plateaus, border plains, and mountains. The proportion of religious believers among the national minorities ranges from fairly high to very high, while in some groups virtually every person is a religious believer—clearly a situation with a specific "mass nature."

Religious beliefs, minority group feelings, and customs are integrated into an organic whole among these national minorities. Religion sets the norms for their core culture and morality. In the old society, while religion was used by the dominant class to maintain control, it also functioned as a means of resisting oppression from outside. Today, while the situation of all religious believers has undergone certain changes, the fact is that religion and the national minorities are still intimately related. We must respect and take seriously their religious beliefs, or else it will affect the unity [with the nation] of the national minorities.

Religion is a product of human society. There is scarcely a nation on earth without at least one national minority that has its own religion. According to statistics in the 1980 edition of the *Encyclopaedia Britannica* ("A Summary of Religion in the Nations of the World"), there are 2,578,049,960 members of the world's religions, which is 60 percent of the world's population. Many nations once had a state religion, so that even today religion and politics are closely related.

Now that China has initiated an "open policy" toward the outside, religious questions are often involved in matters concerning our international relations, making it imperative that we understand how to deal correctly with such questions. Before Liberation, some of the religions in China were controlled by foreign mission organizations and were used by the imperialists as tools for their penetration of China. Today this situation is basically changed, and religious enterprises are managed entirely by Chinese religionists. The opening up of international exchanges among religious circles on the basis of equality, friendship, independence, and self-governance has helped to advance understanding and friendship between the people of China and the people of other nations, and will help the movement for world peace. But in the course of opening up international exchanges we must, at the same time, be on guard and resist any actions by hostile foreign forces to use religion against China.

Religion is a social phenomenon with a long history. Why do we speak today of religion's "long-lasting nature"? We do so because even after the overthrow of the exploiting system that had lasted several thousand years, and after establishing a socialist society, there are still some people who believe that religion has lost the objective social conditions for its existence. They say that we can count the days until it disappears altogether and should adopt simplistic methods of force and coercion to try to wipe out religion.

In this book we will write about the bases for the long-term persistence of religion in the socialist period from every aspect. There are laws about the emergence, growth, and withering away of religion. Religion will naturally wither away only after passing through a long-term preparatory stage while socialism and communism evolve to the point where class distinctions have disappeared, where mankind has greatly strengthened its powers to control the forces of nature and society, and people have a universal scientific world view and outlook on life. This step-by-step process will take a long time, and anyone who uses coercive means to wipe out religion will surely harvest bitter fruit.

Besides the complex and intricate relationships between religion and society, history, and so forth, there is a complex system embodied in religion itself. The forms and manifestations of religion are manifold and varied. There are different religious teachings, different rules and doctrines, different rites, liturgies, and organizations. Even within a single religion, numerous sects emerge for historical and sociological reasons. The enormous complexities of religious thought, the proliferation of religious sects, and the many levels of religious believers all make it difficult to understand clearly all sides of every religious question.

In the early years after the founding of our country, the complex nature of religion was seen in the relationships between questions of religious belief and political questions. The key task was how to discern the contradictions between these two disparate natures, and, under the protection of [the constitutional guarantee of] freedom of religious belief, to educate and unite the religious believers and eliminate the political influence of the imperialists and counterrevolutionary elements in our country who were using religion to maintain their control. Religion is still influenced today by the complex international environment and the class struggle that prevails in certain regions. But the main question is how to deal properly with religion, unite the large numbers of religious believers, and promote vigorously the development of China.

The special features of religion in new China are summed up in the "five natures" mentioned earlier. More than thirty years of actual experience have proven over and over that the main reason for the success or failure of our religious work has been how well we understand the "five natures" of religion. We must increase and deepen our understanding of these "five natures" if we are to give clear and practical guidance to this work during the new period of socialist construction.

III

We should adopt a scientific world view and use the methods of Marxism and dialectical materialism as guiding principles and methodology if we are to make progress with research on religious questions in the socialist period.

In the nineteenth century, Marx and Engels criticized the absurdities of idealism shrouded in the religious fog of Western Europe. They overcame the one-sided nature of the old materialism, lifted the mysterious outer cover of religion revealing its inner nature, and made a great contribution to the history of man's understanding of religion.

Basing his views on valuable practical experience, Lenin also contributed important opinions from Russia on how to understand and deal with religious questions in the midst of socialist revolution.

Marx used the viewpoint of historical materialism to guide people to investigate the changes in religious development that came with changes in society and economic life. He wrote: "It is, in reality, much easier to discover by analysis the earthly core of the misty creations of religion, than, conversely, it is to develop from the actual relations of life the corresponding celestialized forms of these relations. The latter method is the only materialist method, so it is the only scientific method" ("Capital," in *Collected Works of Marx and Engels*, 23:410, n. 89).

Marx's analysis of religion was linked to social and economic forms. Natural, primitive religions of ancient times were the reflection of the narrow [restricted] relationships between man and man and between man and nature.

Protestant Christianity was the most appropriate religious form for capitalist economic relations. Because of the different forms of material production, religions, as their reflection, are also different. Speaking precisely to this, Marx and Engels said, "Religion itself has no nature and no kingdom. . . . We have to go to the material world at each stage of religious development to find out its nature" ("The German Ideology," in *Collected Works of Marx and Engels*, 3:170). Religion is a reflection of social existence, and its reflection will be different in various societies. We have to go deeply into the specific social forms and social relationships of each society to research the characteristics and functions of religion.

Marx and Engels lived more than one hundred years ago. Although the scientific world view and methods of argument that they established have universal meaning that we should continue to follow, their writings about religion in that time and place are not necessarily appropriate for the religious situation in China today. In the course of our research on religious questions in the period of socialism in China, we felt we had to follow these guidelines: adhere to basic Marxist principles; seek truth from facts; follow the principle that "everything proceeds from reality"; never mechanically copy or quote out of context the opinions and judgments of revolutionary leaders about religion; and, most important, never form opinions based on inferences from certain historical situations as a substitute for actual research on questions about religion in the socialist period in China.

We must proceed from facts, which is to say: establish an analytical and systematic research program for comparing China's present-day situation with its religious heritage, and learn about the development and laws of change from the facts of religion during the socialist period. In our investigations of religion we should rely on the strength of society and the collectives, penetrating into every level of religion, down to the grass-roots level of religious believers and their activities. To obtain rich, living, firsthand information on the current situation of religion, culture, traditions, ethnic habits, and customs, we should continually carry out religious surveys and investigations with both breadth and depth. To judge conscientiously and digest these primary source materials, modern scientific methods of systematic analysis should be used. Since society continues to develop, we have to keep on collecting new information, raising new questions, and using new materials to test and deepen our knowledge of the laws of development of religion in the socialist period. If we do this, the results of our research will help to carry out China's religious policy and unite the hundreds of millions of religious believers. It will also help in dealing with religious matters and will promote the building of a socialist material and spiritual civilization.

Over the past three years, we have conducted field investigations and surveys in more than ten provinces, including cities and towns in coastal areas, the interior, and the border regions. We contacted many religious believers, people in religious circles, nonbelievers, and cadres at the grass-roots level. We talked with them separately and together, collecting many firsthand materials. Subsequently we collected theoretical studies based on Marxist principles, exploring some questions that came out of these investigations. This book gives some initial opinions on questions such as historical characteristics of Chinese religion and fundamental changes of religion after 1949; the reasons for its long-lasting existence; and the relations among religion, socialist society, and the policy of freedom of religious belief. We consulted people doing theoretical research on religion, cadres involved in religious affairs, and friends in religious circles. This book will serve as a reference work for other people concerned with religious questions. We "cast a brick to collect jade," hoping that this book will be helpful for the exploration of religious questions in the socialist period in our country.

2 | History and Characteristics of Religions in China

The earliest concepts of religion came into existence in the Old Stone Age in China, about fifty thousand years ago, during the period of the "upper cave men." Flints, stone artifacts, and beads scattered among animals' teeth, grains of iron ore, and fossil bones showed that there was soul worship at that time.

The development of religious concepts throughout history has passed through the stages of nature worship, spirit worship, totem worship, ancestor worship, and the worship of gods and ghosts, just as in other countries. Even today, certain primitive religious ideas and customs are still popular among the people.

At about the beginning of the Christian era, Buddhism entered China from India. That marked the beginning of systematic religion in China, about two thousand years ago. Daoism appeared sometime later, while Islam and various Christian denominations (Nestorian, Catholic, Orthodox, and Protestant) spread one after the other into China, where they have long circulated, exercising their influence on Chinese society and culture. Therefore it is very important to understand the general history and characteristics of these religions in China in order to understand certain religious traditions and changing conditions since Liberation.

The Origins and History of the Great Religions

Buddhism

It is said that Buddhism was founded in the fifth or sixth century B.C. by Sarva-Siddhartha (Sakyamuni), a prince of a kingdom in India. Its basic doctrine sets forth the four truths: suffering; the cause of suffering; the extermination of suffering; and cultivation according to doctrine. Suffering refers to the "bitter" nature of human life, with its "eight bitternesses." The cause of suffering refers

15

to "temptation" as the ultimate source of human suffering (stemming from greed, anger, stupidity, etc.). "Extinguish" refers to the extinguishing of all temptations, the freeing of oneself from the cycles of birth and death, and achieving the way to Nirvana. "Cultivation" means to follow the Eight-Fold Path, to study the Buddhist creeds (dharma), to follow the commandments, and to restrain oneself in order to achieve full consciousness. The original meaning of the word *fo* in "Buddhism" (*fojiao*) means consciousness.

Ancient India had already developed into a slave society when Buddhism appeared. There was a rigid social hierarchy with sharp class contradictions. Society was divided into four castes: priests, nobles, farmers and artisans, and slaves and hired laborers. There was, in addition, an "untouchable" caste. Brahmanism was the orthodox religion of India, and the Brahman caste formed the ruling class. The emergence of Buddhism was representative of a rising tide of anti-Brahmanism. Siddhartha (the original name of Sakyamuni), who came from the aristocratic class, advocated "equality among the four castes" and opposed "Brahmans at the top," thereby winning support of the nobility, farmers, and artisans. This contributed greatly to the spread of Buddhism.

Buddhism split into many schools and sects in the course of its historical development, due to various interpretations of its doctrines and beliefs. In the first century A.D., Hinayana Buddhism emerged, stressing that every person could become a boddhisattva, while Mahayana was the branch that preached self-liberation; but Mahayana called itself the higher, orthodox Buddhism. In the third century B.C. (during the Qin dynasty), monks were sent from India to preach Buddhism. There were Buddhist believers in many parts of China during the Western Han dynasty. Although the Wu Emperor of the Han dynasty had opened up communications to the outside world, making the travel of Indian monks to the East possible, these travels were not recorded until the end of the Western Han dynasty. In 2 B.C., a Buddhist monk came from the West and gave Buddhist scriptures to Jinglu, a Chinese scholar. It was at this time that Buddhism achieved formal recognition and the beginning of its legal status in China. (Another legend says that Buddhism came into China in 67 A.D.)

The preaching of Buddhism in China and the translation of its scriptures began during the Western and Eastern Han dynasties. At first the scriptures of both Hinayana and Mahayana Buddhism were translated and circulated; some Hinayana sects were formed, but they disappeared, and Mahayana became the mainstream of Chinese Buddhism.

Buddhism continued to proliferate during the Wei, Jin, and Northern and Southern dynasties. All of the emperors of the Southern dynasties were Buddhists, the most outstanding being the Wu Emperor of Liang, who required that everyone, from the upper classes to the common people, should become Buddhists. The emperor himself entered the temple four times to undergo monastic discipline and wrote many essays promoting Buddhism.

Buddhism achieved its highest point during the Sui and Tang dynasties. There were many famous monks; Buddhist sects, including Tiantai, Lu, Jing, Jingtu, Faxiang, Huachan, Chan, Mi, and Sanjie, emerged during this period. These sects competed with each other and the temples and monasteries thrived, while Buddhism spread from China to its eastern neighbors, Japan and Korea.

After the Song dynasties, Buddhism went into a gradual decline. In more recent years, Yang Wenhui set up the Jinling printing house, printing scriptures from hand-engraved blocks. After the 1911 Revolution people such as Taixu and others tried to revive Buddhism by opening a Buddhist college and publishing Buddhist books, but they were never able to bring back the past prosperity of Buddhism. Nevertheless, Buddhism still exercises a far-reaching influence upon various aspects of the social and cultural life of socialist China.

The Buddhism that came into China was divided into two branches, northern and southern. The main sect of the northern branch is Mahayana Buddhism, and its scriptures, written in the Han language, circulate among the Han people, so it is known as Han-language Buddhism. Another sect of the northern branch merged with native Tibetan religion and is called Tibetan Buddhism (Lamaism). It belongs to the Tibetan language system and has spread among the nationalities of Tibet, Mongolia, Yugu, Naxi, and so on. The main sect of the southern branch is called Hinayana Buddhism and is popular among the Dai and other minority nationalities. Its scriptures are written in the Pali language, so it is called Pali-language Buddhism.

Daoism

Daoism, a religion that originated in China and can be called a "native religion," appeared in the Western Han dynasty (second century A.D.). Daoism can be traced to ancient concepts of ghosts and gods, and the magical practices of the Qin and Han dynasties, using the ideology of the five elements and *yin* and *yang* that emerged before the Qin dynasty, together with some mystical elements of the philosophy of Huang and Lao. Some of its concepts come from the ideas and methods of Fangxiandao and Huanglaodao, who maintained that man can gain immortal life and become a celestial being by means of certain practices. Its main scripture is the *Daodejing*, and [its founder] Laozi, is deified and treated as a god.

Daoism was popular among the people and has served as the banner for peasant uprisings. At the time of the Shun Emperor of the Eastern Han, Zhanglin and Zhangheng, father and son, set up the Wudoumidao (Five Pecks of Rice) sect in the region of Bashu; during the reign of the Lin Emperor of the Eastern Han, Changjiao founded the Taipingdao sect. The dao doctrines of both sects were basically the same, all treating Laozi as the founder and adopting the name "Dao" for the religion. Thus Daoism was established. Zhanglu, the grandson of Zhanglin, set up a regime in southern Shaanxi Province that was integrated with religion and was welcomed by the people for its benevolent government. Zhangjiao aroused the broad masses of the peasants and launched the Huangjing Uprising, which shook the regime of the feudal nobility by using the ideology of the *Taipingjing*, which opposes the accumulation of wealth by the rich, advocating living on one's own labor and helping the poor.

Later, Daoism gradually split up. On the one hand it survived among the common people, while on the other hand the ruling class tried to reform original Daoism and create a complete Daoist system by mixing it with the ideologies and practices of Buddhism and Confucianism. The two volumes of *Baopuzi*, written by Ge Hong during the Eastern Jin dynasty, set up a theory and practice for achieving immortality and advocated the integration of Daoist magical practices with the well-known teachings of Confucianism. During the Northern Wei dynasty, Kou Qianzhi said that he had received instructions from Laozi to clear away the "falsehoods of the three Zhangs" (Zhanglin, Zhangheng, Zhanglu), and to "give priority to rites and to practice [ritual] exercises and take [magic] medicines."

In the time of the Ming Emperor of the Southern Song dynasty, Lu Xiujing assembled a large collection of Daoist scriptures, assimilated the ceremonial rituals of Buddhism, and compiled books about rites and fasting. In the time of Qiliang of the Southern Song dynasty, Tao Hongjing further developed the system of Daoist mysticism and promoted the integration of Buddhism, Confucianism, and Daoism. Through the reforming work of Ge Hong, Kou Qianzhi, Lu Xiujing, and Tao Hongjin, the doctrines and rites of Daoism were brought to completion.

During the Sui, Tang, and Northern Song dynasties, many emperors were Daoist believers. Rulers of the Tang dynasty said they were descendants of Laozi and gave their support to Daoism in various ways. Emperor Wu even abandoned Buddhism in his enthusiasm for Daoism, and the Song dynasty rulers expended much effort in promoting Daoism. Because of the support of the Tang and Song rulers, Daoism flourished, with many famous Daoist scholars and priests.

As for their religious activities, Daoists can be divided into two sects, Fulu and Danding. The Fulu sect worships ghosts and gods. The Danding sect focuses on the practice of outer-elixir [*waidan*] (drug of immortality) and inner-elixir [*neidan*] (refining spiritual essence, *jin* and *qi*, within the human body). A number of "new Daoist" sects appeared after the Northern Song dynasty, of which one, the All-True Daoism, which attempted to integrate Daoism with Buddhism and Confucianism, survived. This sect, which advocated concentration on the practice of *neidan* and separation from secular life in order to seek the truth, set up a system for doing this, and reached its peak in the Yuan dynasty. Different *waidan* sects gradually came together, forming Zhengyi Daoism, resulting in the parallel existence of two large Daoist sects, Quanzhen and Zhengyi.

From the middle of the Ming dynasty through the Qing and Republican periods, Daoism declined. But the ongoing influence of some Daoist doctrines and rituals among the customs and habits of the people must not be underestimated.

Islam

Islam, founded by Mohammed, came into being on the Arabian peninsula in the early seventh century. Its basic doctrines consist of belief in Allah, the holy books, angels, prophets, predestination, and the life hereafter (day of judgment)—the Six Beliefs. To believe in Allah (the True Lord) is to believe that Allah is the one God in the universe, the creator of all things and creatures. To believe in the prophets is to believe that Allah has sent many messengers, or prophets, since the creation of the world to spread "the word of Allah," and that Mohammed was the last prophet, the one whose words and deeds embodied the will of Allah. Belief in angels means that Mohammed received his "revelation" for the founding of Islam from angels. Belief in the holy books means accepting the doctrine that the Qur'an is the "word of Allah," the last of the holy books, and that this "holy teaching," this "revelation," is the record of Mohammed's words and deeds. Belief in predestination means that everything on earth, including the fate of human persons, is prearranged by Allah. Belief in the life hereafter means that all human beings will experience resurrection and be judged by Allah at the time of the end of the world, the good ones going to paradise and the evil ones to a fiery hell.

All Muslims (Islamic believers) must recite the words of testimony, "There is no other god but Allah, and Mohammed is the Messenger of Allah," in order to demonstrate their faith. Besides this, they should offer prayers five times a day, fast during the month of Ramadan, give the legal alms (*zakat*), and make the pilgrimage to Mecca, if possible, once during their lifetime. These are the five religious duties, the "five basic practices," required of every Muslim—reciting, worship, fasting, offerings, and pilgrimage.

The Arabian peninsula was in a chaotic condition in the early seventh century, with politics in confusion and separate tribes fighting one another. At the same time, foreign powers invaded the region, trading routes were destroyed, the people suffered heavy exploitation and high interest rates, and social conflicts and class rivalries deepened. The only way out was to break down the tribal fortresses, abolish polytheism, bring about unity among the Arabs, join with one heart to resist the foreign invaders, and scramble for outside commercial markets. In this way, social contradictions could be reduced. Mohammed conformed to the needs of the times, putting forth slogans such as "ban usury," "free the poor," "only one God," and "peace and security." These represented the interests of the merchant class, and, in some degree, the wishes of the broad masses of the people. Islam, born in these conditions, grew in popularity.

When Mohammed began his religious work in the early seventh century, the existing polytheism could not immediately be replaced. It was not until he moved to al-Medinah in the year 622 and set up a religious community integrating religion with government that he could overcome the influence of polytheism in civil organizations, systems, and the military. By the third decade of the seventh century, Islam had become the ruling religion of the Arabian peninsula, bringing about unification of the region. After unification, wars of conquest were launched, a caliphate [theocratic nation] was established, and

Islam spread to three continents: Europe, Asia, and Africa.

Historians usually agree that Islam first came into China in the mid-seventh century. In A.D. 651, the Third Caliph sent his emissary to pay tribute to the Emperor Gaozong of the Tang dynasty at [the capital] Chang'an, introducing Islam. An important reason for the spread of Islam in China was the development of commercial trade between China and the Arabians. Arabian and Persian Muslim traders traveled to China by land and by sea between the seventh and thirteenth centuries. The sea route, beginning in the Persian Gulf, traversed the Arabian Sea to the port of Guangzhou [Canton]. The land route from the Arabian peninsula crossed the southern or northern Tianshan Mountains in Xinjiang and terminated in Chang'an. The Muslim traders were given residences in Guangzhou, Quanzhou, Hangzhou, Yangzhou, Chang'an, and other places and had their own Muslim temples and cemeteries. Over time, Chinese Islam emerged from these beginnings.

Military expansion of the Arabs and Mongols was the principal means by which Islam spread into China. From the tenth to the twelfth century, the Arabs carried on incessant warfare in Central Asia, which led to the acceptance of the Islamic faith by peoples who dwelt along the northwestern borders of our country, south and north of the Tianshan Mountains. After the first Yuan emperor, the Mongols fought their way westward for half a century, forcing various ethnic peoples of Central Asia, as well as Persians and Arabians, to move eastward. These people were organized into the vast "Western Army" as soldiers and artisans, usually called "Hui Hui," who gradually spread over China. They settled in various places, some marrying Chinese but retaining their Muslim traditions, building Muslim mosques as their cultural and religious activity centers, and forming religious residential neighborhoods. This is how the Hui nationality came into being in China.

Islam continued to develop in China after the Yuan dynasty, and by the seventeenth century there were at least ten ethnic nationalities that had converted to Islam: the Uyghur, Kazakh, Hui, Kirgiz, Dongxiang, Tajik, Uzbek, Tartar, Sala, and Bao'an. Because Islam is intimately linked to the traditional culture, life, and customs of these nationalities, it has strong nationality characteristics in China today.

There were many Islamic scholars and well-known *ahongs* (imams) during the Ming and Qing dynasties after the expansion of Islam in China. On the one hand, they promoted religious education in the mosques, maintaining and spreading Islamic learning and culture; on the other hand, they introduced and spread the history and teachings of Islam by translating and publishing the Arabic- and Persian-language holy books.

Most Chinese Muslims belong to the Sunni [Ahlal-Sunnah] sect, while religious law studies come under the Hanafiyah sect. Many other sects emerged during the growth and spread of Islam in China.

Christianity

Christianity had its beginnings in Palestine in the first century. Legend says that it was founded by Jesus of Nazareth in Judea. Believers call Jesus the "Christ," that is, savior. The fundamental doctrine of this religion is that there is in the universe an "all-wise, all-kind, omnipotent, and omnipresent God." He created and rules over the world. Humans have been guilty of sin (original sin) since their first ancestor and have suffered for their sins. The only way to be redeemed is to believe in God and his son, Jesus Christ. The spirit of God, called the Holy Spirit, is present on earth among humankind and can bring persons to acknowledge their sins, repent, and be forgiven [literally, "obtain holiness"]. God, Christ, and the Holy Spirit, also called the Holy Father, Holy Son, and Holy Spirit, form the Christian belief in God as the "Trinity." The Christian scriptures are the "Old Testament" (inherited from the Judaic classics) and the "New Testament."

In the first century A.D., Palestine and Asia Minor were under the tyrannical rule of the Roman Empire. At that time not only were the slaves oppressed, but also some free people who had been bankrupted became slaves. In their attempt to exterminate the indigenous political and social features of the subject nationalities, the Roman Empire spared no effort in wiping out their religions as well, forcing them to worship Roman gods and even Roman emperors. The acute class and nationality contradictions brought about rebellions among the nationality groups along the eastern Mediterranean coast, particularly the Jewish nationality. But when all uprisings were defeated, some of the dissidents placed their hope in God, expecting that a Messiah (savior of the world) would come down from heaven to destroy injustice on earth and relieve them from suffering. The idea of a Messiah had long been popular among the Jews, but the savior had not yet come. Some of the Jews began to believe that Jesus was this savior sent to earth by God. They gradually separated themselves from Judaism and established a new religion, spreading the "gospel" everywhere. Early Christianity was thus a movement of the oppressed against the "authorities," and very quickly it spread outward among the lower-class peoples along the eastern shores of the Mediterranean Sea. Christians suffered severe persecutions under the Roman rulers.

When middle and upper elements of society had permeated the [Christian] religion, securing a dominant position, they changed and sought to be loyal to the rulers. Some Christian communities gradually changed from their original fanatical and chaotic state, forming organized groups by the end of the second century with professional leaders, rules, and scripture canons. Roman authorities also changed their attitude from one of persecution to cooptation, adopting Christianity as the state religion of the Roman Empire in the fourth century. In the European Middle Ages the orthodox church became a pillar of feudal society, placing philosophy, politics, law, and so on under the control of theology. Some of the peasants, poor people, and town dwellers used heretical Christian sects as banners and bonds of unity in fomenting struggles against feudalism. In the year 1054 a great split took place between the church in the East and West. The Eastern branch called itself the correct religion (Orthodox), and the Western branch called itself the universal church (Catholic).

In the sixteenth century a reform movement against the feudal rule of the Pope again split the Western church. New sects broke off from the Catholic church, forming the "New Religion" [Protestant]. Protestants [*xinjiao*—new religion] believe that the faithful can communicate with God without going through a priest. Organizational changes were made in the church (such as the system of bishops, elders, congregations, and so on). The main denominations are the Lutheran, Presbyterian, Anglican, Baptist, Congregational, Methodist, and others; many other denominations were derived from these.

Christianity first came to China early in the seventh century. In the year 635 Alopen, a missionary of the Nestorian Christians, came from Persia to Chang'an. He translated scriptures and set up a "Da Qin Temple" for his religion, called Nestorianism [*jingjiao*]. He was received with respect by the Emperor Taizong of the Tang dynasty. During the following two hundred years, Nestorianism spread across the nation. In the year 835, Emperor Wuzong issued an order banning Buddhism and sending monks and nuns back into secular life. Nestorianism was banned as well, and about two thousand missionaries were banished. Nestorianism could no longer be found in China proper, but it continued on in Khitan, Mongolia, and elsewhere.

After the Mongolians became masters of China in the thirteenth century, Mongolian Nestorians came into China, and Nestorian Christianity was quite popular in the Yuan dynasty. At the same time, the Roman Catholic church sent Franciscan missionaries to evangelize in China, and they were well received by the Yuan rulers. Both Nestorians and Catholics respected the cross, so they were called the "religion of the cross," and their churches were called "cross temples." Some missionaries and believers were also called Manicheans. After the Yuan dynasty, Christianity again disappeared from China proper.

Catholicism again came into China at the end of the Ming dynasty. In 1582, the Italian Jesuit missionary Matteo Ricci came from Macao, which was in the hands of the Portuguese, to Zhaoqing, near Guangzhou. His preaching methods included adapting Christian teachings to Chinese customs and culture and introducing Western science. In this way he made a good impression on the Ming rulers and officials, giving a foothold from which the Catholic church could propagate the faith. Later, Dominican and Franciscan missionaries joined the work and disputes arose, resulting in the "Rites Controversy" over the question of Confucian rites and worship of ancestors. In the early eighteenth century, the pope's order banning participation in these rites by Christians was followed by the Kangxi Emperor's order to the missionaries either to obey the "Matteo Ricci regulations" [approving the rites] or to leave China. Subsequently, the Yongzheng Emperor issued a further order banning Catholicism, and most of the missionaries were driven out of China. From that time until the early nineteenth century, the preaching activities of the Catholics were at a low ebb.

The Russian Orthodox church began preaching in the mid-seventeenth century in places like Heilongjiang and Beijing. In 1715, the government of the Russian Czar sent a Russian Orthodox mission to Beijing. In 1727, with the signing of the Treaty of Kiakhta, the mission became permanent. In the nineteenth century, the Russian Orthodox clergy set up churches in Xinjiang, Inner Mongolia, Harbin, Shanghai, Tianjin, Qingdao, and other places.

Protestantism entered China about the time of the Opium War, and its preaching activities went forward on a large scale. The first Protestant missionary was Morrison of the London Missionary Society, who came to Guangzhou in 1807. He translated the Holy Bible into Chinese. Later, missionaries of various denominations from North America and Europe came into China. At the same time, Catholic missionaries also swarmed in. At first the foreign missionaries worked only in the commercial ports along the coast, but later, protected by the unequal treaties, they went deep into the interior. They expanded their Christian influence by means of schools, hospitals, and charitable organizations, not only preaching among the Han Chinese, but also pressing into the regions inhabited by minority nationalities deep in the interior and border regions. (Note: Christianity includes the Catholic, Russian Orthodox and Protestant churches, but [in Chinese] Christianity generally refers to Protestantism only. For literary convenience, the term Christianity [jidujiao], in accordance with custom, will refer to Protestantism only in later chapters of this book.)

The Influence of Religion on Chinese Culture

Throughout its long history, religion not only has had a profound influence on the life and culture of the Chinese, but also has become part of Chinese traditional culture.

All religions, when viewed epistemologically, are merely the illusory reflections in the human mind of external influences that control people's daily lives. All religious world outlooks are based on erroneous and distorted understanding of the objective world. But religions are also the way that man tries to understand objective alien forces, and his efforts to make use of those forces. They have often drawn wrong conclusions, but, in the course of their explorations, they have also often discovered the laws of development of certain objective things, thereby advancing early scientific knowledge. Ancient peoples believed that the movement of the stars through the skies could determine the fate of people on earth, and thus astrology was born. In the course of observing astronomical phenomena, they discovered certain laws governing the movement of celestial bodies, and thus developed ancient astronomy. All Chinese religions produced a certain number of astronomers who produced almanacs. Searching for ways to prolong life, ancient peoples melted and combined certain minerals, hoping to produce an elixir of immortality. Quite a number of people, including some kings and emperors, lost their lives by taking such potions. In the course of their experiments, however, they observed the chemical and physical changes of various ingredients and thus advanced the early understanding of chemistry. This can be seen in the Cinnabar Sect of native Daoism. When the people, as a result of certain religious practices, discovered ways to preserve their health, ancient medical science was born.

Religious ideology is part of the idealist ideological system. But, because of its studies of man's awareness of "self," "heart," "nature," and "spirit," and of the process of human cognition and other subjective activities, it has played a significant role in the development of philosophical thought. While criticizing mechanical materialism, Marx also appraised the historical function of idealistic ideology. He pointed out that, "Of course, idealism does not know real, sensuous activity as such," but in earlier materialism "the thing, reality, sensuousness, is conceived only in the form of the object or of contemplation, but not as human sensuous activity, practice, not subjectively. Hence it happened that the active side, in contradistinction to materialism, was developed by idealism—but only abstractly" (Marx, "Theses on Feuerbach," in *Selected Works of Marx and Engels*, 1:16). Dialectical discussions of certain religious concepts, such as *kong* (emptiness) and *you* (having), *sheng* (coming into being) and *mie* (dying out), *yin* (feminine, negative) and *yang* (masculine, positive), and *gang* (firm) and *rou* (flexible) are a precious hereditary treasure. Religious believers speaking in defense of religion sharpened people's logical thinking. The Buddhist study of *yin* (cause) and *ming* (enlightenment) is a good example.

Since religious faith is the illusory reflection of objective reality, producing all kinds of myths, the power of rich, varied, and imaginative thinking is developed, exercising strong influence upon the creative arts, such as painting, sculpture, music, architecture, literature, and poetry. Despite their focus on gods and the other-world, the religious arts represent artistic creativity inspired by the real life of humanity. Therefore, when the mystical mask of religious art is removed, it does, in fact, reflect man's pursuit of a perfect humanity and an ideal realm. Many of these works have become everlasting cultural treasures. Novels and plays based on religious myths have long been part of the literature and art loved by the broad masses of the people.

Except for Daoism, all of China's religions came from abroad. As they spread into China, these religions brought with them foreign cultures, thus promoting cultural exchange between China and the West. Buddhism brought the culture of India and the Western regions. Islam brought Arabic culture. Christianity brought the cultures of America and Europe. These cultures mixed with Chinese traditional culture, thus bringing many influences into our culture. Missionaries such as [the Jesuits] Ricci and Schall at the close of the Ming dynasty used the advanced science and technology of their country as a stepping stone to open the way for evangelism, so that even when the Kangxi Emperor expelled large numbers of foreign missionaries over the "Chinese rites" controversy, some missionaries working as astronomers, palace painters, royal medical specialists, and watch and clock makers were allowed to remain in the capital and kept up certain Catholic influences.

All these imported religions had to translate their scriptures while propagating their faith. As they pursued accuracy, precision, and elegance in their translations, these religious translators made important contributions to linguistics and phonology, linking the cultural and psychological traditions of different nations and ethnic groups, and promoting the interflow of ideologies among different peoples. The contents of these various religious scriptures were not limited to religion. The *Dazangjing* of Buddhism and the *Daozang* of Daoism are encyclopedic collections containing treasures for the study of Chinese culture.

All Chinese religions have had their ups and downs through history, and they all have had lasting and far-reaching influence upon Chinese culture. Most of the ancient buildings still preserved in China are Buddhist temples and pagodas, such as the brick pagoda of Yueyang in Songshan, Henan; the Tang dynasty wooden buildings of the Nanchan and Foguang temples at Wutaishan, Shanxi; the great wooden pagoda in Ying County; and the East and West stone pagodas of the Kaiyuan Temple in Quanzhou, Fujian. These all are precious subjects for those studying the ancient architectural technology of China. The Buddhist sculptures and frescoes preserved in the stone caves of Dunhuang, Yungang, and Longmen are world-renowned art treasures. Combining Indian and Chinese sculptural traditions, they are a great cultural heritage. Others, such as the Potala Palace in Lhasa and the Ta'er Temple in Qinghai, with their magnificent buildings and elegant and beautiful sculptures and paintings, are characteristic of Tibetan culture.

Buddhist scriptures have high literary value and have influenced the history of Chinese literature. Such Buddhist scriptures as *Fahua*, *Weimojie*, and *Baiyu* influenced the novels written in the Jin and Tang dynasties; *Banruo* and the ideology of the Chan sect influenced the poems of Tao Yuanming, Wang Wei, Bai Juyi, and Su Shi. The writings of the Chan sect of Buddhism influenced popular forms of narrative literature and were closely related to Chinese folk literature. Materials from Buddhist scriptures have often provided subjects for paintings. Certain freehand brushwork is related to Chan ideology. As for music, Sanskrit was popular in the second century A.D., and various types of Tang dynasty music all had their origins in Buddhist countries. According to legend, there are still a few Tang musical scores preserved in certain Buddhist temples.

The practice of medicine, astronomy, and health exercises came with Buddhism. Eminent Tang dynasty monks created the *Dayanli* (a kind of calendar), surveying the meridian lines and making outstanding contributions to astronomy. More than ten books of medicine and pharmacology that had been translated from Indian originals can be found in Tang and Sui books. Tibetan Buddhism also had its own kind of medical studies. Buddhist wood-block carving advanced the printing industry of China. The oldest books printed with woodblocks still extant in the world are nearly all Buddhist relics. Legend has it that the well-known "Shaolin Boxing" came from the "Xinyi Boxing," which was first taught by the Indian Buddhist, Damo, when he came to China to found the Chan sect, and was later developed by successor monks.

Buddhist philosophy has unique views in studying man, the universe, and formal logic. In his "Natural Dialectics," Engels praised Buddhist believers for their higher level in the development of dialectical thought. During the well-known Chinese culture of the Wei, Jin, Six Dynasties, Sui, and Tang dynasties, Buddhist learning become the principal mode of Chinese philosophical thought. Absorbed by the new Confucianism, Buddhist thinking helped the idealist philosophy of the Song and Ming dynasties to prosper.

The arts and music of Daoism fill a brilliant page in the cultural history of China. Daoist sculpture and painting was first influenced by Buddhist arts, but their creativity had characteristics of Daoist philosophy and beliefs, and their skills were directly inherited from ancient Chinese bronzes, pictorial tiles and ancient figure painting, which resulted in a distinctive Daoist style. Many artists throughout history were Daoist priests. Daoist murals extant today, such as the Song dynasty murals in Lingfen and Hongtong counties in Shanxi Province and the huge mural in the Tiankuang Hall of the Dai Temple on Mount Tai, belong to the precious heritage of Chinese art. The Daoist Quanzhen Sect prospered during the Yuan dynasty, while the Daoist murals in the Shanxi Yongle Palace are masterpieces of Chinese art history, epitomizing the Tang and Song dynasties' Daoist painting traditions. After the Song and Yuan dynasties, scholars and painters, using Daoist subject matter for inspiration, pursued "quietness and letting things take their own course." They created an elegant style, free and natural, not seeking fame and wealth. On the other hand, Daoist patterns and decorations became part of the people's folk art, and the statues of gods symbolizing auspiciousness were popular.

The music used in Daoist rites was said to be able to "move the gods." Daoist music consisted of singing, reciting, and playing musical instruments, with solos, chorus, chanting, drums, wind and percussion instruments, and ensembles. Some music theory and musical scores are preserved in the *Daozang* and other Daoist works. Chinese Daoist music, by continuing and developing this ritual heritage, and nourished by popular folk music through the years, reached a relatively high level. Up until the middle of the twentieth century, Daoist rites and ceremonies had provided rich spectacles for the farm people in Jiangsu, Zhejiang, and other parts of south China.

Daoist alchemy, long practiced, made contributions to Chinese *materia medica* and ancient chemistry. For example, Daoists in the Tang and Song dynasties, drawing on the experience of their forbears, produced quite a number of Chinese medicines. The liquid made according to a prescription recorded in the *Baopuzi jindan* by Ge Hong, a Daoist of the Eastern Jin dynasty, could melt gold. While experimenting with alchemy, Daoists discovered a combustible mixture of nitre, sulphur, and carbon that led to the invention of black gunpowder.

Daoist gymnastics (*jianshenfa*) (the old name was eight-part or twelve-part exercises) accelerated the development of ancient Chinese *wushu*; Daoist acupuncture and acupressure are closely linked to ancient Chinese medical science. Ge Hong and Tao Hongjing were famous medical specialists. Ge Hong collected folk remedies and tested recipes, writing "handy emergency aids" that were convenient, inexpensive, and effective. The account of smallpox in this book is the earliest scientific record in medical history. His knowledge of tuberculosis was a thousand years ahead of that in foreign countries. Tao Hongjing, drawing on the medical and clinical experience of his predecessors, pushed ancient medical first aid farther ahead. He classified and annotated "Shengnong Herbs" and "Records of Famous Physicians," and compiled "Collected Annotations on Herbs," an important document about Chinese herbal medicine. Daoism promoted the exercise of internal organs by breathing exercises, and founded an important school of *qigong* health exercises.

Although Islam came into China in the Tang dynasty, it was not until the Yuan emperors moved large numbers of Persians, Arabians, and Central Asians to the east that it spread widely. Arabian and Central Asian culture were brought in and gradually became part of Chinese culture. Arab craftsmen brought to China the skills for weaving golden silk. Military artisans manufactured the Hui-Hui gun, a cannon that mechanically fired stone projectiles. A number of medical scientists and almanac astronomers were given important positions. In the Yuan dynasty there was a Hui-Hui office of astronomy side by side with the official astronomical office. Zamaludin, the Hui-Hui astronomer, compiled the ten-thousand-year calendar and made seven kinds of astronomical instruments. Three medical institutions were set up in the Yuan dynasty under the imperial medical office. Stories about the medical treatment given by Hui-Hui physicians and surgical operations by "Old Hui-Hui" were recorded in nonofficial writings. When he held a position with the Yunnan government, the famous politician Saidianchidansidin of the Yuan dynasty gave great attention to developing agricultural production, teaching skills in planting sorghum, rice, and hemp, promoting methods for building reservoirs to guard against drought and flood, and dredging six rivers in Kunming. During the Yuan dynasty, Muslims brought their science of astronomy, calendar calculation, *materia medica*, agriculture, and water conservancy; they contributed both to our scholarly culture and the development of production.

There was still a Hui-Hui calendar office under the Office of Astronomy in the Ming dynasty. Zhu Yuanchang believed that "The Westerners are better in astronomy." Some Hui-Hui masters cooperated in translating books about the calendar, longitudes and latitudes, and astronomy. Their traditional crafts continued to develop, of which the most outstanding (related to their traditional commerce) were the spice industry, medicine (combined with their *materia medica*), and the porcelain industry (with the discovery of "Hui blue" and the adaptation of their geometrical patterns and Arabic characters). The Hui-Hui of the Ming dynasty were well known in trade and commerce. Overseas trade began to wither away at the end of the Ming dynasty. Among the Hui-Hui of the Ming, Zheng He, the great navigator, "sailed to the Western oceans" seven times in the twenty-nine years between 1405 and 1433, as admiral of a fleet of vessels, visiting more than thirty Asian and African countries. He went on pilgrimage to Mecca as well. Many of his subordinates were Hui-Hui, such as Ma Huan and Hasan, the chief imam of the Xi'an Mosque, who served as interpreters for the ocean expeditions. Their unprecedented ventures made lasting contributions to advancing communication between East and West and economic and cultural exchanges.

Jesuit missionaries came to China at the end of the Ming dynasty and won the friendship of Chinese rulers and officials by introducing Western science and technology. Upon arriving at Zhaoqing, Ricci invited people to look at his "Maps of Mountains and Seas" and European clocks, sundials, and an armillary sphere. When he arrived in Beijing in 1601, he offered clocks, a steel-string fiddle, and a world map to the Emperor Wan Li. With the help of his colleagues he translated *Geometry in the Original*, *Methods of Surveying*, and other books, introducing Western knowledge of astronomy, geography, and mathematics. After Ricci, other Jesuit missionaries, including N. Longabardi, S. de Ursis, A. Schall, J. Terenz, J. Aleni, and J. Rho, made further contributions to the introduction of Western astronomy, calendar calculation, and so forth. They won the confidence of the court in the late Ming and early Qing dynasties, and some were given official positions in the Office of Astronomy, helping the government to revise the calendar. They helped the last Ming rulers cast dozens of cannons, and later, under the Kangxi Emperor, continued the calendar revision and sent out a number of Jesuit colleagues into the provinces to survey the physical features and make a precise map of China.

When their mission activities took them deep into the interior of China, Catholic and Protestant missionaries set up educational and cultural projects on a large scale, introducing Western knowledge of astronomy, geography, mathematics, physics, and chemistry. Their Western educational system also attacked the feudal educational system with its examinations based on the eight-legged essays, and raised a large number of new intellectuals quite different from the old-style scholars and officials. Chinese *materia medica* had enjoyed a long history, but Western medical science was not brought into China, complementing Chinese traditional medicine, until the church hospitals were set up.

The churches also opened orphanages, homes for the elderly, leprosy hospitals, and schools for blind children. The Protestant YMCA and YWCA pioneered in introducing modern sports activities and various service programs for social reform.

The goal in disseminating modern Western bourgeois culture in China was to carry out cultural imperialism by raising up a generation of comprador Christians with a sense of national inferiority. On the other hand, the conservative, traditional Chinese culture and feudal society came under attack. Some intellectuals, hoping to change China's destiny, imbibed ideas about Western bourgeois democracy and modern science from books and magazines printed and distributed by Christian organizations, such as the Society for the Diffusion of Knowledge. But even more informed people wondered why, in the semifeudal and semicolonial state of old China, if they turned to the West to learn, "the teachers impose cultural aggression on the students" ("On the People's Democratic Dictatorship," in *Selected Works of Mao Zedong*, 4:1475). They hoped they could find ideological weapons, starting from China's real situation, to free themselves from foreign oppression and enable their country and people to set out on the road to independence and prosperity. In the end, however, the Western science and culture brought in by Christian missionaries did force Western culture and Chinese culture into a new stage of mutual contact and assimilation, objectively stimulating, to a certain extent, the course of China's history.

Special Characteristics of Religion in Chinese History

Religions have been present in China throughout history, exercising significant influence on various aspects of Chinese culture. But most Chinese have been indifferent to religion, and the number of true religious believers has been only a small proportion of the total population. There has never been a religious power (except among the ethnic minorities) that could control the political situation and take a ruling position. This is because all of the religions in China developed and expanded in the traditional Han Chinese culture areas, forming characteristics that differ from those of other nations and peoples.

1. The concepts of "heaven," the "mandate of heaven," and "unity of heaven and man" in our traditional ideology have inhibited the development of the notion of a personal God.

The concept of the "unity of heaven and man" has been present in our nation for a long time. Long after the Stone Age and the early age of agriculture, humans, in order to survive, had to accommodate themselves to nature, such as the weather, land, and the availability of water. Although there were concepts of "heaven" and "gods" in ancient times, favorable weather had to be matched by the hard work of the people. The will of heaven and the work of man complemented each other. When the *Shanshu: Hongfan* says, "Consult the village people, consult the common people, and consult the sorcerers and shamans," it gives the same importance to human knowledge as to the will of God. This concept of an interflow between heaven and man that developed into the idea of "matching heaven with morality" and "the unity of heaven and man" is an important characteristic of Chinese traditional ideology.

In ancient times, the concept of "heaven" meant nature, as well as "sovereignty." It was neither a personified God with absolute control over the world, nor [an impersonal] nature that had to be conquered. Heaven and man were not completely at odds but were able to make some mutual accommodation.

Confucius, Mencius, Laozi, and Zhuangzi all supported the concept of the "unity of heaven and man," emphasizing that "man" must acknowledge and be in harmony with "heaven." They tended to weaken the sovereignty of "heaven," giving prominence to the functions of nature. "The mandate of heaven is nature, nature can be called doctrine, and cultivating doctrine can be called religion" (*Zhongyong*). "Man models himself on the earth, the earth models itself on heaven, heaven models itself on doctrine, and doctrine models itself on nature" (*Laozi*, chap. 25). These references show the ideological trends during the time before the Qin dynasty.

The "unity of heaven and man" proposed by the Han Confucian school came from the search for a cosmology that accounted for "responses" between heaven and man, enabling man to have external freedom for his actions. The "heaven" mentioned here actually means "atmosphere" (*qi*), that is, nature and the body. The "unity of heaven and man" as understood by the Song Confucian school was, from an ontological viewpoint, the result of their search for internal freedom for human nature. Their "heaven" actually means "reason," the mind or spirit. The cosmology of the Han Confucian school and the ontology of the Song school prevented the concept of "heaven" from developing into a religious personification of God. Chinese traditional ideology always found solutions to questions that elsewhere were usually treated religiously, by means of philosophical reflection, as with the question of the "unity of heaven and man." In this way, religion could never develop widely among the Han Chinese. Religious theology in China also shifted toward philosophy and reason, weakening the sense of mystery and transcendence. This accounts for the great difference between Buddhism in China and elsewhere.

2. The people of China are indifferent to religion because Confucian ideology, with its emphasis on ethics, has long been dominant.

Confucian ideology, which held its dominant position through all the dynasties, neither negates nor supports religions, ghosts, or deities. Confucius many times mentioned the concepts of "heaven" and "destiny" and observed some sacrificial rites, but his ideas were focused upon the ethical relations of this world. When asked by Zilu about "serving ghosts and gods" and the afterlife, he said, "How can you serve gods and ghosts when you cannot serve man?" and "How can you know about death when you do not know about life?" Confucius's attitude toward gods and ghosts was to "offer sacrifices to the gods if they exist," and "respect the gods and ghosts, but keep away from them." So it can be seen that the Confucian school had an ambiguous attitude, with no specific religious beliefs.

"Benevolence" (*ren*), the kernel of the thought of Confucius, means "do not do unto others what you would not have done to yourself." He also said, "benevolence means to love people.'' It can be seen that he attached great importance to human relationships. ''Benevolence'' takes ''filial piety'' as its foundation. ''Isn't what is called filial piety the foundation of benevolence?'' In ancient society, filial piety was one of the elements that brought social stability. ''There are few filial persons who would offend the ruler.'' That is to say, ''filial piety'' could lead to ''loyalty,'' and thus the ''king as king, subjects as subjects, fathers as fathers, and sons as sons'' became the basic moral force regulating ethical relationships in the feudal society. This was quite different from the history of medieval Europe when feudal sovereignty relied on religion.

Despite the fact that some Chinese emperors promoted religion, they did not use religious ideology as a basis for their rule. Even during the Tang dynasty, when Daoism and Buddhism both flourished, the government still gave examinations and chose officials based on Confucian theory. In a very basic sense, they still used the Confucian ideology with its patriarchal ethical code to support their reign. The Taizong Emperor of the Tang dynasty in the year 628 ordered the Confucian Temple to be built in the Taixue Ministry, and in 630 he ordered that the Confucian classics and annotations be taught there, and that Confucianism should become the official ideology. Zhuxi of the Song dynasty edited the ''Four Books'' as the main subject for the national examinations, and his works became the official notes, which continued until the imperial examinations were abolished at the end of the Qing dynasty.

The traditional ethical concepts of the Confucians were an important historical factor inhibiting the growth of religion.

3. Feudal dynasties in China both supported and restricted religions, subordinating religion to political power; therefore, among the Han Chinese, no religion has ever been a state (national) religion, nor has there been an ''integration of politics and religion.''

Religion benefited the rulers in different dynasties. Emperors in every dynasty called themselves ''the son of heaven'' to show that their ruling power was divinely given. They said that their royal power came directly from ''heaven'' and that they would, therefore, not need a ''pope,'' ''archbishop,'' or ''high priest'' to crown them, subordinating the royal power to religious authority.

The dynastic rulers never allowed religious influence to contend with imperial authority or to affect their absolute rule. There never has been a ''national religion'' or a regime that ''integrated government and religion.'' Furthermore, some of the religious teachings of Buddhism that conflict with the patriarchal social order, such as to give up one's parents, renounce the supreme rulers, and separate oneself from the world, increasingly came under attack from officialdom. In his book *Yuandao*, Hanyu condemned Buddhism and Daoism, saying that ''they abandon [the relations between] the sovereign and subjects, give up [the relations between] father and son, and ban the doctrine of nurturing and providing for each other, in order to seek so-called quietness.'' Zhuxi went further, saying that ''it can be clearly understood that Buddhism and Daoism are guilty of the great crime of abolishing the three guides [ruler guides subject, father guides sons, husband guides wife] and five constant virtues [benevolence, righteousness, propriety, wisdom, and fidelity], as well as other doctrines not mentioned.'' Catholics and Protestants encountered the same charges when they first came to China.

Moreover, monks and Daoists, whose temples and monasteries owned large tracts of land, would not take part in productive labor. When Buddhism and Daoism prospered, the temples became wealthy, adversely influencing the income of the imperial courts. One of the main reasons for the repeated suppression of Buddhism and Daoism by the emperors of the Tang and the Northern and Southern Song dynasties was economic contradictions, leading them to confiscate temple lands and force the monks and nuns to go back to secular life. Some rulers, while supporting religion, set limits on the number of persons allowed to become monks.

4. The rulers of every dynasty have shown religious tolerance, avoiding religious wars, resulting in an assimilation of all religions.

To protect the benefits of life in this world, our traditional culture has emphasized ethical relationships rather than looking ahead to an illusory world of ghosts and gods. This ideological tradition with its stress on the here and now is characteristic of the Han culture and affects Chinese religions. The sayings "never go to the temple for nothing," and "embrace Buddha's feet when you have a need" are vivid examples. Most people think they can pray to any of the gods, spirits, and supernatural beings when they need their protection.

There has never been a "national religion" in China, and the rulers have always followed a policy of tolerance toward all religions. Daoism is our native religion, while Buddhism, Islam, Nestorianism, and Manicheanism were imported from India and the West during the Han and Tang dynasties. The Chinese rulers treated them all impartially and did not drive them out. The city of Chang'an became the center for the interflow of Asian religions and the exchange of scriptures during the Tang dynasty.

There have been disputes among the different religions at times in our history, but they always reflected struggles between social groups or different blocs inside the ruling class. Assimilation among religions and between religions and Chinese traditional culture has been widespread. There was even the phenomenon of the "integration of three religions"—Confucianism, Buddhism, and Daoism, at one time.

Catholic and Protestant Christianity were partially inculturated in the course of their expansion into China. The Jewish people, who have scattered to the four corners of the world in the past two thousand years, always hold onto their Jewish religious traditions. But today, the distinct characteristics of their religion and nationality can scarcely be seen among the descendants of the Jews who long ago moved to Kaifeng in China, as they merge with Chinese culture. This unique phenomenon is worthy of speculation, as it may not be unrelated to the policy of tolerance of the imperial dynasties.

Of course the tolerance of the rulers is limited at the point where it touches on their own benefits as rulers, or threatens the official ideology. The historical coexistence and fusion of Confucianism, Buddhism, and Daoism was due to the assimilation of Confucianism by the other two religions, which was the reason that they all could coexist for so long. By the end of the Ming dynasty, when the Jesuit missionaries first arrived in China, they were welcomed by Chinese officialdom because they could adapt to Confucian ideology and Chinese rites. But when the Pope would not allow Chinese Catholics to participate in the Confucian rites and sacrifices to ancestors, the Kangxi Emperor issued the order banishing those missionaries who opposed the rites. The Yongzheng Emperor continued the policy of coexistence among Buddhism, Daoism, and Confucianism. At that time some people "asked that tonsure be banned, temples be changed into schools, and monks be banned with reason, even requiring that monks marry nuns to increase the population." The Yongzheng Emperor rejected all these requests, saying that "these preposterous ideas would result in confusion." He held that these three religions "all had different external characteristics but were similar in their inner essence . . . with the same purpose of leading people to be good." However, he still banned the Catholic missionaries who opposed the Chinese rites. The antiforeign movement of later years also reflected the rejection of foreign influence, thought, and customs. Yet, because of the traditional attitude of tolerance in China, there has never been armed conflict among our nation's religions, as occurred during the "wars of religion" in Europe.

5. The religious notions of the Han Chinese have long remained at the primitive stage, such as popular beliefs in gods and ghosts, fatalism, superstition, and ancestor worship.

Beliefs in ghosts and gods and worship of supernatural beings appeared early in the Yin and Zhou dynasties. As society developed, there were different categories of gods and ghosts, and some tribal chiefs and heroes were venerated as gods after their death. People offered sacrifices to their souls in the hope that the "hero's soul" would protect their tribal interests, just as they had done before they died. After the patriarchal clan system based on kinship relationships was formed, people worshipped their ancestors, both for their protection and out of fear of punishment by their spirits. Along with the notion of "heaven" and "Supreme Being" (*di*) came the idea of the "mandate of heaven" (fate).

These primitive concepts about gods, ghosts, and worship were quite popular. In the long course of Chinese feudal society, they intermingled with the patriarchal ideology of venerating [respecting] "heaven, earth, monarch, parent, and master," remaining static, without growth or change. These concepts are common in a religious, idealist world outlook, and they could have been the ideological soil for further development of religion. But these concepts hindered religious development, because the people were satisfied with the protection given by the spirits of their ancestors, and their notions about personality were suppressed. The people's belief in "do your best and obey fate" and "everything is predestined'' also held back the development of the Buddhist idea of ''cause-and-effect retribution,'' and the paradise and hell of the Catholics and Protestants. We have discovered in our investigations that some people believe that everything is determined by fate, so what use is there to pray to Buddha or believe in Jesus? This is one of the main reasons that Han Chinese religious believers have always been few in number.

6. Because of social and economic differences, the religious characteristics of our ethnic minority nationalities are different from those of the Han Chinese.

First, the whole population of minority nationality groups believes in the same religion. For example, among the members of a dozen minority nationalities, such as the Hui and Uyghur, almost all are Muslims. Almost all Tibetans and Mongolians believe in Tibetan Buddhism. All the Dai people believe in Hinayana Buddhism, and other minority nationalities have their own primitive religions. The proportion of religious believers among the Han Chinese is small, and they believe in various religions.

Second, religion is closely connected to nationality questions. Religious belief, fused with traditional customs, forms part of their national culture and psychology. There have been, during the feudal period, instances where politics and religion of some minority nationalities were merged, and some still consider their temples as symbols of their national identity. Although the religions of the Han Chinese are a component of their traditional culture, they are not so closely combined with culture, customs, and psychology as among the minority nationalities.

Third, religion plays a large social function. Religion, among the minority nationalities, always plays an integral role in traditional spiritual civilization. Children's rudimentary knowledge usually begins by reading religious books in mosques and temples. Religious creeds, doctrines, and commandments form the common moral norms undergirding social life. The social function of religion among the Han Chinese is far less important than it is for the people of ethnic minorities.

To sum up, a great deal of information shows that, except for the ethnic minorities, religions have varied historical characteristics in China. This is quite different from countries where there is a ''national religion'' or a government where religion and politics are integrated. These characteristics are also quite different from nineteenth-century Prussia, where Marx and Engels lived, and from czarist Russia in the early twentieth century.

The period when Marx and Engels began to develop their revolutionary theories was ''the year 1840, after orthodox pietism and absolutist feudal reaction ascended the throne with Frederick William IV'' (''Feuerbach and the End of German Classical Philosophy,'' in *Selected Works of Marx and Engels*, 4:216). When the bourgeois revolution began in Europe, this Prussian king tried hard to turn back the wheel of history. As Engels said in 1842, ''when, in the name of 'realizing a Christian nation,' the ruler concentrated the supreme power of both the nation and the church in his own hands, this earthly god reached the highest peak of a religious nation'' (*Complete Works of Marx and Engels*, 1:537–38).

Therefore, in the year 1843, Marx stated clearly that "as far as Germany is concerned, the critique of religion is prerequisite to the critique of everything else" (ibid., p. 1). He meant that in Germany the religious cloak of the ruler had to be stripped off before the profound, revolutionary critique of its reactionary political essence could be carried out.

The czarist Russia of the early twentieth century, in similar fashion, made the Russian Orthodox Church its official, that is, national, religion. "The church relies on the state, just like a peasant serf, and the citizens rely on the state church, just as peasant serfs do. The law of the medieval religious courts (a law that even today is listed in the criminal law and code of our country) is still in effect. This kind of law investigates a person's religious belief, destroys his conscience, and links official position and salary with the bad wine of the state church." This is what Lenin disclosed in 1905, "that shameful, cursed phenomenon" that existed in Russia at that time (*Complete Works of Lenin*, 10:63–64). The leaders of the Russian church, a special social ruling stratum that enjoyed feudal privileges, continuously changed their strategies for confronting the revolutionary tide that even then was surging upward. These Russian Orthodox leaders still held their hostile attitude toward the Soviet regime even after the victory of the October Revolution.

The situation in our country is obviously different. Our traditional official ideology was not religious, but based on concepts of the Confucian patriarchal ritual ethic. In our nation, "the prerequisite for criticism of everything else" is not the "critique of religion," but the critique of feudal patriarchal ritual ideology. The May Fourth Movement used the slogan "Down with the Confucian Shop!" to open the way for a new democratic revolution. Religions in China have been used and manipulated by reactionary ruling classes, but they were not closely tied to reactionary regimes as was the Russian Orthodox Church. Moreover, some religious leaders, under the oppression of reactionary rule and foreign aggressors, could even ally themselves with the revolutionary camp. Religious believers are only a minority of the Chinese people, and no religion (except in the areas of the minority nationalities) has ever been able to take control of political power. Therefore, in our country there has never been a time when religion could influence the political situation. Our religions were restricted by various traditional cultural and psychological factors; therefore, even with "support," they never developed to the stage of "overflow." This describes our national situation. If we are to study the laws that govern the existence and change of religion in our country, we must base our work on reality.

The Status of Religion on the Eve of Liberation

Incomplete data give the following figures for the number of religious believers and places of worship on the eve of Liberation. There were about 40,000 Buddhist temples and monasteries among the Han Chinese, with 500,000 monks and nuns and uncounted numbers of practicing Buddhist laypersons, both men and women. In addition, there were about 4,600,000 Buddhists among the minority nationalities. There are no statistics for Daoist temples and believers. Ten ethnic minority nationalities, with a total population of 8,000,000, were Muslims. The Christians included 3,000,000 Catholics, with 15,000 churches in about 140 Catholic dioceses, and 700,000 Protestants among seventy Protestant denominations, large and small, with 121 foreign mission societies (of which half were American), and about 20,000 churches. Orthodox Christians were mainly Russians residing in China, with few Chinese members.

1. The misery of old China was the soil on which religion proliferated.

The people could barely survive in semicolonial, semifeudal old China, with internal and external troubles, frequent wars, and natural and man-made disasters. Religion was an expression of and protest against these very real sufferings. Here is a typical example as recorded by a foreign missionary:

> A poor illiterate farmer named Chai was dispossessed of a piece of land on high ground by a rich man who built a tomb on it. Chai destroyed the tomb and was imprisoned for it. [When he was released] he again destroyed the tomb, which had been rebuilt, and this time he was placed in shackles. He was in despair. The sense of wrong suffered goaded him to madness. He refused to have his hair cut and went about the prison yard looking like a maniac. He declared that he would wear the garb of mourning until the end of his days unless he got his case redressed. . . .
>
> He escaped and lived as an outcast for some time, venturing home in the dead of night.
>
> The wronged and wretched outcast one evening wandered by a [Christian] chapel where a native evangelist was preaching. In the course of his discourse he frequently spoke of the "living God in heaven." . . . Chai was stirred to the depths of his soul and, filled with unspeakable joy, soon declared himself a believer. He now went to a barber and had his head shaved and took pains to make his shabby clothes appear as respectable as possible.
>
> His few friends were naturally astonished at the change. "You have shaved and dressed yourself again. Have you got back your land?"
>
> "Oh, no," he replied, "but I have found something worth a myriad farms. I have found the living God and his Son Jesus Christ, and am an heir to possessions worth more than the whole world."(Price, *Christian Missions and Oriental Civilizations* [Shanghai, 1924], pp. 386–87; quoted in Bantry et al., *Well-Known Chinese Christians*, pp. 25–27)

Buddhism thrives in the Zhoushan region. Putuo Mountain, located on an island, is one of the four most famous Buddhist mountains. Buddhism is popular among the many fishermen who earn their living in the waters around the Zhoushan islands. This, as an influence on their daily lives and work, cannot be separated from factors related to nature and society. Before Liberation there was a saying, "There are three swords hanging over the heads of fishermen: pirates, merchant tyrants, and storms at sea." Oppressed by the forces of nature and other evil forces, the fishermen could not be masters of their own fate. When they went to sea, they were vulnerable to the whims of nature. Before Liberation, it is said, the death rate of strong fishermen in the prime of life, because of the perils of the sea, was as high as 75 percent. Therefore, fishermen always prayed, asking for Buddha's protection before setting out to sea. Some even offered whole pigs as a sacrifice. Those who could not afford that would offer the head or the tail of a pig as a token. Family members prayed earnestly for their kinsmen while they were at sea. When they returned with the fruits of their labor, they would be plundered by pirates or exploited by merchant tyrants. For these reasons it is still quite common for many people in the Zhoushan region to pray for Buddha's protection and to believe in retribution. Moreover, not a few of these people become monks or nuns. When husbands are lost at sea, wives think this was predestined [fate], so they shave their heads and accumulate virtue by living the hard, disciplined life of a nun, praying for happiness in the next life.

Guanyin is the most popular Buddha in China. There are statues of Guanyin, large and small, in many temples around the country. Some have specially built halls for Guanyin, called "Great Mercy Pavilion," "Guanyin Pavilion," and so on. Guanyin can also have different names, such as the "Buddha in White," "Buddha of the South Seas," "Buddha of Merciful Navigation," "Great Mercy Guanyin," and the like. Guanyin, in the hearts of believers, is the "Buddha of infinite mercy who helps the needy and relieves the distressed." One who is in distress has only to say her name and Buddha will follow the sound of his voice to bring relief. Therefore, the number of worshippers of Guanyin surpasses even those of Buddha Sakyamuni. In Zhoushan, where fishermen suffered so grievously, Putuo Mountain has become a center for rites to Guanyin, and it is not accidental that more pilgrims make their way there than to any of the other well-known holy places. Facts have shown that the sufferings in society before Liberation provided the rich soil on which religion germinated and grew.

In old China, all religions were engaged in charitable works. These good works broadened religious influence. Before Liberation, because of their poverty, many parents gave their babies to Catholic foundling hospitals or orphanages. Due to the poor management of these charitable institutions, the death rate of the babies was quite high; but still a good many orphans grew up in a Catholic environment, married, and had families—orphanage Catholics. For example, among the Catholics belonging to the nationally known Xujiahui Cathedral in Shanghai, one-fourth were men or women who had grown up in Catholic orphanages and lived in the Wuditou and Tangjiexi districts.

Medical services provided by churches were also a means of attracting poor people with health problems. Sermons were preached in church hospitals and clinics during the treatment of patients, and quite a few of the patients were converted. According to the report in the second issue of *Shengjiao* (Holy religion) magazine in 1932, "every day five or six hundred patients" sought treatment in a corner of Yangshupu district, Shanghai, where Franciscan Catholic

Sisters treated patients and handed out medicines. "The fathers preached" in the Hongkou Church and "quite a few" persons were converted.

Other than working people, there were a number of intellectuals in old China who plunged into the embrace of religion when they felt depressed and hesitated at the crossroads because of the darkness of society. There were also people who, believing that only religion could reform society and people's hearts, put forth slogans such as "moral character will save the nation." Their activities could not change the dark reality of the old society, but their indignation and concern for the people and the world expressed their discontent with society as it was.

In semicolonial and semifeudal old China, peasants and poor people who were heavily oppressed had a powerful spirit of revolt. Before guidance in progressive revolutionary ideas was available, they frequently used religious ideology as their banner of rebellion, with religious organization as the network. The Taiping Heavenly Kingdom movement is an example. Hong Xiuquan got his ideas from the pamphlet, "Good Words Exhorting the Age," a Christian tract preaching that people should worship God, and that, since all human beings are children of God, all men are equal and should "enjoy everlasting happiness" in the "Heavenly Kingdom." Hong opposed idol worship, saying all persons should worship God. He regarded all idols as monsters and all rulers as "*yama*" [Kings of Hell]. "The whole world as one family enjoying everlasting peace" would be realized only after these monsters were exterminated. He maintained that all persons were equal, saying, "God, the Heavenly Father, is for everyone; how can emperors hold power only for themselves?" and "All men are brothers, dear children in the eyes of God." These ideas became the call to arms, mobilizing peasants for attacks on the monsters who represented all feudal powers. Hong Xiuquan also organized the sluggish peasants into the Society of God Worshippers. The total number of [Protestant] Christians at that time in the whole country was about 1,400, but the Society of God Worshippers grew from several hundred into the Taiping Army, which was said to number one million. Certain Christian doctrines thus formed the banner for a mammoth peasant uprising.

2. The reactionary ruling class controlled and made use of religion.

Despite the fact that religion played different roles under different conditions among various social groups, its pessimistic teachings about this world and about a life hereafter, and its ideas about fatalism and the will of God played into the hands of the ruling class who always controlled religion, propping it up and using it to consolidate their rule.

Throughout feudal society, the rulers supported and promoted Buddhism and Daoism. For example, from the end of the Tang dynasty through the Song, Yuan, Ming, and Qing, its temples were built and maintained at the expense of the national treasury, the so-called Five Dynasties Beneficence. Puji Temple, the largest on the mountain, was built with funds granted by the Shengzong Emperor of the Song dynasty. Because of these imperial grants, these islands all became temple property and were exempted from paying the royal tax. Putuo Mountain became the "Buddhist Kingdom by the Sea" and enjoyed political privileges under the rule of the temple.

During the thirty to forty years following the 1911 Revolution, many warlords, bureaucrats, politicians, traitors, and leading Guomindang [KMT] figures claimed they were Buddhist converts and used Buddhism to cover up their reactionary nature. Although he was a Christian, Chiang Kai-shek tried every means to rope in the Buddhist leadership. Buddhist leaders, supported by the KMT, held a news conference at the Bilu Temple in Nanjing following the victory over Japan, where they announced plans to reorganize Buddhism by registering temples and believers and encouraging Buddhists to take part in politics, to spread Buddhist teachings among the people, and to reform society. In fact, what they really wanted was for Buddhism to serve the reactionary rule of the KMT. There had been other monks before who had been led on by the reactionary government to preach Buddhism to political prisoners in the hope that they would become obedient to the KMT.

Before Liberation, Daoism was also closely linked with the ruling classes and always supported by warlords and the KMT government. The Quanzhen Daoist sect held the "Fang Jie" (a Daoist ceremony) six times in the years following the 1911 Revolution. Those who lent their support included Li Yuanhong, Chang Jinhui, and a number of provincial governors, generals, and other officials. In 1944, to curry favor with Japan during the military invasion, a ceremony, "Prayers for a Sure Victory in the Holy War," was held at the Taiqing Temple in Shenyang [Manchuria], including such nonsense as, "Our close neighbor, the Japanese empire, spares no expense to fight and bleed in order to spread oriental justice, and the works of Laozi and Zhuangzi are holy books of oriental justice." They even hoped to follow the iron heels of the Japanese invaders and "propagate Laozi and Zhuangzi everywhere, both east and west." Some Daoists in Shanghai and elsewhere, aided and abetted by traitors, organized such reactionary activities as "mourning over dead Chinese and Japanese officers and soldiers," "mourning over Wang Jingwei [a puppet official]," and so on.

The main source of funds for Chinese Buddhist and Daoist temples in the past was exploitation of their lands. The big temples among the Han Chinese usually owned large tracts of land which provided more than half their total income. For example, one of the four great temples, the Jinshan Temple at Zhengjiang, Jiangsu, had more than 10,000 mu of land before Liberation, scattered in Taizhou, Yizheng, Yangzhong, and other counties. A great deal of land was owned by the several temples on Jinhua Mountain, one of China's four most famous Buddhist mountains. Four of them alone—Baisu, Zhiyuan, Ganlu, and Dantanlin—owned more than 4,000 mu of land in three provinces—Jiangsu, Zhejiang, and Anhui. Huacheng Temple had land spread across Anhui and Jiangsu provinces. Legend has it that the Tianning Temple at Changzhou, one of the four big temples south of the Yangzi River, had more than 10,000 mu of land at its peak of prosperity. Besides land in four townships of Wujing County, this temple also owned land that was rented out in Yixing, Jintan, Kunshan, Changsu, Wuxian, and other places. Some of the temple properties were given by the rulers in various dynasties; some were taken over by temples with the support of the rulers; some were purchased at very low prices; and some were donated by Buddhist believers. The temples usually bought land from the peasants at very low prices. The Tianning Temple of Changzhou bought land from the peasants at the time of the 1911 Revolution for prices ranging from 5,000 to 10,000 coppers per mu. Some peasants mortgaged their land (meaning they could redeem the land when they had money), but when they could not pay the rice rent or interest, the land became "dead"; even if they should have money to redeem it at a later time, they could not. Although the land rents charged by the temples, 200 jin of rice per mu, were quite heavy, the peasants had to pay that much, no matter whether their harvests were good or poor. Sometimes their rice was seized while it was still in the fields unharvested. Some peasants' homes were even searched for rice to pay the land rents. A struggle against excessive rents broke out in 1927 and continued for several years in protest against the cruel rents charged by the Tianning Temple. Some temples located in big cities also made money by lending at high interest rates or from building rents.

Tibetan Buddhism in the past was closely linked to the system of feudal slavery, a [theocratic] system of "integrating politics and religion" under the joint dictatorship of monks and aristocrats. The leading figures of Tibetan Buddhism throughout dynastic history were the large slaveowners, who concurrently held local political power. The supreme ruling power of the three Tibetan feudal lords was held in the name of the god Buddha. They could make, interpret, and implement the law, based on Buddhist doctrines and the "will of the god Buddha." Temples could use their religious privileges to control the courts, prisons, and armed forces. The degree of feudal exploitation by Tibetan Buddhism, which owned large areas of land and many slaves, was more extensive than that of Buddhist temples and monasteries among the Han Chinese. Due to the rigid hierarchy of ranks inside the temples, ordinary monks were totally powerless, virtually slaves. But lamas in the upper ranks enjoyed feudal privileges, imposing heavy exploitation on their subordinate lamas and farm slaves. Farm slaves rented land from the temples and were required to turn in as much as half of the harvest or more. The temples and monasteries also owned a great number of livestock which were cared for by slave shepherds, who each year were required to turn in a high percentage of their product. The temples and monasteries were the greatest usurers in Tibet. For example, data show that the total amount of barley loaned out by the three big temples at Lhasa (Zhebeng, Sela, Gandan) was as much as 1,430,000 ke (one ke is about twenty-five jin), while silver loaned out at interest amounted to 990,000 chen, the equivalent of about 14,780,000 silver dollars.

Besides this, the temples and monasteries practiced another form of exploitation through charging fees for dispensing of religious services to the believers.

High-ranking lamas also used their wealth and feudal privileges to oppress and insult their subordinates, even to the point of persecuting and killing some.

As the religion of a minority nationality, Islam was always politically oppressed, manipulated, and utilized by the Han ruling classes; and, particularly in regions where they lived together as an ethnic community, it was also controlled by their own ruling class. The Yuan dynasty rulers used the upper-class Muslims to consolidate their political control. Qing dynasty rulers, on the one hand, cruelly suppressed the Muslim uprisings and, on the other hand, controlled and manipulated the Islamic mosques, requiring that the mosques in the Northwest keep their believers under control and prevent further uprisings. By the end of the Ming dynasty, some of the Muslim sects in the Northwest where Muslims lived together in their own communities were integrated into the feudal system, forming *menhuan*. The head of the menhuan, called the *jiaozhu*, was acknowledged by believers, who gave him absolute obedience, as the one who would lead them into paradise. The tombs built for the jiaozhu in the Muslim cemetery were called *gongbei*; believers had to worship and recite scriptures at these tombs. The jiaozhu, who appointed his subordinate imams (*ahongs*), ruled over many mosques. He used the money contributed by the faithful to buy land and livestock and to set up ranches and businesses, and he generally became the wealthiest man in the area.

The position of jiaozhu was hereditary, passing from father to son, which resulted in the accrual of feudal privileges and power. Muslims who belonged to the menhuan had to farm the land or mind the livestock of the jiaozhu, creating a heavy economic burden. In addition to farming and serving the jiaozhu, they had to take part in various services to honor the dead in the jiaozhu's family, not only giving money, provisions, firewood, and fodder, but also losing time that should have been used for their own productive work. They were heavily exploited.

After the 1911 Revolution, some warlords in the Northwest used the local Muslim sect to serve their reactionary rule. Another sect served Chiang Kai-shek by spreading anti-Communist propaganda. In 1949, a few Muslim reactionaries engaged in counterrevolutionary activities, secretly accepting orders from the Guomindang on Taiwan and setting up "Independence Branch Units" in Gansu, Ningxia, and Qinghai provinces to carry out counterrevolutionary subversive activities. They were wiped out by the People's Liberation Army.

Catholic and Protestant Christianity entered China on a large scale after the Opium War. At that time they were closely related to the Western colonial powers. The earliest [Protestant] missionary to China was Morrison, a British staff person for the East India Company, which specialized in the opium trade. While preaching and translating the Bible, he bruited the idea of "consular jurisdiction," and later he became a deputy consul for Britain to China. This is sufficient evidence to show the close relationship between the colonialists and missionaries. Morrison's son later joined the British invasion army and took part in drafting the first of the unequal treaties, the Treaty of Nanjing, in 1842. Parker, one of the first American missionaries to China, took part in the signing of the first of the unequal treaties between America and China, the "Treaty of Wangxia" of 1844. Later, Parker became an American envoy to China.

A number of other missionaries participated in signing various unequal treaties in the hundred or more years after Morrison and Parker, some putting forth suggestions for exterminating China. For example, at the end of the nineteenth century, the British missionary, Timothy Richard, interfered, on the one hand, with the "constitution reform movement" and, on the other hand, suggested to high officials, such as Li Hongzhang and Zhang Zhidong, that certain departments of the Qing government be placed under the control of foreign countries, attempting to demote China to the status of a British colony, like India and Egypt. Another British missionary, Hudson Taylor, the founder of the "China Inland Mission," advocated ensnaring people by handing out relief assistance after natural calamities in order to quench the resistance of the Chinese people aroused by the British invasions. He said, "Through calamities, God gives us good opportunities to show what the British have done for the good of China."

A number of missionaries served colonialism, and the forces of colonialism supported missionary work with their armed might. Article 17 of the Treaty of Wangxia stipulated that missionaries had the right to establish churches and to buy land in the five commercial ports. Other countries competed for these same rights. Missionaries were still not allowed to go into the interior of China, but the French Catholic missionary, Chapdelaine, entered Guangxi Province without authorization and was later arrested [and killed] by the local government. France started the second Opium War under the pretext of the "Father Chapdelaine Incident." As a result, the "Treaty of Tianjin" and "Treaty of Beijing" stipulated that missionaries were allowed to go into the interior to preach and would be "free to rent or buy land and to set up churches." Prior to that, Article 29 of the "Treaty of Tianjin between China and the United States" said that China "should protect all preachers and believers, and should not interfere with them." Article 13 of the "Tianjin Treaty between China and France" stipulated that "local officials should provide good treatment and protection for those missionary preachers who go into the interior with proper identification papers."

Under protection of the unequal treaties, foreign missionaries could go deep into the interior, traveling where they wished and ignoring Chinese laws. They could even give orders to Chinese officials. Missionaries could set up churches anywhere, putting up signs that said, "X [name] Church of Great Britain," or "X Church of the United States," paying no heed to the local government. Even the prime minister of the Qing dynasty was forced to admit that "It's just like so many independent enemy countries here in our country" (Fan Wenlan in *Chinese Modern History*, vol. 1, book 1, p. 348).

As a result of the highhanded treatment by missionaries and some Chinese Christians, the people's hatred was aroused, resulting in many "missionary legal cases.'' The Western powers made use of these missionary cases to demand large sums in reparation, and more privileges. The Boxer Uprising of 1900, which followed the earlier missionary cases, was the most widespread explosion of the anti-imperialism movement. The spears of the peasant insurgents were directed against the imperialist powers who had made use of religion to invade China. The Boxer Movement was defeated because of the combined forces of the Western powers and the treasonous surrender of the Qing government. The Western powers took advantage of the situation to force the Qing government to sign the ''Treaty of 1900,'' which was a national humiliation.

After the May Fourth Movement [1919], the anti-imperialist, anti-feudalist struggle of the Chinese people entered a new stage, and after the birth of the Chinese Communist Party, the revolutionary movement daily surged to higher levels. The imperialists speeded up their support for the anti-Communist and anti-people activities of the comprador bourgeoisie so they could hold onto their rule. Religion was still one of their important tools. Three of the four big families (Chiang, Soong, Kong) that ruled over old China had close relations with Christianity. Chiang Kai-shek was baptized and joined the Christian church in Shanghai in 1930. According to Chiang's official biography, *The Personal Lives of the Generalissimo and His Wife*, ''his conversion to Christianity was a political act which came through the influence of his mother-in-law and his wife'' (taken from ''Examples of How American Imperialists Made Use of Religion,'' in *Patriotic Movements in Christian Circles*). By becoming a Christian, Chiang Kai-shek tried to strengthen his ties with the American ruling group, the principal foreign supporters of Christianity. A number of American missionaries shouted at the tops of their voices that Chiang Kai-shek was the only leader of China.

Chiang Kai-shek employed a staff man from the Christian YMCA to head up his ''New Life Movement.'' Once, while giving instructions to his subordinates, Chiang said: ''In carrying out the 'New Life Movement,' contact the local YMCA where there is one, or the church where there is no YMCA.'' He believed that the program would suffer ''heavy loss if we don't make use of'' the YMCA and the church (quoted from ''Condemn American Imperialism which Makes Use of Reformism Inside the YMCA to Invade China,'' Wu Yaozong in *Wenhuibao*, July 20, 1951).

The Vatican supported all Chinese reactionary regimes. When Chiang Kai-shek set up the ''Nationalist government'' in 1927, the Vatican was the first to cable its diplomatic recognition, ordering Chinese Catholics to ''respect and obey'' this government. When Japanese militarists triggered the September 18 [1931] Incident and occupied the three northeastern provinces of China, setting up a puppet regime in Manchuria on March 9, 1932, the Vatican granted it diplomatic recognition on March 9, 1934. In October 1938, Pope Pius XI wrote a letter to the puppet emperor of Manchuria, saying that ''Catholics are not willing to lag behind in rendering their patriotic respect and obedience to the state power" (*Journal of the Paris Foreign Mission Society*, no. 206, 1938, pp. 118–19).

At the height of the War of Resistance against Japan, Zanin, the apostolic delegate in China, ordered Chinese Catholics "to lean neither to the right nor the left" during the conflict, and to show as much kindness toward the enemies of China as to the Chinese people (*Gongjiao jiaoyu*, May 1939, p. 434). The Catholic bishop of the Shanghai diocese held a large "memorial mass" for the Japanese invasion army and the puppet troops of Wang Jingwei in the Yangjingbin Cathedral in October 1942. Some Christians claimed that "China has reached the life and death crisis point. . . . Every Chinese must confess his sins" (*Guonanzhongdi xinxi*). In Beiping [Beijing], which was controlled by the Japanese, there were even preachers who used religious doctrines to support the criminal acts of the enemy; an article in a religious magazine said, "Those who have done harm to us are simply passing on the [bitter] cup for God" (referring to those who fulfill God's will); "Not only do we not hate them, we thank them" (*Spiritual Food Quarterly*, Winter 1944), and so forth.

Catholic and Protestant reactionaries always regarded the Communist Party as the fierce enemy of the church and slandered the Communists, saying they "scorned their fathers, superiors [*jun*], and the five human relationships." *Suggestions for Prayers* (February 1932), a publication endorsed by the Vatican, in its main topic, "Exterminate the Communists in China," called on "all believers to pray for the extermination of the Communists" (*Sacred Heart*, no. 2, 1932, p. 38). The American pastor Gongside [translit.] early in the Anti-Japanese War preached "Heavenly Kingdomism" to fight against Communism in China. And the American Cardinal Spellman, during a visit to China, while speaking at a welcome dinner given by the mayor of Beiping [Beijing], went so far as to say that the Communists were the "devil incarnate," and that the United States should "suppress the rebellion." Leighton Stuart, who had been preaching religion in China for many years when he was appointed American ambassador to China, spared no effort in following the American policy of supporting Chiang Kai-shek against Communism. In July 1947 he instigated the leaders of the National Christian Council of China to go to Nanjing to encourage Chiang Kai-shek and tell him that the Christians trusted him and were willing to help him. Chiang said that he hoped that Protestant Christians would clearly express their support for the "general mobilization for suppressing the rebellion," just as the Catholics had done. Price, the American missionary who had been an adviser to Chiang, published an article in September 1948 entitled "The Challenge of Communism to Democratic Christianity," in which he called on the people to "use Christian renewal of the heart [*gexin*] to cope with Communism's revolution [*geming*], and to use Christian [communal] sharing to cope with Communism's sharing of property."

An atmosphere of fear and anti-Communism swept throughout Catholic and Protestant Christianity on the eve of Liberation, spreading such rumors as "religion will be wiped out in the liberated areas,'' and that priests and Sisters would be persecuted, and Protestant pastors ''nailed to crosses.'' Some Christians shouted at the tops of their voices that ''the last days were coming.'' One Protestant sect, proclaiming that ''World War III would soon break out, and that would be the end of world civilization,'' published American books in Chinese, such as, *The Atom Bomb and the End of the World* and *The Last Page of History*, selling as many as 100,000 copies. Their position was that the mission of the church ''was not to change the government, but to change the hearts of the people; not to resist imperialism or to support democracy, but to preach the gospel everywhere on earth.''

A reactionary leader of another Protestant sect in 1948 plotted secretly ''to put down the revolution by preaching the gospel'' and stirred up believers to go into the streets and to ''parade in white clothing,'' preaching that the great affliction was just ahead. Just prior to the crossing of the Yangzi River by the PLA, he incited believers to pray that ''God would make the Yangzi River the demarcation line and prevent the Communist Party from crossing, and that if they tried to cross, they would all be drowned, just as the Bible said that Pharaoh's army drowned in the Red Sea.''

In addition to anti-Communist sentiment stirred up inside the Catholic church, an organization of armed counterrevolutionary spies appeared. After the victory in the Anti-Japanese War, a Belgian Catholic priest, de Jaegher [Lei Zhengyuan], set up the ''Church National Salvation Youth Corps'' in North China, enlarging its scope and activities from 1946 to 1948. This youth corps repeatedly contacted the ''Command Headquarters of the Eleventh War Zone,'' the highest Guomindang unit in North China, the ''Beiping Field Headquarters,'' and the ''North China Bandit Suppression Headquarters.'' Under their command, this youth corps received financial aid and direction for organizing counterrevolutionary armed units. In July 1947 this corps, plotting with Catholic priests and bishops in Zhengding and Shijiazhuang, organized more than five hundred Catholics into local units and stirred up trouble in the Zhengding liberated area, one time even occupying the city and setting fires; they also robbed, raped, and looted in the countryside, and provided important intelligence information for Guomindang air bombing of the liberated area.

These facts about ways in which the religions were supported, controlled, and used by imperialism and the domestic reactionary ruling classes have shown that in the semicolonial and semifeudal old China, religion as a social force was closely related to the ruling classes and to the political struggles of society. Religion played a large, negative role as it was used by imperialism and domestic reactionary ruling classes.

3. A patriotic tradition existed among religious circles in modern China.

In old China there were numerous reactionary elements in religious circles who threw in their lot with imperialist and feudal forces. Nevertheless, during the past hundred years, there were also a number of knowledgeable leaders who, complying with historical trends and the demands of progressive patriotic religious believers, joined the patriotic movement in opposition to foreign invasion, and the movement to reform society and save the country. This is related to certain aspects of our history and to the complex contradictions in our society.

First, no religion has ever been in a ruling political position, nor has there ever been an integration of religion and politics as occurred in European history. Most of our religious leaders attached themselves in some degree to reactionary regimes, but concurrently they maintained their relative independence. They were both afraid of and unhappy with those regimes. Many religious leaders had links with middle-level and lower-level religious believers, and, through these contacts with social reality, were aware of the demands of the masses of the people. Quite a few of them sympathized with, supported, and even took part in activities opposing reactionary rule.

Second, by adopting a policy of supporting and making use of religion, the KMT regime was no different from earlier ones, causing conflicts between the KMT political powers and some religious leaders. The KMT issued successive sets of regulations controlling and restricting temples and monasteries. Those who violated the regulations would be "expelled from the temples or taken to court." The regulations placed temple properties under the control of local officials, giving opportunities for local warlords, politicians, and tyrants to occupy the temples, which often happened. Some warlords seized and occupied temple properties and even sold them to supply their troops. Some of the buildings of the Shaolin Temple in Henan Province, which was the earliest location of Chan (Zen) Buddhism, burned to the ground after being set afire by warlords.

Most temples and monasteries on the eve of Liberation were in disrepair. The KMT, while manipulating Islam and roping in its upper circles, suppressed and massacred Muslims who were opposed to their rule. In the two or three years following 1928, Muslims at Hezhou (Gansu Province) were repeatedly slaughtered. Later, Muslims in Cangxian and Yuanshan, Hebei Province, and Geping in northern Shandong Province were frequently robbed and killed by soldiers of reactionary warlords. Reactionary troops occupied mosques and ate pork there, even in some cases destroying the mosques. Many incidents of profanation of religion occurred. The violent Haigu Muslim uprising was triggered by Guomindang troops under Chen Cheng who, under the pretext of recruiting soldiers, extorted money, forced Muslim recruits to eat pork, and assaulted women. More than 20,000 Muslims took part in the uprising.

Third, Catholic and Protestant churches gained ground under the umbrella of the aggression of the colonial powers. This aroused the opposition of the masses, resulting in numerous religious legal cases. Using these cases for their own advantage, foreign powers increased their aggression. All this greatly upset those believers who had a strong national sensitivity. They hoped that the church could free itself from foreign influence and control, and that they could be freed of the opprobrium attached to sarcastic name-calling like "believers in foreign religion'' and ''second-class foreigners.'' The internal struggle to free the church from foreign control began in the latter half of the nineteenth century, gaining force along with the growing patriotic, anti-imperialist people's movement.

Fourth, during the profound suffering of our country, most religious leaders shared the same fate as the masses of the people. When Japanese militarism invaded our country, churches, temples, and monasteries were destroyed by the enemy's guns, kinsmen were killed and wounded, normal life disappeared, and religious leaders, in varying degrees, threw themselves into resistance activities. Similarly, some leading Catholics and Protestants, because of sharp conflicts between Japan and certain American and European countries, were drawn into the anti-Japanese resistance.

Many facts from the history of the past hundred years show that there were always progressive religious persons in old China who were part of the patriotic anti-imperialist forces of the Chinese people.

First, informed Protestants and Catholics advocated getting rid of foreign control and took part in activities opposing the foreign invasion of China.

Early in the 1870s, there were a number of people inside the Protestant churches who had strong national awareness and believed that their church should be independent and self-managed. Chen Mengnan from Guangdong, a scholar, had studied the Bible and converted to Christianity. He held that since the teachings of Christ were the word of heaven, Chinese believers should have their own church so as not to be called a foreign religion. In 1873 he set up the ''Guangzhou Gospel Church of Eastern Guangdong,'' the first indigenous Chinese church.

After the failure of the anti-imperialist Boxer Movement, the resulting national humiliation was a strong stimulus to a number of patriotic Christians. Shanghai pastor Yu Guozheng was the first to oppose ''including the article on protection of religion in the unequal treaties.'' With powerful emotion, he said that ''evil people sought protection under religion, and that was the reason why so many religious law cases occurred . . . leading to the great humiliation of 1900.'' In 1903 he founded the Independent Presbyterian Church, and in 1906 the ''China Independent Jesus Church,'' advocating ''doing away with the protection of religions by the unequal treaties . . . and arousing churches and believers everywhere to strive to be independent, self-managing and self-propagating . . . and totally free of control by Western churches.'' The church's general regulations pointed out that ''this church was established because the members of various churches are greatly concerned about the gravity of the religious legal cases, are saddened by the acceleration of foreign invasion, and organize this church in order to change the situation with the idea of loving both one's nation and one's religion, in the spirit of independence and self-government, hence the name, ''China Independent Jesus Church'' (*Annual Report of the Protestant Churches in China*, no. 11, 1931, pp. 92–94).

After the 1911 Revolution, and particularly during the First World War, the

Independent Church grew, and by 1920 it had spread to sixteen provinces. Besides this, a number of Christians in Shanghai, due to the religious legal case of 1902 in Zhengzhou, Henan, and the resulting "harsh compensation demanded by the Western government, proposed an independent Chinese Christian Church," winning responses from many people in many provinces. After the 1911 Revolution, the independence movement of patriotic believers also appeared in North China.

Along with the growing national and democratic revolutionary movement after the May Fourth Movement [1919], and particularly after the May 30 Massacre [1925], many patriotic religious people plunged into the mass movement to abolish the unequal treaties, protesting against imperialist aggression and advocating that the Chinese churches break away immediately from foreign missions and become independent. After the May 30 Massacre all of the members of the China Inland Mission church in Kaifeng said that they wanted to strive for the independence of the church in order to gain the "dignity of the nation, of the church and of the Christians." The Jieyang Church in Guangdong proclaimed that it would "break away from the British mission which was under the protection of the unequal treaties" and called for a self-governing church. In the Wenzhou region of Zhejiang Province, in addition to the China Independent Jesus Church, there were forty churches that broke away from the control of British missionaries. When a British missionary of the China Inland Mission gave false testimony after the May 30 Massacre, the indignant Chinese members of that church broke away and set up the Zhonghua Christian Church, later renamed the "New Fellowship of Shanghai Christians." In the wake of the victories of the Northern Expedition [1926–27], the independence movement of the Christian churches gained strength. For example, Christians in Xiangtan, Hunan Province, called for a "Movement for a Self-Governing Church," saying that "all the rights of the present Chinese church, that is, self-ownership, self-government, and self-enjoyment, should be transferred to Chinese Christians." The Hushan, Shunyou, and Yesu churches in Hangzhou joined together and organized an independent church that broke away from foreign missions. At that time there were more than six hundred independent churches in China.

The colonial powers made use of "divine authority" inside the Catholic church and exercised strict control over the believers. But there still were patriotic Catholics, such as Ma Xiangbo, who dared to stand up to the foreign missionaries. He founded Zhengdan, a church university, in Shanghai in 1903, giving great emphasis to patriotic education for the students. But he was opposed by Jesuit missionaries and was forced to leave Zhengdan. He then founded the Fudan Public School at Ligongci in the Xujiahui district of Shanghai (which later became Fudan University). He appointed Chinese as teachers and school administrators, thereby demonstrating his integrity as a Chinese and his protest against the Jesuit missionaries.

During the May Fourth Movement, Tianjin Catholics actively responded to the call for all Tianjin workers to go on strike. Catholics at Rencizhuang organized the first "National Salvation Church Corps," calling on compatriots in the church to "brace up and save the country . . . to give help to the whole nation" (*Tianjin Yishi Daily*, June 11, 1919). After that, other Tianjin churches organized similar units, bringing people from all walks of life together, participating in the patriotic anti-imperialism movement and going to the streets and the countryside, speaking and parading everywhere.

After the May Fourth Movement, patriotic students from the Catholic schools of Shanghai, such as Zhengdan College, the Shanghai Sino-French School, and the Xuhui Public School, participated in three strikes (walkouts from factories, schools, and markets). Patriotic students from Catholic schools in Beijing and Guangzhou also took part, in varying degrees, in the patriotic movement. When Japanese invaders attacked Jinan and slaughtered Chinese compatriots in May 1928, students from Catholic schools broke through the closed gates of their campuses and took to the streets in the patriotic struggle against the invaders. These accounts show the enthusiastic patriotism of the Catholics, particularly Catholic youth, at that time.

Second, patriotic religious people played an active role in the National Salvation Anti-Japanese Movement. They provided support for frontline troops, fought Japanese invaders, rescued wounded soldiers, helped refugees, and contributed to the victory in the War of Resistance.

In the 1930s the Japanese intensified their invasion of China, and patriots in the Christian YMCA joined the national salvation movement. They initiated singing activities in Shanghai, compiling, printing, and teaching songs about resistance to Japan and arousing the patriotic fervor of young people. They went into shops, factories, and schools to lead young people in singing these songs of national salvation. On June 6, 1936, more than five thousand young people at the public athletic field outside the west gate of Shanghai, led by Liu Liangmo, the YMCA secretary, in a great chorus of voices, expressed their determination to defend the motherland and fight to the death to avoid enslavement by another country.

After the outbreak of hostilities, patriotic members of all religions actively supported the war against Japan. A number of Christian organizations issued manifestoes calling on Christians to join in the war effort and halt the Japanese violence. Christian churches and organizations all over China organized refugee shelters, collected money, gave solace to the frontline fighters, rescued the wounded, and gave assistance to students and compatriots fleeing into the interior from occupied areas. The Christian patriot Dr. Liu Zhanen, president of Hujiang University, was murdered in Shanghai on April 7, 1938, by traitors and spies, because he took an active part in national salvation activities. He died a glorious death for the liberation of the Chinese nation.

The then president of the Buddhist Association, Yuan Ying, organized the monks into first-aid units in Shanghai, Hankou, and Ningbo. They rescued refugees and wounded in the battle zones under the rain of bullets and were called the "Enemies of the God of War." Yuan Ying also traveled to Singapore and Borneo to raise funds to support the War of Resistance, sending back to China large sums contributed by overseas Chinese. When arrested by Japanese military police he stood erect, never bowing his head.

Maoshan in Jiangsu, a famous Daoist scenic place, was a major base for the New Fourth Army. The army headquarters was located in the Daoist Quanyuan Temple. With the help of Chen Yi, patriotic Daoists, in the spirit of "we abandoned family life but not our country," plunged wholeheartedly into the fight to save their country. Some of them actually took part in armed fighting; others served as army guides, collected information, passed messages, cared for the sick and wounded, raised food and money, and so on. On August 13, 1939, Japanese militarists in retaliation burned down 90 percent of the Maoshan temples and killed twenty-four Daoist monks.

"Muslims, also, have responsibility for whether the nation will live or die." Muslims from the national minorities also rose up against the Japanese. For example, not long after the Lugouqiao Incident [July 7, 1937], Beiping Muslims organized the "Beiping Muslim Support Committee for Anti-Japanese Resistance." Together with other units, they went into the streets and lanes, giving out resistance propaganda. They organized a fund-raising corps, army comfort corps, nursing corps, and battle zone first-aid units. In February 1938, a "Chinese Muslims National Salvation Association" was organized and issued a "Resist Japan and Save the Nation" manifesto, calling for mobilization of the Muslim spirit of "courageous sacrifice and resolute unity" in the fight against the Japanese invaders, saying, "Be a foundation [stone] of religion, be a battlement for the nation." In these ways Muslims showed how they loved both their religion and their country.

In Gansu Province the Muslim anti-Japanese national salvation movement spread like a prairie fire. Muslims in Henan, Hubei, Hunan, Guangxi, and other provinces organized branches of the Muslim National Salvation Association, resistance support units, Muslim first-aid youth units in the battle zones, Muslim save-the-nation youth units, and others who engaged in propaganda activities, mobilization, and fund raising. (These references are taken from Ma Yunshan, "Brief Stories of the Muslim Anti-Japanese Movement during the War of Resistance," in *Gansu Nationalities Studies*, no. 2, 1985.)

The well-known Muslim economist from Ningxia Province, Hu Songshan, disseminated anti-Japanese resistance propaganda in Muslim mosques and schools. Many Muslim anti-Japanese resistance units were organized in North China. The central Hebei unit of about 2,000 fighters was formed in July 1939. Part of this unit later became the Muslim Branch Unit, fighting in the border areas of Hebei, Shandong, and Henan, dealing heavy blows to the Japanese invaders. People called it the "Invincible, Undefeatable Iron Brigade." Da Pusheng, the leader of Shanghai's Muslims, traveled in Islamic countries for over eight months telling about China's War of Resistance and winning international sympathy for China. Another leader, Ha Dechen, never stopped his anti-Japanese activities, although he was repeatedly threatened by the Japanese and their puppets.

The Catholic "elder patriot," Ma Xiangbo, shouted in protest at the top of his voice when the Japanese occupied the northeastern provinces after the September 18 Incident. He said, "In just one year, the mountains and rivers have changed their color. Our countrymen should rise up against this great humiliation and save ourselves. We shall not stop until our mountains and rivers are taken back." After the December 9 Movement he plunged with all his strength into the Shanghai National Salvation Movement led by the Chinese Communist Party and was elected to the standing committee of the nationwide National Salvation Association, which included people from all walks of life. When Sheng Junru and others were followed and closely watched by KMT secret police and these activities became extremely difficult, important meetings were held secretly in Ma's residence. After the Japanese occupied Shanghai, Ma moved to Guilin and other places to continue his anti-Japanese activities. This Catholic patriot died at age 100 in Liangshan, Vietnam, on November 4, 1939; still deeply concerned about the progress of the war against Japan, he shouted, "News, news!"

Third, progressive religious believers cooperated with the Chinese Communist Party in the patriotic democratic struggle.

Under imperialist oppression and KMT reactionary rule, progressive religious persons, aware of the sufferings of the people, responded to the policy of national independence and people's democracy put forth by the Communist Party and willingly cooperated with the party, supporting and taking part in the revolution in varying degrees. Some even sacrificed their lives. The living Buddhas, the Mongolian Xini and the Tibetan Geda, were just such progressive religious leaders. During the first revolutionary war, the living Buddha Xini of the Yikezhao tribe commanded the Twelfth Regiment of the Mongolian People's Army under the leadership of the Chinese Communist Party. He persisted in the struggles that followed the failure of the revolution in 1927, and he finally gave his life to the revolution. In 1935 during the Long March, the Red Army helped the Tibetan people to organize the government of Ganziboba, and the living Buddha, Geda, was elected vice-president. After the Red Army moved on northward, he gave protection and medical treatment to the army's sick and wounded. In 1949, Geda worked hard for the peaceful liberation of Tibet, but he was murdered by secret agents on his way to Changdu. The deeds of these progressive religious leaders, like the countless other martyrs of all Chinese national minorities over the past hundred years, should be recorded in the history books of the glorious people's revolution.

Wu Yaozong, chairman of the publications department of the national YMCA, was an outstanding patriot among Christian leaders. He had originally been a pacifist, but he changed his mind when the Japanese imperialists invaded

China. He maintained that religious believers should stand for justice and oppose the invasion. After the September 18 Incident, he joined the National Salvation Association. Later, through his communications with Zhou Enlai, he gradually came to see that only the Communist Party could save China. After the victory over Japan, he played an active role, along with others from many walks of life, in the patriotic democratic movement opposing persecution and civil war. In June 1946 he went to Nanjing, together with representatives of various patriotic democratic circles, to appeal for peace. He was nearly beaten by agents of the KMT, but still handed the memorandum expressing his opposition to civil war to General Marshall, the special envoy of the American president. In 1947 he delivered speeches at Jiaotong University in Shanghai and Zhejiang University in Hangzhou, publicly supporting the democratic struggle of the students and calling it a "powerful movement for justice." In 1948 he published an article in the Christian periodical *Tianfeng* entitled "The Present-Day Tragedy of Christianity," in which he pointed clearly to the way in which Christianity had become a tool for American imperialist cultural aggression. Together with patriotic Christians such as Chen Yisheng, Sheng Tilan, Ding Guangxun, and others, he helped organize the "China Christian Democratic Research Institute," which promoted democracy, opposed civil war, and expressed progressive ideas.

Liu Liangmo, a staff member of the national YMCA, while still in the United States, joined General Feng Yuxiang in speaking out against Chiang Kai-shek and against the civil war. Deng Yuzhi, chairperson of the labor section of the national YWCA, went to the American General Wedemeyer after the victory over Japan and told him that Chinese Christians were opposed to the support given to Chiang's civil war by the American government. Patriotic Christians in Shanghai and Nanjing voiced their objection to the KMT suppression of students. The student relief agencies, professional youth organizations, and workers' night schools run by the YMCA and YWCA in varying degrees gave their support and protection to revolutionary young people.

Even more religious believers took part in the patriotic democratic movement against Chiang and the United States. Many young believers in church schools participated in the struggle against hunger, persecution, and the civil war. Many Muslims also fought against the suppression and humiliation imposed by KMT reactionaries. Muslim fighting units in the liberated areas were reactivated, and units in the triangular area formed by Beijing, Tianjin, and Baoding carried on armed struggle. Armed Muslims in Shandong performed heroically. Muslim units in the Northeast, collaborating with brother units in the battle to retake Changchun in 1946, were a major force in the attack on the airport. They were later reorganized into a railway engineering brigade, repairing railroads and bridges during the War of Liberation and making significant contributions. A Muslim revolutionary guerrilla unit in Zhaotong, Yunnan Province, assisted the PLA in its march into Yunnan.

Patriotic leaders and members of all religions made their contributions to the overthrow of the dark rule over China throughout the whole period of the Chinese people's revolution.

It should be emphatically pointed out that in old China, each of the religious organizations was controlled by the imperialists and reactionaries, and that the patriotic activities of the progressive elements could never become the mainstream, nor could they change the situation in which the reactionaries manipulated and controlled religion. Nevertheless, before Liberation, the patriotic ideas and activities of some religious leaders were in line with the trends of the Chinese revolution and had far-reaching influence on the struggle by which the various religions freed themselves after Liberation from the control of reactionaries, both domestic and foreign. Their patriotic heritage has become the important internal factor bringing about fundamental changes in our nation's religions since Liberation.

3 | Fundamental Changes in the Status of Religion after the Founding of the Nation

THE BIRTH of the People's Republic of China on October 1, 1949, put an end to the history of hundreds of millions of working people ruled by a few exploiters, as well as to the history of the enslavement of the Chinese people by imperialism and colonialism.

In the first three years after the founding of the People's Republic of China we completely wiped out the surviving forces of Guomindang reactionaries and bandits, accomplished the peaceful liberation of Tibet, established people's governments at different levels in various places, set up the Planning Committee of the Tibetan Autonomous Region in 1956, completed land reform in newly liberated areas, suppressed reactionaries, launched the "Resist America, Aid Korea" and the "Three-Anti" and "Five-Anti" movements, and rapidly restored the national economy. Our planned economic construction began in 1953, and the social reform of privately owned means of production was accomplished in most areas of the country by 1956. As the result of sweeping social changes, we basically eliminated the exploiting classes and established a socialist system in the seven years from 1949 through 1956.

Profound social reforms led to great changes in religion in new China. The series of changes in politics, organizations, and ideology kept abreast of the changes in the country and society and conformed to the wishes of the masses of religious believers and patriots in religious circles. Our country adopted a correct religious policy that supported the patriotic and just actions of progressive persons in religious circles and the masses of believers. The patriotic anti-imperialist movement launched by Catholic and Protestant churches eliminated imperialist influences and upheld independence and self-government of the churches, placing religious enterprises under the full leadership of Chinese believers. Buddhist, Daoist, and Islamic circles abolished their internal feudal privileges and oppressive, exploitative systems and began to function normally.

Changes in the Political and Organizational Status of Religions

In old China religion was used and controlled by domestic ruling classes and by the imperialists, with many negative effects. After the founding of new China, the conditions by which the ruling classes controlled and made use of religion no longer existed. Through patriotic and democratic reforms in religious circles, religions were now run by Chinese religious believers.

    1. Christianity, both Protestant and Catholic, has been freed from the domination of colonialism and imperialism and is now run by Chinese religious believers themselves.

The Protestant Three-Self Patriotic Movement

The Three-Self Manifesto and opposition to control by foreign missions. In the early days after the founding of new China, Christian churches and church schools and hospitals were still under the control of foreign missions, and imperialism still attempted to sabotage new China through those foreign missions. At that time three situations characterized the state of affairs inside Protestant Christianity.

First, various reactionary rumors sprang up, some denigrating the Communist Party, others clamoring in vain for restoration of the reactionary rule and the return to power of the U.S.-Chiang clique. Some clergy persons used the term "red horse" to attack the Communist Party by innuendo and slander, saying they were "addicted to killing and blood-letting," while some clergy attacked the Resist America, Aid Korea Movement, saying it was "incited by demons."

Second, some Protestant Christians, seeking to adjust to the new situation, and thinking they could modify certain ways by which foreign missions controlled Chinese churches so as to continue their dependence on foreign missions, instituted measures to bring about these changes. On the one hand, in November 1949 they wrote letters to North American Protestant mission societies asking that the power to make policies and handle funds be transferred to Chinese church leaders; on the other hand, they emphasized the need for foreign missionaries to "come to work and serve in difficult situations."

In May the following year, the China Committee of the Associated Mission Boards sent a tricky reply in which they wrote: "Missionary work has never been directly connected with the government (note: the U.S. government)." They went on to say that if "the Chinese churches can be loyal to the spirit of Christ, the mission societies are willing to continue to help." This shows that the North American Associated Mission Boards had not changed their hostility toward China and would not give up their control over Chinese churches, but would attempt to maintain control by economic means.

Third, some insightful persons in religious circles were aware of the way in which imperialist aggression had made use of Christianity and felt that if Chinese churches continued to rely on foreign missions they would not be able to adapt to the independence and self-government of new China, and there would be no future for Christianity in China.

People like Wu Yaozong were representative of this group. In June 1949, Christian patriotic democrats Wu Yaozong, Sheng Tilan, Deng Yuzhi, and others participated in the preparatory meeting for the new Chinese People's Political Consultative Conference (CPPCC), which convened in Beijing. At this meeting Wu Yaozong spoke with emotion, saying, "It is time now that Christians should free themselves from capitalist and imperialist traditions." Later he published an article, "Reform of Christianity," in the newspaper *Dagongbao* [*Ta kung pao*], pointing out: "In the past as well as in the present, the imperialists have been making use of Christianity against China." He held that "Christianity must struggle to free itself from capitalism and imperialism. Chinese churches must practice the principles of self-government, self-propagation, and self-support, which have been advocated for many years."

In September 1949, five persons, including Wu Yaozong, attended the first session of the CPPCC where Wu spoke in support of the "Common Program" and expressed his determination to uproot "corrupt and evil traditions inside religion" and the "connection between imperialism and religion." At that time certain patriotic believers wrote to newspapers exposing and opposing imperialists who used the church for aggression. Their position expressed the desire of a great number of patriotic religious believers to free themselves from the control of colonialism and imperialism, and to bring about independence and self-government in the churches. This heralded the beginning of the patriotic anti-imperialist movement by Protestant Christians after the founding of new China.

In the spring of 1950, Wu Yaozong and others organized a team to visit various places around the country to communicate to the churches the gist of the CPPCC meeting and the "Common Program" and to learn about the actual situation of the churches. In May that year, together with some Protestant Christians from Beijing and Tianjin, they called on Premier Zhou Enlai. They told him about the contradictions and difficulties the churches were facing at that time and asked for help to solve these questions. In those talks the Christians, edified and inspired by Premier Zhou, came to understand that Christianity in China had long been under the influence of imperialism, which was the basic reason why it could not fit in with new China.

Later, they decided to launch an innovative Three-Self Movement (later called the Three-Self Patriotic Movement), basing their decision on the stand of patriotic Chinese Christians for self-government, self-support, and self-propagation. Their action immediately won the approval and support of Premier Zhou Enlai. He said, "Firmly hold to the principle of national anti-imperialism, cut off links with imperialism, and let religion restore its true features. Today religious circles have begun a national movement of their own to settle accounts with the links to imperialism that prevailed for the past hundred years." He praised them, saying, "Religious units must be independent, they must be self-reliant and establish churches that are self-governing, self-supporting, and self-propagating. In this way Christianity will become a truly Chinese Christian church" ("Four Rounds of Talks Regarding Questions about Christianity," in *Selected Works of Zhou Enlai on the United Front*, pp. 181–82).

Soon after this round of talks, Wu Yaozong took responsibility for drafting "The Way for Chinese Christianity to Give Itself to Construction of New China" (usually called the "Three-Self Manifesto" in Christian circles). This document "called on believers to be clear about the evils done by imperialism in China, to learn the facts of how imperialism made use of Christianity, and to eliminate completely imperialist influences inside Christianity." It urged them "to be alert for imperialist plots, particularly those of American imperialists cultivating reactionary influences by means of religion." The manifesto demanded that Christian churches and organizations "make concrete plans to achieve the goal of self-reliance within the shortest possible time." This document was sponsored by forty well-known Christians; within a month or so, echoing those leaders, it was signed by about 1,500 other church leaders. *Renmin ribao* (People's daily) published the manifesto and the list of signatures in its issue of September 23, 1950, and expressed its enthusiastic support in a special editorial.

Of course, the Three-Self Manifesto did not have smooth sailing thereafter. From the very beginning it encountered obstruction and sabotage from clergy who upheld the imperialist stand and from people under their influence. Patriots from Christian circles were slandered. Struggles focused on the China Christian Council, a nationwide Christian organization that had been under the control of imperialist influences for years.

At the council's fourteenth annual meeting in October 1950, a number of top clergy attempted to write another manifesto to counter the Three-Self Manifesto. After this failed, they tried to manipulate from behind the scenes, hoping to prevent the conference from discussing the Three-Self Manifesto and to exclude Wu Yaozong from joining the leadership committee of the council. Their attempts failed, however. The participants not only discussed church reform and the three-self goals, but also made the decision to call on all Christians to sign the Three-Self Manifesto.

Cutting off links with foreign missions and setting up a Three-Self Patriotic Organization. In June 1950, American imperialists started the war of aggression against Korea, at the same time dispatching troops to invade and occupy Taiwan, which is Chinese territory. In September they bombed and strafed our northern provinces, a serious threat to China's security. A movement to Resist America and Aid Korea to protect our homes and country was launched in China on a grand scale. That movement provided a good education for Christian circles. It led them to understand imperialism better and aroused their patriotic fervor. The shameless slander against China made by Austin, the American delegate to the

United Nations, in September 1950 insulted the Chinese people and particularly enraged patriotic religious believers. He described the cultural aggression of American imperialists as "friendship" and "a measure of good will." Christian units, schools, and hospitals held meetings and parades, expressing strong protests.

On December 12, 1950, the American government made the outrageous announcement that it would seize public and private properties of China in the United States, and that no ships registered in the United States would be allowed to enter Chinese harbors. That provocation further enraged the Chinese people, including patriotic religious believers.

On December 28, the Chinese government announced the "control of American properties in China and freezing of bank deposits." This new situation accelerated the "three-self" process of the Christian church.

In April 1951, the State Council convened a "Meeting on the Disposition of Christian Units that Received Subsidies from the United States" in order to solve the economic difficulties of Christian units in China, and to discuss and decide on ways of resolving the situation. At the meeting patriotic Christians, including quite a few top leaders who had determined to draw a line of demarcation between themselves and imperialism due to the influence of the "Resist America, Aid Korea Movement," exposed the evils and plots of the imperialists to make use of foreign missions for aggression against China. A preparatory committee for the Chinese Christian "Resist America, Aid Korea Three-Self Movement" was organized, and a "Joint Manifesto of Representatives from Chinese Christian Churches and Units" was issued as an expression of the determination finally, completely, and totally to cut off links with American and other missions in order to achieve self-government, self-propagation, and self-support for all Chinese churches.

After the conference, Christian churches and units in many cities across China held meetings to accuse imperialists of using Christianity for aggression against China. Foreign missionaries were returning at that time to their home countries, and one after another foreign mission organizations stationed in China pulled out.

As a consequence of the solidarity of all branches and units of the church, the Protestant Three-Self Movement Committee was organized in August 1954. Wu Yaozong was elected chairman, with Chen Jianzheng, Wu Yifang, Chen Zonggui, Jiang Changchuang, Cui Xianxiang, and Ding Yuzhang as vice-chairmen. The constitution stated that the aim of the organization was to unite Christians all over China, led by the Chinese army and people's government, to love the motherland, to abide by China's laws, to adhere to the policy of self-government, self-propagation, self-support, independence, and self-management of the churches, and to defend the achievements of the Three-Self Patriotic Movement. Since then, Protestant Christianity in China has become a self-managed religious enterprise belonging to Chinese believers. Regional Three-Self Patriotic Associations have been established in one place after another all over the country.

Eliminating counterrevolutionary influences inside Protestant Christianity. After Chinese Protestant Christianity cut its links with foreign missions, a few counterrevolutionaries inside the churches continued to fan the flames of disorder and to commit sabotage. Some of them used their status as clergy to confuse the masses, to swindle money, and to jeopardize people's lives and health. Using both preaching and publications, some attacked the Chinese Communist Party as "Satan," slandered new China as the "Dark Ages," and labeled patriotic believers as "Judas." Others seized control of churches or certain religious sects, deceiving and harming the masses and secretly carrying on counterrevolutionary activities. For example, certain counterrevolutionaries under the guise of religion not only deceived the masses and swindled money out of them under the pretense of "healing illness by prayer" but also in their "preaching" spoke nonsense by saying that the American invasion forces were "troops from heaven," and that the bombing and killing of Koreans was "punishment for their crimes."

Those few remaining counterrevolutionaries in various places who used the guise of religion were arrested by the government during the nationwide movement against counterrevolutionaries in 1955, and counterrevolutionary influences inside the churches were basically wiped out.

The Shanghai Public Security Bureau arrested the Ni Tuoshen (Watchman Nee) counterrevolutionary clique who were hiding inside the Shanghai Christian Assembly Places (Juhuichu) in January 1956 and exposed their counterrevolutionary crimes. Before Liberation, Ni Tuoshen, the head of the clique, had continually colluded with the America-Chiang spies, plotting against the Communists and, after Liberation, providing Guomindang spies with important military and political information. For instance, he offered plans to bomb power plants and plotted how to prevent nationwide liberation and undermine social stability. He also stirred up religious believers in an attempt to undermine the land reform and Resist America, Aid Korea movements, and to steal Chinese scientific and technological information.

An unprincipled and mean person, Ni raped numerous women. Since they were hiding under the guise of a mystical "spirituality," these counterrevolutionaries poisoned many believers, particularly young ones. Therefore, the public exposure of their various crimes produced wide repercussions inside the churches. Believers in Shanghai and elsewhere around the country, particularly those of the "Juhuichu" groups, rose up one after another to bring their evildoings to light, saying they would sharpen their vision in order to distinguish right from wrong, and would draw a clear line of demarcation between themselves and the counterrevolutionaries. The victory of this movement basically wiped out the counterrevolutionaries inside the Protestant Christian churches and placed religious activities on a normal road, enabling the Chinese Protestant Three-Self Patriotic Movement to move forward victoriously.

The Anti-Imperialist Patriotic Movement in the Catholic Church Opposes the Vatican's Interference in Our Nation's Political Affairs and Publishes the Patriotic Manifesto

Catholicism in old China was used and controlled for a long period of time by imperialism. The attitude of the Pope and the Vatican was habitually hostile to China.

After the Chinese People's Liberation Army (PLA) liberated Nanjing in April 1949, the Vatican, through its internuncio to the Guomindang government, Riberi, distributed the July 1 papal letter, "An Order from the Roman Holy See," to all parishes in China. The papal letter incited Catholic believers to oppose the people's government, stipulating that those believers who "registered their names to join the Communist Party or helped that party" or "issued propaganda and read or published articles in the party's books, magazines, and newspapers" should all be "banned from participation in the sacraments."

Having received this order, all parishes immediately called emergency meetings for transmitting and arranging plans sent down from the hierarchy. For example, Joannes de Vienne, the French archbishop of Tianjin diocese, immediately called a meeting to transmit the order and prepared handwritten instructions entitled "How to Observe the July 1 Order from the Vatican," which were distributed to the churches, schools, and philanthropic organizations under control of the diocese. Some additions were made to the original document: "Those who accept Communist theories will be expelled from the church," "It is not permitted to explain Communist books to Christian believers," "It is not permitted to read theoretical articles in the Communist newspapers," and "Believers are not allowed to attend the Huabei University, the Revolutionary University, the Public Security School, the Military-Political University, or the Staff and Workers' School." In addition, Catholics were "not allowed to join labor unions, the Women's League, or the Youth League, or to give names to the Communist Party, etc." (Gu Changsheng, *Missionaries and Modern China*, p. 428).

In 1950 Riberi, again in the name of the "internuncio," distributed the "warning" from the Roman Holy See, dated July 28, with the threat that all Catholic believers who joined organizations set up "with instructions or with help from the Communist Party," no matter under what pretense, should be punished according to the order issued by the Holy See on July 1, 1949. That is, they would "forfeit the right to attend Mass" and even "be expelled from the Catholic Church as an extraordinary punishment."

The actions of the Vatican and the imperialist influences inside the Catholic churches meddling with our country's internal affairs aroused the opposition of many patriotic Catholics. For example, a number of Catholic intellectuals from Shanghai church schools and Catholic workers from the Tushanwan workshops in the Xujiahui [Ziccawei] parish mounted anti-imperialist struggles.

In another case an agent of the [Catholic] Furen University in Beijing forcibly intervened and infringed on our educational sovereignty by threatening to stop educational subsidies and to expel certain teachers without any reason. The president of the university, Chen Huan, led the patriotic teachers and students, including religious believers, in a determined struggle against this man, finally cutting off the links between the university and imperialist influences and welcoming the government to take over the university. Among the university staff there were a number of patriotic persons who resented imperialist intervention in our domestic affairs and held that the university should get rid of imperialist control.

Fr. Wang Liangzuo of Guangyuan County, Sichuan Province, together with five hundred other Catholics, issued a "Manifesto of Guangyuan Catholics for a Self-Reliance Movement" on November 30, exposing the relationship between Catholic missionary work and colonial aggression. The manifesto called on the church to "cut off all relations with imperialists." This manifesto was echoed by Catholics in many areas. In an editorial of January 8, 1951, *Renmin ribao* said "Welcome to the Patriotic Movement of the Catholics" and gave warm support to the patriotic views of Fr. Wang Liangzuo and others.

After that, Catholics in various places issued a number of manifestoes concerning this problem. On January 13, 1951, Tianjin Catholic circles issued a "Manifesto on Self-Reliance and Innovation." On March 31 the auxiliary bishop of Nanjing Diocese, Li Weiguang, issued a manifesto calling for "firm opposition to the Vatican's intervention in China's domestic affairs and severance of all political and economic relations with the Vatican." On September 17, Catholics in Beijing and Shanghai issued a manifesto expressing their anti-imperialist stand and calling for severance of the church's links with imperialists.

Exposing and denouncing the use of the Catholic Church by imperialists for their evildoings. In the course of the Catholic anti-imperialist patriotic movement, imperialism and its agents used "ecclesiastical power" (*shen quan*) to engage in disruption and sabotage. They tried to win the hearts of young Catholics by deceit and organized so-called religious doctrine groups to spread the "three don'ts" (that is, do not read Communist newspapers, do not listen to Communist propaganda, and do not acknowledge the presence of imperialists in the churches). These groups also preached the "irreconcilability of theism and atheism" and tried to stir up antagonism between believers and the government. Some patriotic believers were threatened with "excommunication" (the most severe punishment given to religious clergy and believers in the Catholic Church, that is, expulsion from the church and not "going to heaven" after death).

In certain Catholic churches in Shanghai there were occasions when believers were dragged away as they were going to "receive Holy Communion." To deceive the masses, the imperialists in the churches tried every possible means to deny the existence of relations between the missionaries' work and the colonialists. Two examples are the "Statement from All Bishops of the Chinese Catholic Church" drafted by de Vienne and distributed by Riberi, and the church-approved "References for Study," which said, "Our Catholics have had no relations with imperialism so there are no links to cut off."

After the auxiliary bishop of Nanjing Diocese, Li Weiguang, issued the declaration of independence in March 1951, Riberi at once wrote to the bishops in every diocese expressing his objection and urging them to "thoroughly understand and bravely fight against the enemy's plotting." They went so far as to call the Chinese government and the Chinese people who supported the anti-imperialist movement in Catholic circles "enemies."

Patriotic believers were indignant over the evildoings of the imperialists and their agents who made use of religion to oppose new China and interfere with our domestic affairs. They rose up to expose and denounce them. In response to the just demands of the patriotic believers and the broad masses, a number of notorious foreign missionaries, such as de Vienne from Tianjin and Riberi from Nanjing, were expelled from China. After that the cases of other groups of foreign missionaries who made use of the Catholic Church for sabotage activities were investigated and disposed of on the basis of the testimony of patriotic believers. These cases took place in Beijing, Nanjing, Wuchang, Yangzhou, Shenyang, Kunming, Anqing, Wuhu, Xi'an, Kaifeng, Jinan, and elsewhere. Not only had these missionaries long colluded with reactionary elements, sabotaging our revolutionary cause, but after Liberation they continued to collect information for the imperialists, spread rumors against new China, and obstructed and damaged the anti-imperialist movement in Catholic circles. It was natural for these missionaries to be punished by our government and to be banished from China.

In response to the just actions of our patriotic Catholics and government, the Vatican, shouting at the top of its voice, continued its acts of sabotage. Pope Pius XII issued a "Public Order to All Chinese Catholics" on January 18, 1952, claiming that these criminals who had brought detriment to the Chinese people were "wronged and slandered"; it urged Chinese religious staff and believers to be "courageous for righteousness" and "not to fear or waver, to scorn danger and difficulties," and to stand against the people and the government to the very end. On October 17, 1954, they issued another "order," continuing to slander patriotic believers "who have recently joined in the sinister movement sponsored by those who hate religion and hate the church set up by our heavenly Lord Jesus Christ," urging Catholics to be "brave and fearless and to press ahead" in their opposition to new China.

However, this perverse "order," when placed alongside the many evidences of the criminal activities of imperialists using the Catholic church for sabotage, could only serve as a negative teaching example that made Chinese Catholics understand them even better, raising their anti-imperialist and patriotic consciousness. Patriotic religious personnel did not fear the "loss of divine power."

Patriots were not afraid of being refused "holy communion," or even the threat of "ultimate punishment." They held meetings, made denouncements, and supported the government in its move to banish the foreign missionaries who worked for imperialism. The anti-imperialist patriotic movement among Catholic believers went forward.

Eliminating counterrevolutionary influences inside the Catholic church. Although numbers of imperialists using the guise of religion had been sentenced to imprisonment or banished, their agents hidden among the Catholics had not stopped making use of religion for sabotage activities. They not only continued to spread falsehoods, such as "there is no imperialism inside the Catholic church," "atheism and theism are irreconcilable," and "the policy of religious freedom is not true," but also put forth the new "three no's": "no retreat, no betrayal, no surrender." They continued to abet and incite certain believers to stand against new China. They went so far as to set up counterrevolutionary organizations to gather military, political, and economic information for imperialist espionage agencies; they planned and spread counterrevolutionary rumors; they caused damage to the building of the motherland; they attacked and persecuted patriotic believers; they even spread the word "to fight to the last" against the people's government.

Confronted with this situation, a struggle was started in 1955 to eliminate the counterrevolutionaries in the Catholic church, and a group of counterrevolutionaries hidden inside the Catholic church was exposed. The masses of believers held meetings in which they exposed and denounced various criminal sabotage activities of the counterrevolutionaries. On September 25, 1955, the Shanghai diocese convened a gathering of ten thousand people to denounce the [Bishop] Gong Pinmei counterrevolutionary clique. Many Catholic believers, priests, and nuns who had never dared to attend any meeting since the founding of new China were present at the gathering. They shouted the slogan they had never dared to shout, "Long live the People's Republic of China." On National Day that same year the flag of the People's Republic of China was hoisted in front of the Shanghai Cathedral at Xujiahui. Decorated archways were set up for the occasion, and for the first time patriotic priests held a "solemn high Mass" to pray for the blooming and prosperity of new China. After nightfall about twenty thousand people, believers and nonbelievers alike, assembled in the square before the Cathedral. This fully displayed the patriotic unity between Catholics and people in other walks of life. The anti-imperialist patriotic movement once more achieved a victory.

Breaking free from the control of the Vatican and independently electing and ordaining bishops. According to 1948 statistics there were more than 110 foreign bishops in the 140 Catholic dioceses. After the founding of new China these foreign bishops eventually left the country and could no longer carry out their church duties, but the Vatican still kept them in their positions by "remote control" from outside China, imagining they would come back some day. In the meantime the Vatican was persecuting patriotic Chinese bishops. For example, in February 1952, the Congregation of Propaganda Fide of the Vatican made the decision to expel auxiliary Bishop Li Weiguang of Nanjing, who had issued a manifesto calling for independence and self-reliance. The resolution was formally announced on March 16, 1955.

Due to the lack of bishops in most dioceses, there were difficulties in administering the sacraments, and the religious life of believers was seriously affected. The bishops, priests, and masses of believers who had been tempered in the furnace of the anti-imperialist patriotic movement were determined to free themselves from the control of the Vatican and to elect and ordain bishops by themselves. The Shanghai diocese elected Zhang Shilang auxiliary bishop on March 16, 1956, and cabled the Vatican. This reasonable, lawful, and patriotic action was unreasonably denied by the Vatican's Congregation of Propaganda Fide, but it won the support of Shanghai Catholics and believers all over the country.

At that time about two hundred regional or local patriotic committees had been set up in different places. In 1957 the first representative meeting of Catholics was convened in Beijing and adopted the decision to ''firmly free ourselves from the control of the Vatican, and realize an independent, self-reliant and self-governed church.''

In the meantime the [national] Chinese Catholic Patriotic Association was formally established. Pi Shushi was elected chairman, with Yang Shida, Li Boyu, Li Weiguang, Wang Wencheng, Zhao Zhengsheng, Dong Wenlong, Li Depei, and Cao Daosheng as vice-chairmen. Local Catholic patriotic committees were set up one after another around the country. In March 1958, the Catholic priests of Wuchang and Hankou elected two bishops. The sacred ceremony of ordination was held in April and won the support and congratulations of Catholic churches in various places.

The Vatican responded with rude interference to this act of electing and ordaining bishops themselves; speaking nonsense, they said that the elections that took place in Wuchang and Hankou were ''invalid'' and ''without value,'' and that those who took part would be threatened with ''excommunication.'' Catholic believers in China were not frightened by this unreasonable threat and interference. Priests from every diocese (and in some cases including nuns and laypersons) subsequently took part in the election of their own bishops and freed themselves from the control of the Vatican.

2. Buddhism, Daoism, and Islam have freed themselves from being used and controlled by the domestic reactionary classes.

The Democratic Reform Movement in Buddhism and Daoism

Eliminating feudal privileges and the system of oppression and exploitation. Buddhism and Daoism had long been used and controlled by the ruling classes that gained their feudal privileges this way. In old China the temples and their properties were under the protection of the ruling classes. The abbots of large temples had the right to enslave and punish lower-ranking monks and tenants. These privileges were acknowledged by the ruling class.

The founding of new China enabled Buddhists and Daoists to free themselves from subordination to the ruling classes. Through democratic and land reforms the feudal privileges of Buddhism and Daoism were abolished. Buddhists and Daoists, like ordinary citizens, now enjoy citizens' rights and fulfill citizens' obligations according to the constitution. Abbots are no exception. The only difference between Buddhists and Daoists and ordinary citizens is their religious belief.

In old China the main source of income for Buddhist and Daoist monasteries came from exploitation in the forms of land rents and usurious loans. Some temples and monasteries owned large tracts of land and exploited farmers and poor people by means of heavy land rents and usurious loans. Land owned by temples in rural areas was confiscated during land reform and usurious loans were abolished, destroying the Buddhist and Daoist system of feudal exploitation.

In January 1950, the government issued "Instructions on the Question of Suburban Land in Old Liberated Areas," which stipulated that all land belonging to temples and churches was to be confiscated by the state and properly distributed. "Monks and nuns who were willing to engage in agricultural production would be eligible to receive a share of cropland."

"Land Reform of the People's Republic of China," issued in June 1950, called for the "confiscation of land of temples, churches, schools, and collective units in the countryside and other public land," except for the buildings and halls of temples, which would be reserved according to the law. Buddhist and Daoist monks and nuns would receive their shares of land the same as the peasants. The document "Land Reform in Suburban Areas" contained the same provisions. During land reform those abbots who had blood debts [guilty of murder] and had earned the bitter hatred of the people, as well as those abbots who had ridden roughshod over monks of inferior rank, would be given their due punishment. Thus, Buddhism and Daoism were freed from feudal exploitation.

Since 1950, Buddhist circles have carried on the tradition of paying attention equally to agriculture and to religious meditation. Productive-labor organizations were set up in various temples under the policy advocated by a number of well-known Buddhists. Able-bodied monks and nuns now engage in agriculture, forestry, handicraft work, and social services.

Beijing monks and nuns opened the Daxiong Gunnysack Factory in 1950, with 265 young Buddhists taking part in manufacturing. In 1951 the Daren Gunnysack Factory and six hemp-weaving groups were set up in Beijing. Later the First Printing Cooperative, a weaving factory, and the Biqiuni Sewing Unit were established.

In 1951 and years following, Fujian Buddhists also opened up weaving, handicraft, bamboo, shell, sewing, metalwork, bindery, paper box, and cord-making factories and workshops. About five hundred monks and nuns took part in these projects, organizing productive-labor projects in agriculture and sideline industries in suburban counties.

After the founding of new China, monks and nuns in Shanghai started handicraft workshops to make stockings and towels and opened up farms as well. Several hundred monks of Wutai Shan in Shanxi Province, in addition to farming several hundred acres of land, came down from the mountains to help farmers with the autumn harvest and at other busy times. Monks of Emei Shan in Sichuan Province raised funds and set up a tea factory in order to support themselves. In 1953 Changsha Buddhists organized the first weaving and dyeing cooperative of Changsha, the old Kaifu Temple Horticulture Group, and the Liuhe and Jinlao weaving factories, with a total of 105 Buddhists in the work force.

Buddhists and Daoists of Nanyue, Hunan Province, jointly organized the Nanyue Religious Believers Agriculture Mutual Aid Group, which later developed into an agricultural productive cooperative. Monks of Lingyan Temple of Suzhou, in addition to planting trees to reforest the area, had more than enough food for their own needs. Generally speaking, Buddhists and Daoists freed themselves from the shackles of the feudal economy through land reform, eliminating the exploitative and oppressive feudal system of Buddhism and Daoism and enabling vast numbers of able-bodied monks and nuns to start a new life of physical labor and self-support.

Purifying the ranks of Buddhists and Daoists. In old China the majority of Buddhist and Daoist monks and nuns came from the working people. They became monks and nuns because of personal misfortune or loss of livelihood. Some evildoers, however, had sneaked into Buddhist and Daoist circles due to the control of reactionaries. For example, a counterrevolutionary who had long colluded with local tyrants and evil gentry and was guilty of monstrous crimes while savagely oppressing the country people had sneaked into the Buddhist temple at Jiuhua Shan. This man was arrested and punished during the movement to suppress counterrevolutionaries.

In another case, a few Guomindang and Sanqingtuan (Youth League) core members who had served the reactionary ruling classes infiltrated the staff of the Jinshan Temple at Zhengjiang and the Dinghui Temple at Jiaoshan where they utilized Buddhism to sabotage the revolution and national construction after Liberation. They were sorted out in the movement to suppress and eliminate counterrevolutionaries.

At the beginning of the anticounterrevolutionary movement, some of the Buddhists and Daoists, influenced by religious ideology, did not do very much to help, and some even hindered the movement. Through education and taking part in social activities, particularly when counterrevolutionaries and evildoers among Buddhists and Daoists were uncovered, they became clear-sighted and better informed.

For example, they based their new understanding on some sayings from Buddhist scriptures, such as "Justice does not show itself unless injustice is crushed" and "Resisting tyranny to save the good is surely what Buddha does." Buddhists came to know that without suppressing and eliminating counterrevolutionaries, there would be no healthy atmosphere, and Buddhist ranks could not be purified. Only with the counterrevolutionaries and evildoers wiped out could the cause of Buddhism develop normally. With a better understanding of the situation, having come to the realization that suppressing and eliminating counterrevolutionaries was not contradictory to the teaching of Buddhism and Daoism, and now able to distinguish right from wrong, Buddhists and Daoists everywhere plunged into the movement to suppress and eliminate counterrevolutionaries.

Before and after the founding of new China, and quite apart from these developments, members of some reactionary superstitious sects and secret societies, using the cover of Buddhism and Daoism, not only engaged in superstitious activities, defrauding people of their money and possessions and harming some persons' lives, but also colluded with Guomindang reactionaries and feudal landlords to spread rumors in order to sabotage the cause of the people's revolution. In the course of the banning of reactionary sects and secret societies, Buddhists and Daoists all over the country supported the correct measures adopted by the government.

The heads of the reactionary sects and secret societies who sneaked into Buddhist and Daoist temples were basically eliminated. For example, among those sects and societies was the so-called Datong Buddhist Association. Another was the World New Buddhist Association, which was unearthed in Tianjin in November 1950. Members of these and other reactionary sects and secret societies who had infiltrated Buddhist organizations were eliminated.

In July 1953, the Buddhists of Shantou, Guangdong Province, cleaned out a batch of "Xiantiandao" members who had sneaked in among the Buddhists. With the suppression and elimination of counterrevolutionaries and the banning of reactionary sects and secret societies, evildoers inside Buddhist and Daoist circles were removed, their ranks were purified, and they returned to a normal way of development.

Setting up patriotic religious organizations. In old China, Buddhist and Daoist monasteries were usually independent of one another, each with a strong sectarian bias. Before Liberation the Buddhist Association of China was a nationwide organization in name only; it had never achieved real unity and was full of internal contradictions. Daoism had attempted many times to set up a nationwide organization but had never succeeded. Guided by the party's united front policy, patriotic unification had been strengthened after the founding of new China. Since 1950, local patriotic Buddhist organizations and Buddhist academic organizations such as the Buddhist Preparatory Association, the Buddhist Preparatory Committee on Unification, the Buddhist Committee, and the Buddhist

Studies Society were all set up with the aim of uniting Buddhists for participation in patriotic movements.

To keep pace with the developing situation, Buddhists and Daoists felt the need to establish nationwide patriotic organizations. In November 1952, on the initiative of twenty well-known living Buddhas, Buddhist masters, and lay Buddhists, a preparatory meeting for the Chinese Buddhist Association was convened, and the document "On the Formation of the Chinese Buddhist Association" was adopted.

In May 1953, the Chinese Buddhist Association was formally established in Beijing. The first council of the association was formed, with Yuan Ying elected as chairman and Xiraojiacuo, Gongdelin, Jingneijicun, Nenghai, and Zhao Puchu as vice-chairmen. The aim of the association was to unite Buddhists all over the country, to enlist them for participation in the movement of loving the motherland and protecting world peace under the leadership of the people's government, to help the people's government to implement its policy on religious freedom, to maintain contact with Buddhists in different places, and to carry forward the good Buddhist traditions. Since then, regional Buddhist associations have been set up all over the country.

In November 1956, on the initiative of twenty-three nationally known Daoists, a conference was held in Beijing and the preparatory committee of the Chinese Daoist Association was set up, adopting a "Document on the Formation of the Chinese Daoist Association."

In April 1957, the first national Daoist representative meeting was convened in Beijing, and for the first time in history a "Chinese Daoist Association" representing Daoists nationwide was established. The conference adopted regulations and elected the first council, with Yue Zongdai as chairman and Chen Yinning and Wang Yueqing as vice-chairmen. Its aims were to unite all Daoists, to educate them to love the country and love Daoism, to take active part in socialist construction, to carry forward the good traditions of Daoism, to report on the situation and problems of Daoists in China, and to make proposals and help the government implement its policy on religious freedom. Since then local Daoist associations have been formed one after another.

The Chinese Buddhist Association and the Chinese Daoist Association (including the local associations) are patriotic religious organizations. They have played an active role in uniting Buddhists and Daoists for participation in socialist construction.

Reforming Tibetan Buddhism and separating religion from politics. In old China, religion and politics were commingled in Tibet. The Dalai Lama was the head of both the government and Tibetan Buddhism. In April 1951, after the founding of the People's Republic of China, the plenipotentiary of the central government and the plenipotentiary of the Tibetan local government held talks in Beijing. In May that year they signed "The Agreement of the People's Central Government and the Tibetan Local Government on the Peaceful Liberation of

Tibet.'' On October 26 the PLA units sent into Tibet reached Lhasa and were welcomed by Tibetan monks and laymen.

After the peaceful liberation of Tibet, the Tibetan local government, basing its position on relevant items of the agreement, still kept religion and politics together. After long preparation and discussion, a preparatory committee for the Tibetan Autonomous Region was formally set up.

In October 1956, the Patriotic Chinese Buddhist Association was set up. Socialist reform was being carried out in most areas of China at that time. With regard to the special situation in Tibet, the people's central government declared that for the next six years, that is, until 1962, democratic reforms in Tibet could be delayed. The time for reform would depend on future conditions and would be settled by discussions among Tibetan leaders, upper circles, and the masses. Monks and laymen and some of those in higher circles were in favor of unification with the motherland and wanted to have discussions leading to democratic reforms.

Others among the upper circles, however, instigated and supported by imperialists and reactionaries in other countries, were plotting behind the scenes, imagining they could maintain the combination of religion and politics. They used religious activities to spread rumors. In March 1959, they launched armed rebellion, attempting to split the motherland and to gain ''independence for Tibet.''

Because it was against the will of Tibetan monks and laymen and went against the historical trend toward unification of the motherland, this rebellion was quickly put down. Democratic reforms in Tibet speeded up after that; religion was separated from politics, and the preparatory committee for the Tibetan Autonomous Region began to exercise regional government power. The barbarous and backward system of slavery that had burdened the laboring people for thousands of years was overthrown and a million slaves stood up and freed themselves.

The deputy chairman, Bainqen Erdeni Quejijianzan [Panchen Lama], spoke at the second session of the preparatory meeting convened in July 1959, saying, ''in Lamaist temples all things related to feudal oppression and exploitation must be reformed.'' After several years of effort, feudal privileges in the Tibetan temples and monasteries were finally eliminated and replaced by new democratic systems of administration. Tibetan Buddhism achieved a new birth after democratic reform, so that all monks could now engage in various religious activities with a light heart. Since the separation of politics and religion, Tibetan Buddhism has gradually become a purely religious enterprise, and religious belief has gradually become a personal matter for individual believers.

The Islamic Democratic Reform and Patriotic Movement

The ruling classes of old China adopted a dual policy toward Islam. On the one hand, they roped in a few members of the upper Islamic circles, using and controlling the Muslim community ["Islamism"] to maintain their reactionary rule; on the other hand, they adopted a policy of national oppression, refusing to recognize the national minority status of Muslims, plundering and killing them and holding their religious belief in contempt. For these complex historical reasons there existed within the Islamic community a system of severe feudal oppression, exploitation, and feudal privileges, while at the same time there was a history of revolts by the Muslim masses against the oppression and plunder of the ruling classes.

After the founding of the People's Republic of China, oppression of national minorities was abolished, the policy of national equality and unity among the minorities was put into practice, and Islamic believers enjoyed equal rights in the great family of national minorities. At the same time the system of oppression, exploitation, and feudal privileges in the name of religion that had grown up over many years was gradually abolished through democratic reforms.

Abolishing the system of oppression, exploitation, and feudal privileges. The system of oppression, exploitation, and feudal privileges was mainly visible in the mosques where the chief *ahong* [imam] collected religious taxes from the believers and assigned them to unpaid labor. In certain regions where the *menhuan* system prevailed, with a single person (*jiaozhu*, literally, "religious leader") at the center, serving both as *ahong* and landlord, oppression, exploitation, and feudal privileges were more serious. Religion, politics, and economics were combined in the form of a sectarian theocracy. Under this system the hereditary religious head man (*jiaozhu*) had power over the life and property of the believers, forming a kind of economic feudal fiefdom. Their mosques and temples owned much land, livestock, industry, and businesses, had a monopoly on education, collected heavy religious taxes from the believers, and assigned the people to unpaid [corvée] labor.

After the founding of new China the special situation of the Islamic minority nationalities was taken into consideration. During land reform local Muslims were asked to give their opinion concerning the disposal of land owned by the mosques. Democratic reforms among the Islamic peoples were carried out only after full consultation with the people at all levels. During land reform the vast lands owned by members of upper religious circles were distributed to Muslims with little or no land, heavy religious taxation was stopped, and all these measures enabled more than 1,900,000 Muslims with little or no land to share in the distribution of 7,420,000 mu of land.

For various reasons, however, some of the feudal privileges, oppression, and exploitation in the name of religion were not completely abolished at that time. In addition, there was the continuing problem of religious burdens and excessively heavy religious expenses. Burdens refer to taxes paid to the temples; expenses mean regular religious contributions of money or property. Expenses of this kind for Muslims in Northwest China amounted to 20 or 30 percent of their income, and as high as 50 percent or more for some people.

For example, there were over 8,000 members of the Dongtashi Cooperative in Wuzhong City, half of whom were Han and half Hui. All of them were Muslims. The Han Muslims had a mosque, but their total annual expenses were no more than twenty or thirty yuan, which amounted to a few fen per capita. But each Hui Muslim had to pay tens of yuan annually, a burden that affected the living standards of the Hui Muslims (see Li Weihan, *The United Front and the Problem of Nationalities*, p. 550).

Since 1958, in the wake of the intensive development of nationwide democratic and socialist reform demanded and supported by Muslims of all nationalities and by patriotic upper circles, democratic reform was carried out and the system of oppression, exploitation, and feudal privileges basically abolished. As a result, Muslims were greatly encouraged and inspired to take the socialist road.

Cleansing Islam on the inside. In old China certain members of the upper circles inside the Muslim community, cheated and roped in by Guomindang reactionaries, did things that obstructed the people's revolution. After the founding of new China, the people's government adopted a policy of uniting and educating them, with the result that most of them, having raised their consciousness, followed the patriotic road. Of course a few remained antagonistic and continued to make use of religion to engage in activities that jeopardized the revolutionary regime. They made reactionary speeches that deceived religious believers. But the broad masses of Muslims, having improved their understanding as a result of patriotic education, helped to ferret out the few oppositionists who hid themselves inside the Muslim community in order to carry on activities hostile to the socialist motherland.

The establishment of religious patriotic organizations. In old China Muslims were long ruled by a reactionary government that despised and oppressed the national minorities. During the War of Resistance against Japan, Muslims all over China set up organizations such as the Chinese Muslim National Salvation Association (later called the Chinese Islamic Association) and the Chinese Muslim Society. But the circumstances of history did not permit them to function nationwide.

After the founding of the People's Republic of China, the people's government implemented the policy of equality for national minorities, unity, mutual help, and religious freedom. Muslims began to feel the warmth of new China. In 1950 the people's central government stipulated that all local governments could give a one-day holiday to all Muslims on the festival marking the end of Ramadan, which was a custom of the Muslim people. Muslim cadres, workers, PLA soldiers, and students are now given a holiday on Islamic festivals. The people's government respects the customs of the Muslims and gives preferential treatment on food supplies such as beef and mutton. The State Council also stipulated that Muslims are exempt from the tax on slaughtering cattle and sheep for use in the three most important Islamic festivals.

The people's government is also concerned about the employment of

Muslims and provides help in solving their financial difficulties. All of these actions made Muslims understand that their country cared for them, stirring their patriotic enthusiasm to the point where they felt they should establish a new nationwide Muslim organization.

In 1952 the well-known Muslims Bao E'han, Da Pusheng, Ma Jian, Liu Geping, Sai Futing, Pan Shiqian, and Zhang Jie called a preparatory meeting in Beijing for the formation of a Chinese Islamic Association. In May 1953, the first session of the Chinese Islamic Representatives Assembly was convened in Beijing. This conference elected Bao E'han chairman and Yang Jingren, Ma Yuhuai, Da Pusheng, Ma Zhengwu, and Yimin Mahesumu (a Uyghur) vice-chairmen. General regulations for the Chinese Islamic Association were drawn up and approved. The aim of the association as stipulated can be summarized as follows: To help the people's government implement the policy of freedom of religious belief, to develop the good traditions of Chinese Muslims, to love the motherland, and to safeguard world peace.

Ideological Changes among Members of Religious Circles

Members of religious circles (i.e., religious clergy and upper-level believers) do not belong to a unique social class; rather, they belong to different classes and different social strata according to their economic position and political attitudes. They have close spiritual ties with the masses of believers and exercise an influence on their spiritual life that cannot be neglected. Great changes have taken place in the ideology of members of religious circles in the new social environment of China since Liberation, whatever their family background and experience.

1. Splits have occurred among those few persons who had close ties with imperialism and the reactionary ruling class. Before and after Liberation, there were a few upper-class believers in religious circles who had close connections with imperialism and the reactionary ruling class at home. Because of their own private interests, they felt that "the end of the world" was coming with the victory of the people's revolution. Some of them did all they could to hinder the liberation and unification of China, while others spread libel about Communism, hoping in vain for the collapse of the people's government so that the reactionaries would some day come back.

For example, imperialists instigated pro-imperialist elements among Tibetan local rulers to sever Tibet from China under the pretext of "independence" and "complete self-governance," hoping to make Tibet a colony or appendage of the imperialists. The rebellious activities of the pro-imperialist elements reached their peak on the eve of the PLA's march into Tibet. They put on all kinds of ugly shows of "independence" and "anti-Communism," deploying the main force of the Tibetan army at Changdu in a vain attempt to stop the PLA.

Another example is the counterrevolutionary activities plotted by [Archbishop] Riberi, the "envoy" from Rome to China, in which some Catholics took part. In March 1951 Riberi dished out a "letter to all bishops in China," slandering new China as a "miserable age," conspiring to start a "prayer crusade." At that time, some people inside the Catholic church participated in this counterrevolutionary activity. There were also a few people inside Islam in China who spread words against Communism and against the people, opposing various policies of the people's government in the early days after Liberation. Some even spoke out publicly, counterposing "religious law" against "national law."

With imperialism driven out and the feudal ruling class overthrown after the founding of new China, these religious figures lost their political and economic support, so they had to make a decision on "where to go." By adopting the policy of forgiving past misdeeds, the people's government joined with them politically, helped them economically, protected their religious freedom, and thus gradually won over most of them, leading to changes in their political stand. Typical examples are those high-level Christian figures who changed their standpoint. At the beginning of the Three-Self Movement, there were people who first stood against it and later, under the pressure of the situation, gave their signatures to the "Three-Self Manifesto," but only half-heartedly. Only when the movement to Resist America and Aid Korea swelled daily, when people from different circles exposed the political, economic, and cultural crimes of the American imperialists, were the hearts and minds of these Christian figures touched. At the end of 1950, when the United States egregiously froze Chinese assets and China adopted corresponding measures, did these people realize how hopeless it was to rely on foreign power.

In April 1951 the Administrative Council of the national government convened the "Conference to Deal with Christian Organizations Receiving American Subsidies" and announced the severe and just stand of the Chinese government in opposing the use of religion by American imperialism to sabotage new China. The government, deciding to care properly for those religious organizations that had accepted American subsidies and were confronted with financial difficulties resulting from the American action to freeze Chinese assets, reduced or exempted taxes on church buildings and land. Meanwhile the government helped them, by means of education, to see the crimes of aggression against China carried out by imperialists using religion. Certain high-level religious figures, after going through ideological struggles, drew a line separating themselves from the imperialists, denouncing their crimes, and, making a decisive step alongside the Chinese people, liberated themselves from the imperialists. Some high-level Catholics also came to see the facts about the Vatican's unbroken hostility toward the Chinese people, gradually taking the road of opposing imperialism and loving their country.

Of course there were a few people who refused to abandon their reactionary stand and continued to make use of religion for antipeople activities, but they became more and more isolated. Those few high-level Tibetans who instigated armed revolt made use of religion in their criminal activities aimed at splitting our motherland. But the Tibetan Council (Kanbuting), with the Panchen as representative, steadfastly supported the unity of China, denouncing the revolt of the reactionary clique.

2. Most religious figures have personal experience of the invasion and oppression of China by the imperialists, and have also seen for themselves the corruption of the reactionary Guomindang. They did, then, have some feeling of patriotism and democracy and discontent with imperialism and the Guomindang reactionaries. But, because the religious organizations to which they belonged were under the political influence of reactionary forces and financially dependent on foreign mission subsidies and feudal exploitation, some religious figures were fearful, resentful, and suspicious of the Communist Party and the people's revolutionary cause. In particular, when they heard the slander spread about by imperialists and reactionaries on the eve of Liberation, such as "theism and atheism are irreconcilable," "the Communist Party wants to wipe out religion," "pastors in liberated regions were nailed to crosses," and so forth, they doubted the truth of the Communist Party's religious policy.

After Liberation their feelings of discontent were reduced when they saw that the PLA observed strict discipline, religious activities went on as usual, and religious freedom was clearly written into the Common Program. But they still had a degree of fear and suspicion. In particular, some Protestants and Catholics were ambiguous in their attitude, influenced by the idea that there was "no imperialism inside the churches," and were unable to draw a line separating themselves from imperialist agents and reactionaries who used the guise of religion.

Religious patriots and believers, while going through the [political] movements of land reform, anti-imperialism and loving one's country, suppressing counterrevolutionaries, democratic reform, and so on, again and again exposed the crimes of imperialist agents and reactionaries who were hiding inside the churches. Most religious figures could clearly distinguish between friends and enemies. The stability of social order in new China, the recovery and growth of the economy, plus the deepening of education on patriotism and the contributions of patriotic believers all made them feel love for new China, see the superiority of the socialist system, and understand that "there would be no new China without the Communist Party." They also saw that not only the interests of the motherland and the people but also the purity of religion would suffer if they did not draw a line between themselves and the imperialists and reactionaries. Because of their aroused patriotic consciousness, they gained confidence in the religious policy and gradually drew closer to the people. Some of them became activists in the anti-imperialism and democratic reform movements.

3. A few progressive religious figures played a leading role in loving their country and religion. Before Liberation, there were only a few patriotic progressive figures in religious circles. Some of them had taken part early on in the

democratic revolutionary movement, serving the revolution and establishing friendly ties with the Communist Party. They gave firm support to new China after Liberation and were representative of progressive religious circles. For example, Christian patriots Wu Yaozong, Deng Yuzhi, and Liu Liangmo, the Buddhist leader Zhao Puchu, and others all played active roles in the democratic movement before Liberation. In September 1949 they attended the first session of the Chinese People's Political Consultative Conference, supported the Common Program, and hailed the birth of new China. It was at the suggestion of Liu Liangmo that the "March of the Volunteers" was named the national anthem.

In 1950, a group of Christian patriots headed by Wu Yaozong issued the "Three-Self Manifesto" drafted by Wu, which had a profound influence in religious circles. Wu Yaozong, although attacked and slandered by imperialist agents and other reactionaries, courageously kept on fighting despite setbacks and never stopped promoting world peace, thereby becoming a model among Christian circles. In the early years of the War of Resistance, Buddhist Master Yuan Ying took an active part in fighting against Japan. On the eve of Liberation some people advised him to go abroad, but he remained firm, saying, "I am Chinese, I grew up in China, and I will die in China. I will never go elsewhere." After the founding of new China he made particular contributions in promoting the patriotic campaign, in developing international Buddhist contacts, and in the movement to defend world peace. Just before his death he warmly praised new China in his will, saying, "Social morality has improved throughout China, unimagined predestined developments have come about, and I am blessed to see this flourishing time before my death." He also encouraged his followers to be "of one heart and one mind, devote yourselves to the enterprise of world peace, and take part in the patriotic movement. You should think of how to benefit the people, support the country, and be rich in affection; this is the chief good and the beginning of Buddhahood."

The Tibetan Buddhist elder, the Venerable Shirob Jaltso, has been the vice-chairman of the Qinghai provincial government since December 1949. Devoting himself to the unity of the motherland, he made nothing of the hardships of traveling all over Qinghai's farming and herding areas to propagate the government's policies on religion and national minorities. He also worked ceaselessly to maintain the seventeen-point agreement on the peaceful liberation of Tibet. He strongly condemned the fallacy of an "independent Tibet," supporting the unity of China. He was respected for his patriotism and honored as a patriotic elder.

Islamic figures also plunged into the current of resisting Japan and saving the country in the early years of the War of Resistance. They also made their contributions to liberating all China and building up the new regime. For example, Bao E'han issued a telegram in September 1949, during the liberation of Xinjiang, accepting the PLA's "peace terms, consisting of eight items and twenty-four points," crossing over to the people, and making a contribution to the liberation of Xinjiang. Besides these, the chief imam of the Xinjiang Uyghurs, Saimi, and the chief imam of the Hui nationality, Ma Liangjun, also worked for the building of new China and strengthening of national unity.

The contingent of religious patriots continually grew along with the progress of society. These people were the backbone of patriotic religious organizations. They loved their motherland, supported the socialist system led by the Communist Party, and supported national unity. They were also knowledgeable about religion and, being well-connected with the masses of believers, led them on the road of loving both their religion and their country. They also played a leading role in establishing independent, autonomous churches.

In a word, the hearts and minds of religious figures who had been attached to imperialism and feudalism have, in different degrees, greatly changed through the deep social reforms that followed the founding of new China. At present, most religious figures in our country are patriotic, supporting our constitution, socialism, and the unity of the motherland. Of course, we still have to be vigilant against our enemies, both at home and abroad, who make use of religion to engage in sabotage. But there is no doubt that our religious figures have fundamentally changed their thinking.

Changes in Religious Thinking

In old China, imperialists and the feudal ruling class used religion, on the one hand, as a spiritual tool to enslave the people; on the other hand, the masses, pressed down by the three great mountains, were unable to free themselves from their burden of suffering, so they turned to religion for spiritual sustenance. Thus the main reasons for religious thinking were negativism, escapism, and pessimism. Religion wants people to believe that the world is full of suffering, man is vicious, and "salvation" can be found only by religious faith; that human life is illusory, uncertain, and filled with pain, and only "paradise" or the "Buddhist heaven" can give lasting "happiness." Humankind should endure all sufferings in the real world while pursuing "happiness" and "blessings" in the future.

Fundamental changes have taken place in society since the founding of new China. In this unprecedented social environment, religious ideas cannot but change. Marx and Engels have said: "Quite obviously, man's views and concepts change in step with each reform of the social system. That is to say, man's religious ideas also change" (*Complete Works of Marx and Engels*, 7:240). The great social changes of the socialist period are bound to bring changes in religious thinking.

Religious figures and the masses of believers, after the founding of new China, came to realize that certain traditional religious concepts no longer conformed to the reality of the new society in which they were living. For example, the sludge and foul water left over from the old society were cleared away as a result of the victory of the people's revolution and socialist reform. Great changes are taking place in the sphere of social morality—new persons and new things, forgetting self and helping others, are serving the public good. Our long-suffering motherland is turning into a beautiful and happy paradise on earth. Facing this new reality, we can no longer say that the new society is dark and bitter, nor that people are vicious and malicious. To build a new China, to wipe out oppression and exploitation, and to send away poverty and backwardness are closely connected with happiness and benefits for everyone; religious believers can no longer take a passive attitude to escape from their responsibility to help humankind. The religious attitudes of negativism, escapism, and world-weariness were tossed out and replaced with positive concepts, activism, and love for both religion and country. This can be seen in all religions.

Changes in Christian Theological Thinking

In the early 1950s, patriotic Christians whose consciousness had been raised and viewpoint changed realized that they could not go along with certain Western theological concepts and called on Chinese believers to take on the task of "self-propagation." At that time Wu Yaozong explained "self-propagation" as follows: "To achieve self-propagation, Chinese believers themselves must exploit the treasures of Jesus's gospel, free themselves from the shackles of Western theology, clean out the idea of escaping from reality, and create a theological system of their own." Later, patriotic Christians developed clear explanations of the creeds, which had been wilfully distorted by imperialists and reactionaries, that conformed with the real spirit of the Bible and contributed new elements to Chinese Christian theological thinking.

Some Christian ideas, such as "love your enemies," "do not kill people," "Christians do not belong to this world," and "forgive people seventy times seven times," were used in the early years after Liberation to oppose the anti-imperialist patriotic struggles that were carried out in Christian circles, causing some Christians to blur the line between themselves and their enemies and hindering their progress in patriotism. Seeing this, some patriotic Christian figures, again drawing on the Bible, held that all religious concepts must be understood in an all-around way, using the Bible as background for linking all beliefs. They pointed out that believers, according to the teachings of Jesus, should distinguish right from wrong, good from bad, and should oppose evil forces, plunging themselves into the cause of just struggles. The imperialists and reactionaries inside the church had committed many evil acts that brought harm to the motherland and the people. To apply mechanically the teachings of "love your enemies" and "do not kill people" and let them do what they want would be a sin against Christian moral teachings.

In April 1953 the Shanghai Gospel Press published the tract "Purity Without Flaw," which, with ulterior motives, said that the world is under the control of the devil and filled with crimes, but that the church is always sinless, pure, and without flaw. It argues in this way to support the use of religion by the imperialists, oppose the Three-Self Movement, and attack new China. It was refuted at once in articles written by patriotic Christians. To clear away further imperialist distortions, the Christian periodical *Tianfeng* in 1956 published a broad and intensive discussion, using religious ideas, on "how Christians should deal with the world" and "the relation between Christians and secular people." The results can be seen in the following discussion of four theological questions.

1. Does the world belong to the devil or to God? The crux of this question is what attitude should be taken, affirmative or negative, toward the progress and light of the new society. According to basic Christian beliefs held by many believers, "the world was created by God," "human beings act with justice and right according to the will of God," and "the world is not controlled by the devil, but by God."

2. Is human nature entirely corrupt, or does it possess both a "sinful nature" and "the image of God"? The crux of this question is what attitude, affirmative or negative, should be taken toward the masses of the people. Many Christians, from the viewpoint of Christian theology, believe that man should not be seen as totally depraved, because on the one hand he is "fallen and corrupt," and on the other he has "the image of God." They point out that the splendid character, intelligence, talent, and great creative powers shown by the masses of the people in revolution and [socialist] construction cannot be obliterated, because they reflect the "image of God."

3. Are "belief and nonbelief" mutually antagonistic, or should they live peacefully together, even though there are differences in belief? This question involves relationships between believers and nonbelievers, between the church and society. Many Christians believe that if you say "you love God" you have to show it by "love for the people," and that antagonism toward nonbelievers does not conform with the belief that one should "love others as oneself." Christians should do their best not only to live peacefully with others, but also to cooperate with them in building the motherland.

4. Is religious belief antagonistic to social morality, or can the two be integrated? This question is related to one's attitude, affirmative or negative, toward the spiritual changes of the people in the new society, and whether believers should play an active role in building the new society. The great majority of Christians refute those who say "Speak only of [spiritual] life (i.e., faith), not about good and bad, right and wrong." Basing their views on the Bible, they believe that one should be clear about what to love and what to hate, and not only affirm the moral progress of others, but take on moral responsibilities of one's own.

The discussion of these theological issues is, in fact, a new explanation of and probe into certain traditional Christian beliefs, which overcomes the negative side and elucidates the positive side, forcing change and growth on these traditional beliefs. These changes are an objective adaptation to the needs of the new society.

Changes in Buddhist Ideas

Development of the concept of "Buddhism on earth." Buddhism holds that everything is empty, that all human life is suffering, and that happiness can be found only in the "clean earth" of the Western Paradise and the "Kingdom of Buddha." In the old society, a one-sided emphasis on these ideas easily led the believers into escapism, pessimism, and negativism. There have been manifest changes in Buddhism since the founding of new China. The most important change is the recognition that Buddhists not only can pursue happiness in the future life but should also work for happiness here on earth. The early Buddhist classic *Zeng ahan jing* says, "All Buddhas come from the earth." This shows the spirit in which Buddha attaches importance to the world. The *Liuzu tanjing* also says, "Buddhas on earth cannot live out of the world; looking for Buddhas out of the world is like looking for horns on a rabbit." This shows the inseparable relationship between Buddha and the world.

Many patriotic Buddhists have taken over these Buddhist ideas, giving them new meaning. They hold that in new China the reactionary rule of the Guomindang has been overthrown and the people have become masters of the country, so the "world" is our great socialist motherland. To advocate "Buddhism on earth" is to ask Buddhists to observe the five commandments and the ten goods in order to purify themselves; to practice the "four deeds" and the "six trips to the other shore" so as to help the people; to take consciously as one's duty to bring about the "clean earth" and to contribute to socialist construction.

The constitution of the Chinese Buddhist Association (CBA) makes it clear that positive Buddhist beliefs, such as "dignify the land" and "give help with affection" (i.e., to take an active part in building the motherland, to go all out and serve the people) should be observed by the broad masses of Buddhists. This embodies the idea of Buddhism on earth. The first chairman of the CBA, Yuan Ying, made it a priority for all Buddhists to take an active part in all patriotic movements, to support world peace, to help the people, and to love the country. The well-known scholar and patriotic elder Shirob Jaltso, while serving as chairman of the CBA, wrote articles calling on Buddhists to "struggle for the creation of a real Pure Land on earth." Zhao Puchu, speaking at a Buddhist conference, also called on Buddhists to promote the idea of Buddhism on earth. The adaptation and development of the idea of "Buddhism on earth" has given rich new content to the Buddhists' "love of both country and religion."

A new understanding of Buddhist beliefs such as "be merciful" and "don't kill living creatures." With the commandment "do not kill living creatures," mercy is at the heart of Buddhism. In the past, Buddhists held that mercy is the origin of Buddhist practice, so that even those who committed monstrous crimes would not be killed. There have been changes since the founding of new China. During such [political] movements as suppressing reactionaries, cleaning out counterrevolutionaries, and Resist America, Aid Korea, many Buddhists came to see the heavy blood debts resulting from the imperialists' invasion and killing of our compatriots, and the many crimes of the counterrevolutionaries. To be merciful to these persons would be cruel to the people. If these persons were not killed it would be empty to talk about mercy to all living creatures. Patriotic Buddhists, basing their words on Buddhist beliefs, said, "The invasion of American imperialists is contrary to the purpose of Buddhism," and "it was the devil who sabotaged world peace." They stressed that "Buddhist mercy takes the broad masses of the people as its objective. To exterminate the few devils that do harm for the benefit and happiness of the majority of the people has as great significance as the infinite mercy of Buddha." This new understanding of "showing mercy" and "not killing living creatures" pushed Buddhist believers toward active support for the movement to Resist America and Aid Korea and toward exposing and informing against evil persons in Buddhist circles.

This new understanding also brought progress to the agricultural output of Buddhist temples and monasteries. In the past, the commandment "Do not kill living creatures" had been used to protect insects and pests that were harmful to crops. One year, when the crops of Ningde Prefecture in Fujian Province were attacked by pests, a number of monks did not dare to use pesticides, holding to the commandment "Do not kill living creatures." As a result, production dropped, incurring unnecessary losses. Later, some monks said that the crops couldn't be protected without killing insects, and they believed that "killing insects and saving crops is also acceptable Buddhist practice." Later, monks in other places agreed, and now they never consider killing pests and insects to be contrary to the commandment "Do not kill living creatures" when it involves agricultural production.

Changes have taken place in different degrees in other religions. For example, ideas of the Catholic church from the early days after Liberation, such as "irreconcilability between theism and atheism" and religion being beyond politics, class, and nation, have been cleared away. Patriotic Catholics said that they should set up their own independent theological studies, should use the Bible to explain and expound matters of faith, and should write Chinese Catholic theology that conforms with the Chinese context and is in the interest of the masses of the people.

Islamic religious ideas have also changed. Muslims overall no longer spread negative ideas, such as "the end of the world is coming," or oppose the marriage law and birth control. They emphasize the positive aspects of their beliefs. For example, in 1983, the Institute for Research on Religion of the Xinjiang Academy of Social Sciences conducted detailed field studies of two Uyghur villages in the Keshen region. They discovered that these Muslim believers, when comparing their lot with that in former times, had come to see that only the Communist Party could make them masters of their land, and that only the socialist system could bring good times and could create a "heavenly garden" whose fragrant flowers bloomed everywhere. Now 90 percent of the Muslims in these two places take as their code of conduct the Islamic belief that "happiness comes both from one's labor and from Allah"; this is the source of their inspiration for socialist construction. Muslims have also changed their prejudiced attitude toward non-Muslims, strengthening national unity by their belief now that "Han people also receive life from Allah (the true God)." They have also continued and developed the good traditional Islamic belief that "patriotism is part of the Islamic faith," saying that "true Muslims love the nation and the people. Our faith does not permit betrayal of our motherland." This fully demonstrates their spirit of love for the motherland and for socialism. In addition, changes in Islamic religious ideas are reflected in their readiness to accept new culture, science, technology, and life styles.

The religious ideas in our country have changed in varying degrees mainly because they have adapted to the changing social, economic, and political conditions, meeting the needs of believers living under new conditions. By continually modifying their religious ideas, the different religions are gradually overcoming certain negative factors and bringing into play the positive factors they should contribute to new China.

The Far-Reaching Significance of These Fundamental Changes

We have illustrated above the fundamental changes in religion since the founding of new China, based on the political status of religious organizations, the ideology of religious circles, and the religious ideas of the various religions. These changes did not occur by themselves; they came about through fierce political and ideological struggles among religious patriots under the leadership of the Chinese Communist Party in the wake of fundamental reforms in the social system. Since these changes among the various religions and sects have developed unevenly, and in some cases are not obvious, why don't we say, "relatively great changes" or "very great changes" rather than "fundamental changes"? This is because changes involve more than increases or decreases in number or extent; they involve changes in nature as well. We might well say that the fundamental changes in the status of religion under the socialist system are another leap forward in the history of religion with far-reaching historical significance. Of course the religious world view is still idealistic, an illusory reflection of the real world in the human mind. The "leap forward" in the "nature" of religion mentioned here refers mainly to the social nature of religion.

Marx's important thesis, "Religion itself has no nature or kingdom. . . . We have to go to the material world at each stage of religious development to find out its nature," is quoted in the introductory chapter of this book. This thesis teaches us that we should not discuss religion in the abstract but should explore religious questions in the material world and the different social systems where religion is rooted. One leap forward in human social history was the shift from primitive to class society. Another was the leap from class to classless society. This leap forward was fundamentally different from the change of the social system from one class to another (for example, from feudal to capitalist society). Two leaps forward were the rise of the exploiting class as the ruling class and its subsequent abolition. These leaps forward were first reflected at the economic level in the ownership of the means of production and will definitely be reflected in the superstructure, such as politics, law, religion, art, and philosophy.

As for religion, the religion of a class society differs from that of a primitive society in at least three ways: (1) The external forces that are obversely reflected in religion are not only natural, but, more important, also social forces. The sufferings caused by class exploitation and class oppression are the main social sources of religion. (2) "All oppressor classes must have two social functions in order to maintain their rule: one is that of executioner, the other of pastor" ("The Fall of the Second Internationale," in *Selected Works of Lenin*, 2:638). In a class society the ruling class, using various methods and approaches, controls and utilizes religion to lull the people's revolutionary will so as to maintain its rule. Of course, due to different times and situations, the form and degree of control will differ. Sometimes the oppressed nationality or class also makes use of religion as an ideological weapon to oppose exploitation and oppression and as a tie for uniting with the masses. No matter what the condition, however, religion is indissolubly bound to class and to class struggle. (3) In class society, "the ideology of the ruling class is at all times the ideology that occupies a dominant position" ("German Ideology," in *Complete Works of Marx and Engels*, 3:52). Therefore the religious ideas and theological theses created and developed by religious leaders generally reflect the social will of the ruling class. The ruling class usually remolds, distorts, and uses for its own advantage religious ideas that originally reflected the wishes of the exploited and oppressed class. Only when that class becomes strong enough can it represent the revolt of the oppressed class against the ruling class and its future interests. In a word, in class society, the religious ideology and theological theories of complex systems of enormous magnitude are all stamped with the brand of class, and, in the wake of great changes in class strength, bring forth corresponding social effects.

The great victory of the Chinese democratic revolution and socialist reform has built a socialist system, abolishing all exploiting systems and basically eliminating the exploiting class. Our country is now developing social productive forces on a large scale and continually consolidating and perfecting socialist productive relations and the superstructure; on this basis we are moving step by step toward total elimination of class differences, social inequality, and great social differences. Of course, this will certainly take a long time. But the historical reforms that resulted in abolishing the exploiting class and system have led to fundamental changes in the state of religion that make it quite different from religion in a class society.

1. The abolition of class exploitation and oppression has led to the disappear-

ance of class as a social source of religion. Of course there are still social sources of religion under the socialist system, but the disappearance of class as a source must not be overlooked.

2. The leadership of churches and various religious organizations in the socialist period is, of course, no longer in the hands of the exploiting class. Religions are now administered by the working class believers of all nationalities themselves. The history of religion used as a tool of the reactionary ruling class to lull the people's revolutionary will has gone forever. Owing to internal [domestic] factors and influences from abroad, class struggle will still continue within certain parameters for a long time to come. Hostile foreign influences, in collaboration with a remnant of reactionaries still extant in our country, are still dreaming of regaining control of religious organizations and religious affairs in China. They have tried many times since the founding of new China, but, like an ant trying to topple a giant tree, it all came to nought in the face of the strong people's dictatorship and patriotic believers. It will be the same in the future. This shows that the changes in the state of religion conform with the objective laws of historical development and are irreversible.

3. Marx, Engels, and Lenin produced many profound and vivid ideas on the social and political functions of religion in a class society and proletarian revolution. Some of their disquisitions still hold. But Marx and Engels, after all, had no personal experience of a society in which the exploiting classes had been abolished, and Lenin lived only briefly in such a society. Therefore, it was impossible for them to supply any ready-made solution to questions about the function of religion during the period of socialist construction. Many facts since the founding of new China show that the social functions of religion, because it has freed itself from the control of the exploiting class, have greatly changed, so that religion is quite different from that in a class society. This point will be thoroughly discussed in chapter 5.

Speaking with Christian leaders in May 1950, Zhou Enlai made this significant statement: "Let religion restore its true features" (*Selected Works of Zhou Enlai on the United Front*, p. 181). What are the original features of religion? Can we say that religion was originally a personal faith, a personal matter, and that after the exploiting class appeared, it became a spiritual club used to dominate the people? In the wake of the fundamental reform of the social system following the founding of new China, religion freed itself from being used and controlled by imperialism and all exploiting classes. Socialist countries practiced a policy of religious freedom, gradually restoring religion to its original status as a personal matter while making it part of the ideological beliefs of a portion of the masses. Religious believers, living in the great socialist family, personally participate in building the two civilizations. Social existence determines social consciousness. The heat of real life is sure to be reflected in the realm of thinking. Again and again they receive patriotic and socialist education, engendering love for the new society. But they are religious believers with God, Buddha, and the True Lord in their hearts. The negative elements of traditional religious ideology still influence them. Struggles between the two ideologies are inevitable, but most of them do not slacken their efforts to bring about the good life before their eyes because of their religious faith. They have made an accommodation, holding that the pursuit of happiness on "this shore" can be integrated with anticipation of happiness on "the other shore." The antagonism between "heaven above" and "this world" that reflects social contradictions has subtly changed in their minds, shortening the gap between the two. In their eyes, religion is truth and socialism is truth as well; the two can coexist. In their words, "Love for one's country is identical to love for one's religion."

Religion is an ideology far removed from its economic base. It has passed through a long period of elaborate manipulation by the exploiting classes. The class brand stamped on religion will not disappear quickly. Its complete removal depends on the long-term development of socialist society and the persistent efforts of the people. We have to look into this side of things while attaching importance to the far-reaching significance of these fundamental changes. But it is important that, while religious believers hold onto their religious world outlook, these changes are very helpful in strengthening the united front with believers, bringing into play the activity of believers in socialist construction, and helping them to raise their ideological consciousness in practice, under the principle of seeking the common ground while preserving differences. People's ideology always follows along with progress and changes in living conditions, social relations, and social existence. Historical materialists can obtain epistemological enlightenment on this changing objective phenomenon, finding further material for reflection about the laws of evolution of religious concepts in the socialist period.

4 | Reasons for the Persistence of Religion

RELIGION has passed through different social forms on its long journey through history, from primitive society to slave, feudal, capitalist, and even socialist society. Religion still exists in every nation and every ethnic group in the world today.

The French materialist philosophers of the eighteenth century all maintained that the source of religion is human ignorance resulting from "fools meeting swindlers." But Lenin said that this is a superficial, narrow culturist way of looking at it. Although they pointed out that the concept of "God" is fabricated, their criticism of this fabricated concept did not touch on the real bases of religion, but only on metaphysics and historical idealism. Since he did not know that human nature is "the sum of all social relations" (*Selected Works of Marx and Engels*, 1:18), Feuerbach's limitation is seen in his abstraction of human nature.

Marx and Engels analyzed the causes of the emergence and growth of religion from the viewpoint of dialectical and historical materialism, pointing out that the sources of religion "are not in heaven, but on earth" (ibid., 27:436). Religion shares its general characteristics with other ideologies, all being reflections of human social existence. The special quality of religion is its distorted and illusory reflection of social existence. According to the thesis of Marx and Engels, if we want to understand the reasons for the emergence of religious consciousness, we must search out both the subjective factors that influence religious believers, that is, the human brain, and the actual objective society, as well as the specific historical and material conditions of society, since all contribute to the creation of the illusion of religion by humankind.

In our socialist society, social classes as a source for religion have disappeared since the elimination of the system of exploitation and the exploiting class itself. However, since the development of man's consciousness always lags behind social existence, it is impossible for old ideology and customs left over from the former society to be completely wiped out in a short time. It will require a long period of struggle to bring about sufficient gains in material prosperity by raising the social productive forces to the point where a high-level social democracy and highly advanced educational system, culture, science, and technology can be constructed. Because of the complicated international environment and the persistence of class struggle in certain sectors, religion is sure to last for a long time yet. We must follow the Marxist principle of always starting from reality and, observing the methods of social investigation advocated by Mao Zedong, carry out intensive investigations if we wish to find out the reasons why people continue to believe in religion in China today.

This chapter discusses the reasons for the persistence of religion in the socialist period under three categories: the influences of tradition on religion, the social sources of religion, and the psychological factors.

Traditional Religious Influences

The history of the evolution of human society is like an indivisible picture scroll. Ideology is the reflection of a specific social existence that changes along with the transformation of the economy and society, but it also has its own relative independence. Religion is an ideology quite far removed from its material base, and, compared with other ideologies, it changes more slowly and has a more obvious historical continuity. As Engels said, "Once religion is formed, it always contains certain traditional material, for in all ideological realms, tradition is a strong, conservative force" (ibid., 4:253). In the present period of socialism in China, the main religious influences are as follows.

Areas Where Traditional Religious Influences Are Concentrated

All religions have long histories in areas where the Han Chinese live, but their traditional influences are especially apparent in certain places and activities.

All religions, for a variety of reasons, have developed certain regional characteristics in the course of their development. Sacred places are concentrated in these regions, becoming centers of religious life and attracting many believers to their religious activities. Some of them, for complex historical reasons, are only relics of the past, but large-scale religious activities are still carried on in other places.

Buddhism and Daoism have their historically famous mountains and scenic spots. For example, there are many Buddhist holy sites and ancient temples on the famous four great mountains, Jiuhua, Putuo, Wutai, and Emei. According to the *Jiuhua Mountain Annals*, Buddhism came to that mountain in the Jin dynasty and became popular in the Tang dynasty. For the past thousand years the burning of candles and incense has never ceased. A week before the birthday of the Dizang Buddha in 1984, we saw large groups of believers from many places, including people as old as seventy or eighty using canes or helped by other people, climbing the mountain. Some knelt on every step to offer prayers. During the most crowded time, the square at the bus station was so packed with people that a drop of water could not trickle through.

More than eight thousand pilgrims sat through the night at the Puji Temple burning incense on the birthday of the Guanyin Buddha (February 19 by the lunar calendar) in 1984. There is a legend that says that the Mao brothers of Xianyang built a thatched cottage and practiced Daoism in the Eighth Cave of Daoism on Mount Tianmao during the reign of the Jing Emperor in the Western Han dynasty. Later, such Daoist thinkers as Lu Xiujing and Tao Hongjing lived here, forming the Shang Qing Sect, also called the Mao Shan Sect, whose influence spread widely in Jiangsu, Zhejiang, and Anhui. Even now, twenty to thirty thousand believers come here to burn incense during the peak season.

The coming of Catholic and Protestant Christianity to China is linked to the opening up of maritime travel, and particularly to recent historical events, so Christianity has prospered in the coastal regions. In some places, such as Qingpu County near Shanghai, Catholics even now live together in their own communities. According to the *History of Missionary Work in Southern Jiangsu*, there were already believers (who called themselves ''net-boat believers'') among the fishing families in the Jiangnan region at the time of the Qing dynasty's Kangxi Emperor. After the Yongzheng Emperor ordered all Catholic missionary work banned in 1724, missionaries often hid in fishing boats and came out at night to preach. The Catholic fishing families of this region have a history of two to three hundred years.

In the years just after Liberation, there were nine to ten thousand Catholics in the Qingpu region. At present, more than 4,000 Catholics a day go on the annual pilgrimage to the nearby shrine at Sheshan. According to incomplete figures, there were 980,719 [Catholic] Christians in Zhejiang, Fujian, and Guangdong at the end of 1984, 32.6 percent of the total number (3 million) in the entire country. This is directly related to the fact that three of the five treaty ports first opened to commercial trade are in these provinces. According to *Zhonghua guizhu* (China turns to the Lord) (1922), foreign missionaries had been engaged in evangelism in these three provinces since 1842. In 1922 there were 127,784 [Protestant] Christians in these three provinces, 37 percent of all [Protestant] Christians in China at that time (344,974). The number has multiplied in the past sixty years, but the number of [Protestant] Christians in these three provinces as a proportion of those in the entire nation has remained about the same, showing the influence of religious tradition in a given place.

Throughout history, each religion's particular rituals and ways of propagating the faith have been influential, and even now they are attracting people. For example, the religious art in Buddhist and Daoist temples is enjoyed by non-believers while at the same time satisfying the religious feelings of believers. Buddhist beliefs are also propagated through written works and the teaching of Buddhist masters. Many of those taking entrance examinations for Buddhist institutes and training classes in recent years have come to know Buddhism by reading the *Mituojing, Yinguang wenchao*, and other Buddhist classics, or by personal contacts with Buddhist monks.

[Protestant] Christianity has used a variety of ways to spread its faith. In old China, people were drawn to the church because of its hospitals, schools, and street preaching. Nowadays the church no longer runs these institutions, and street preaching has ceased, but traditional evangelism still goes on. Pastors use colloquial language and illustrations from everyday life to preach religious doctrines and expound the scriptures. Nonbelievers are drawn by the novelty of congregational hymn singing. Most of the short hymns sung in village meetings are written by the people themselves, incorporating religious content with popular tunes easily learned and understood. As has been the custom in [Protestant] Christian services, clergymen are not the only ones who preach; laypersons also are encouraged to "bear fruit" (that is, to bring in new believers) and to "give testimony" (to describe one's personal religious experience) in order to bring nonbelievers into the church. The steady growth of interest in Christianity in recent years is certainly related to these traditional methods of propagating the faith.

It should be noted that [traditional] concepts and worship of gods and ghosts common in some places is probably another reason for some people's religious belief. Concepts of gods and ghosts are particularly widespread among the Han Chinese, and worship of gods and ghosts is deeply rooted among the people. Mao Zedong said that there were four powers in old China that formed the feudal patriarchal system and ideology. One of the four was the "supernatural system ranging from the King of Hell to the town and village gods belonging to the netherworld, and from the Emperor of Heaven to the various gods and spirits belonging to the celestial world" (*Selected Works of Mao Zedong*, 1:33); this, together with the power of state and clan, and of husbands over wives, constituted the four ropes that bound the Chinese people. Temples to the town and village gods could be seen everywhere in the vast countryside and cities of old China. People believed that these gods would protect them and bring them peace in their earthly lives.

These ideas about and worship of gods and ghosts are different from religion. People who hold these ideas and engage in these practices are not religious believers; in fact, many of them stay away from religion because they are satisfied. However, one feature of these ideas about gods and ghosts is, after all, their continuity with primitive religious customs and belief in supernatural powers. Under certain conditions, worshippers of gods and ghosts may turn to religion. In the course of our recent investigations, we have discovered two related developments: In one situation, religious belief is looked on as a deepening of ideas about gods and ghosts, which serve as pointers toward religion; or the gods of religion are believed to be more efficacious than the spirits people formerly believed in, so they turn to religion.

For example, there was a family in Fujian whose members were told by a fortuneteller that they had been predestined to become monks and nuns. Believing this, the whole family, including husband, wife, and child, abandoned their family life and entered the temple.

Some villagers who turned to Christianity became Christians because they suffered from mental illness which they believed was caused by the devil. Believing Jesus more powerful than the devil, they asked Jesus to cast the devil out.

The other, more obvious, development is the law in China, which, in order to protect the interests of the people, clearly prohibits the activities of sorcerers, witches, fortunetellers, and geomancers. It also stipulates that protection of the freedom of religious belief is a basic right of all citizens. As a result, people who used to believe in gods, ghosts, and fate have turned to religion, contributing to its growth. We discovered this in our investigations in Jiangsu, Henan, and other places.

Traditional Folk Customs and Culture Colored by Religion

A nation, as defined by Stalin, is "a stable community which has been historically formed by a people with a common language, territory, economic life, and psychological character expressed in a common culture" (*Complete Works of Stalin*, 2:300–301). Religion is included in the fourth of these characteristics, under culture, life styles, and customs of the nation: "a common psychological character expressed in a common culture." The spiritual forms of philosophy, literature, art, music, and so forth were integrated with Buddhism and Daoism throughout the cultural history of the Han Chinese, forming a unique religious culture whose influence was widespread in the broad realm of ideology. Even now, after China has become a socialist society, the ancient religious books and records, the magnificent temples and pagodas, the impressive statues of gods, and the works of art with religious themes convey to the people information about religious traditions. Generally speaking, religious knowledge does not necessarily lead to religious belief, but in the course of learning about religious culture, people's curiosity may be aroused, leading to inquiries and even interest in religion, which may be the first step toward religious belief.

For example, some intellectuals come to believe in Buddhism and Daoism because they have earnestly studied these religions; some youths who enjoy literature and arts become interested in religion when they probe into the scholarly values of religion; others, moved by a sense of religious mystery when reading mythic novels or seeing films and plays with religious themes, adopt a religious world view. A senior high school graduate said that he had never seen a temple or monk but came to respect and admire Buddhism because of impressions from the film *Shaolin Temple*, where the monks were not only experts at martial arts but were upright and honest as well.

Nearly the entire population of some ethnic minority groups in China believe in the same religion. Temples are not only the places for religious functions but are also the centers for transmission of national [ethnic] culture for Tibetans and the Islamic national minority groups. Lamaist temples have extensive collections of Tibetan historical and cultural materials. Since there are few doctors and medicines in the Tibetan regions, the temple doctors are the only hope for the sick. There has been a tradition of teaching in the main hall of the Chinese mosques since the sixteenth century. The chief imam taught the children of believers from the ancient religious classics, such as the Qur'an, as well as subjects of general knowledge. Some changes have taken place since Liberation, when the principle of separating education from religion was instituted, but the influence cannot be ignored.

Religion also permeates the life styles, festival customs, and diet of minority nationalities. For example, in the Northwest, where Muslims are concentrated, newborn babies are taken to the mosque to be given a religious name. In Xinjiang Province, where none of the religious sects except the Yi-chan requires formal procedures for becoming a member, it can be said that all Muslims are born Muslim and receive imperceptible religious influences from their childhood on. Chinese Muslims do not eat the blood of animals or the meat of pigs, donkeys, or mules, or of animals that die of natural causes. Some of these rules are found in the Qur'an, which prescribes what can and cannot be eaten.

Because of the Tibetans' belief that all things come from water, fire, wind, and earth, human bodies should be returned to their place of origin, and religious ceremonies are held for Tibetan celestial, earth, fire, and water burials.

Originally the Water-Sprinkling Festival of the Dai nationality took place on New Year's Day when all the people of the village, men and women, old and young, gathered in the Buddhist temples to wash the statues of Buddha. Later, they sprinkled each other, imagining they would wash away personal disaster and live long lives.

The Torch Festival of the Yi nationality, using fire to cast out demons and evil, was an offering to the god of the fields and the goddess of the earth. These religiously colored festival activities and traditional marriage and burial rites were noticeably marked by their mass [popular] and ethnic natures.

In this socialist nation of ours, the government firmly carries out both the policy on nationalities and the policy on religion. According to the policy of freedom of religious belief, there is freedom either to believe or not to believe in religion in the minority nationalities regions. Religious belief in those places is no longer compulsory, and members of a national minority are no longer naturally considered to be believers in a certain religion. However, since religion is closely connected with nationality cultures and customs among these groups, the traditional ways are bound to carry on for a long time. These traditional influences are stronger in the national minority regions than in regions populated by the Han Chinese.

Family Traditions That Influence the Children

A family is a cell of society. Its changes are closely connected with the progress of the society's economic and political systems. China was a semifeudal and semicolonial society for a long time, and the influence of the patriarchal clan system is deep and far-reaching. The patriarchal system is represented in families by the father's power and the filial obedience of Confucianism, which requires children to obey their parents; therefore, parents have quite a strong influence on children in Chinese family life. Among religious believers, parents usually want the next generation to carry on their religion. To a certain extent, this state of affairs continues today in our socialist society. At the same time, the religious atmosphere in the homes of believers deeply influences family members, especially children, through day-by-day aural and visual impressions.

Our investigations of several Buddhist institutes and training classes for monks and nuns showed that the majority of novices came from Buddhist families. A sample investigation made in 1983 shows that more than half of the thirty students came to their faith through the influence of parents and relatives. Some had parents, followers of Triratna, who offered prayers morning and evening. Their children remembered their parents at prayer. Some began to go to the temple for prayers at the age of seven, some began to practice abstinence from meat with their parents at the age of eight, and others began to chant the scriptures at the age of ten. One made his decision to become a monk while still a child and never changed his mind, even after returning from military service. Here are his own words: "Buddhist belief was rooted deeply in my heart from my childhood onward."

The Catholic faith is called the "religion of one generation to the next." Parents are required by Catholic regulations to provide religious education for their children, so the religious influence of the family on children is obvious. Today's devout believers who are middle-aged and older consist in large part of those who were taken to church for baptism a few days after their birth. The "net-boat believers" of Qingpu County could not afford to go to school in the old days, but having attended "Bible classes" at the church, they were able to recite the "Six Holy Texts" and the "Catechism." They went to confirmation, first confession, and first communion (religious ceremonies) at the age of ten. Religious customs were a part of their daily lives.

In the cities there is a long history of well-educated Catholics who were not only baptized as infants but also raised in Catholic schools where they were trained in religious theory, including doctrine, church history, and keeping the faith. This all had a strong influence on their world view. Most of the young people who have been baptized and entered the church recently are from Catholic families. In the three-year period 1981–84, 150 children from Catholic families in Qingpu County were baptized.

Protestant families similarly influence their children. Some young people living in Christian communities said, "I believed in religion from my mother's womb." Seventy-five of the ninety-one students in a certain theological seminary, ranging in age from twenty to thirty, came from [Protestant] Christian families. In some cases, the parents had dedicated their child before its birth as an "offering to God," promising that the child would become a minister. At a certain church in Shanghai nearly all the young choir members are from Christian families, some of them third- or fourth-generation Christians. Although some had not received baptism or church membership until after 1980, they had all been brought up from childhood in a religious way of life.

These examples show that, although public religious activities were prohibited during the ten years of chaos, religious education continued in the families. In Fujian, some monks and nuns were forced to resume secular life, marry, and have children, but they did not give up their faith. On the contrary, their children were given religious training at home. After the restoration of the policy on religion, they took them to the temples, with the result that some have even become monks and nuns.

A child in a Christian family in Shanghai always said prayers with her family before eating, even during the "Cultural Revolution." On her first day of kindergarten, surprised that other children did not pray before eating, she asked her teacher why they did not. This was a naive question, but it vividly illustrates the strong influence that a family has on later generations, even, in this case, during those "historically unprecedented" times.

Aside from its influence on youngsters, the ideology of the traditional patriarchal family influences adult members as well. For example, other members of rural families usually follow those who turn to religion in their search for healing of an illness, thinking that the sick person will be helped if the whole family converts; they also say that this will avoid "some members of the family going to heaven, while others suffer in hell."

Social Sources of Religion

According to historical materialism, religious phenomena "can be explained by the conditions of material economic life in a specific historical period" (*Selected Works of Marx and Engels*, 2:537). In a specific historical period, the historical traditions from the past are indeed influential, but they can function only when they are part of the social conditions of the time. Therefore, if we want to understand the reasons why a person believes in religion, we have to study the society in which he or she lives.

The reasons for the religious beliefs of primitive peoples were largely found in nature. They began to make simple, abstract inferences about natural phenomena as their thinking ability increased along with the development of social productive forces. Because their powers of thinking were still at a low level, they could not correctly understand natural phenomena and divided mankind and the world into a duality of material and spiritual, of physical body and [spiritual] soul. Because they did not understand physiological phenomena such as dreams, they came up with the concept that the human soul could exist alone without the body and would not die. Because they were afraid of thunder, storms, earthquakes, and natural disasters, they personified natural powers such as heaven and earth, worshipping them as alien powers.

Besides natural causes, which still play a role, social causes are the leading source of religious ideas in class societies; that is, the deepest social sources on which religion relies are the blind forces of class oppression which cause so much suffering. As Engels said, "There are people in all classes who have given up hope of material liberation, so seek spiritual emancipation in order to break free from their state of desperation" (*Complete Works of Marx and Engels*, 19:334).

The exploitative system with its history of several thousand years has been eliminated in our socialist society, allowing working people to free themselves from the misery caused by class oppression and become masters of society. This is an earth-shaking change. Since the elimination of that system and of the exploiting class, the class sources for religion have disappeared. This is one side of the question.

The other side is this: China has just emerged from a semifeudal and semicolonial society and is now in the primary stage of socialism. Therefore, its economic, moral, and spiritual aspects still, in many respects, carry traces of the old society. "After the basic achievement of socialist reform, the major contradiction that remains to be solved in China is the contradiction between the steadily increasing material and cultural needs and the backward social production" ("Decision on Some Historical Problems since the Founding of New China"). It is necessary to devote maximum efforts to raise social productive forces, to reform and perfect productive relations and even the superstructure if we are to develop social production. In following this historical course, all social contradictions will be reflected in the human mind, becoming, under certain conditions, the cause for some people to believe in religion.

The Persistence of Poverty and Backwardness

Lenin said, "The deepest sources of religious bias are poverty and ignorance" (*Complete Works of Lenin*, 28:163). In the thirty-odd years since the establishment of the socialist system as the foundation for the development of production and culture, our country has built up an independent and comparatively complete industrial and national economic system, conditions for agricultural production have undergone remarkable changes, production levels have been greatly raised, and cultural-educational undertakings have made great progress. But, since we were unable for a time to shift our main work to the development of productive forces, the historical heritage of poverty and backwardness that remained in some parts was not fundamentally changed, and a number of people have turned to religion because the basic educational and cultural needs in their lives were not being met.

The mistakes of the "Great Leap Forward" movement brought serious setbacks to the national economy, with serious impacts on people's lives. In the early 1960s our country was confronted with its most severe natural disaster. Later, the ten-year catastrophic "Cultural Revolution" seriously damaged social productive forces, leading to an increase of religious believers in some places.

One reason why some rural young people became religious novices in recent years was poverty. Some of the youths who wanted to study in Buddhist institutes and Christian seminaries came from impoverished places and used religion as their means of livelihood. The rapid growth of Christianity in some places was due solely to the hard life of the masses. For example, in northern Jiangsu Province, the soil became poor due to the overuse of land, lack of fertilizers, and the backward state of agriculture. Because of inadequate flood and irrigation works, there was drought when it did not rain and flooding when it did, so that in some years peasants harvested no grain at all, and their lives were bitter indeed. Until the Third Plenum of the Eleventh Party Congress [1978], peasants often did not have enough to eat, and some fled from famine to other provinces. Some prayed to the gods for a good harvest, hoping to break away from the cycle of poverty and hopelessness. Situations like these could be found throughout the mountain and border regions where production was underdeveloped.

It is hard to develop cultural and educational undertakings when the economy is underdeveloped. According to 1982 population figures, the illiteracy rate in China is as high as 23.5 percent, more than two hundred million people. The rate is even higher in the poorer regions. Take the example of a county in northern Jiangsu, where 37 percent of the people are illiterate, young people as well as elderly. Education in these areas is far from developed. Village primary schools were once called the "three muds," that is, "mud houses, mud desks, and mud children," lacking both teachers and facilities. The people in these areas lack scientific knowledge and are liable to be governed by religious thought and traditional concepts of gods and ghosts, even believing superstitious rumors and causing disturbances.

One example took place in the Old Man Yellow Stone Temple in Pi County, Jiangsu Province (Old Man Yellow Stone is a Daoist god). The temple was destroyed during the War of Liberation, and only a few stone tablets with blurred characters remained. In February and March 1979, the word was passed around that Old Man Yellow Stone was back and wished to bestow "celestial medicine" to people on earth to heal their ailments. Almost overnight, over thirty thousand people swarmed in, not only from the local county and province but from Shandong, Henan, and other places as well, offering sacrifices at the site of the old temple. They made tubes of white paper and waited for the wind to blow dust in, which they collected and took home as "celestial medicine" for sick people. This lasted for more than ten days, seriously interfering with social order.

The people in some remote mountainous villages have a very poor cultural life. Some young people who have received some education, and others who are not satisfied with the monotonous life of working, eating, and sleeping, have become interested in religious books and religious life. A number of young people in Zhejiang Province became religious believers because they had enjoyed singing hymns together. In a certain county young people organized an annual hymn sing, which now attracts a chorus of several hundred who give big performances.

Some Christian meeting points in rural Henan have organized choirs and orchestras with accordions, flutes, three-stringed lutes, and harmonicas, which perform for weddings or funerals of believers. Young people are strongly attracted to these activities.

There are certain jobs, such as seafaring, fishing, mining, and forestry, that, at our present level of productive forces, are dangerous and vulnerable to nature's whims. People who work in these jobs and their family members are liable to fear the threats of nature, so many of them turn to religion to seek protection from the gods. For example, the Zhoushan islands are a national fishery where people engage in aquatic production and fishing. The seas are dangerous, often causing families to lose husbands and sons, breaking up families. Fishing equipment has been modernized, and weather broadcasts and communication equipment make it possible for fishermen to escape from dangerous seas in time; nevertheless, they are at the mercy of the angry waves in a sudden change of weather. Fishermen, before setting out to sea, usually kneel devoutly before the Guanyin Buddha, who helps the poor and relieves the distressed, hoping for peace and safekeeping.

In the mind of most rural people, illness is still a calamity difficult to cope with. Transportation is poor in certain villages and mountainous areas, physicians are few, and medicines hard to get. The sick have to travel long distances to the hospital, and family members have to give up productive work time to escort them. When they see a doctor they have to pay, and some cannot afford it. If the main family worker falls ill, the family finances suffer. One reason for the rapid growth of Christianity in the countryside in recent years is that some people who charge no fees whatsoever are preaching that praying to Jesus can cure illness. So some people resign themselves to their fate and turn to religion for help. A material analysis of the social basis for this situation again shows a complex combination of poverty, backwardness, and underdeveloped health care, leading people to believe in religion in their hope for restored health.

Interaction of Religion and Other Ideological Factors in the Old Society

Engels emphasized that, while the economic base determines the course of the historical struggle, it is not the only decisive factor: "The factors that affect the course of the historical struggle, and the many conditions that decide the forms of the struggle, are a variety of factors from the superstructure; [these include] political, legal, and philosophical theories, and the religious viewpoint and its further evolution into a system of creeds" (*Selected Works of Marx and Engels*, 4:477).

Various ideas and customs left over from the old society still persist in contradiction to the new ideas and customs of our socialist society. These feudal and decadent bourgeois ideas became rampant during the ten years of chaos, and their influence is still felt to a certain degree.

A prominent token of feudalism still found in our social life is inequality between men and women and discrimination against women. For example, there are fewer opportunities for girls to receive an education than boys in the rural areas, with the result that there are more young female illiterates than males. In a certain village in Jiangsu there are about as many girls as boys in primary school, but only 40 percent are girls in junior high school, and 15 to 20 percent in senior high schools. In many parts of Zhejiang Province most of the women are financially dependent on the men because they are not included in the work force. In some cities there is discrimination against women looking for jobs, and young men have more job opportunities.

All this makes it hard for women to take charge of their own destiny. Surveys show that there are more women than men believers in all the religions. Of all the people baptized as Christians in Shanghai between 1979 and 1982, 77.3 percent were women. On the eve of Guanyin's birthday in 1984, of the 1,405 pilgrims who came every hour to the Taxiong Hall of the Putuoshan Temple to worship, 1,116 were women, or 80 percent of the total. There were more women than men among the recent young converts of each religion, which is a function of their social position.

Another factor is the cost of marriages in some places, where expensive betrothal and wedding gifts must be given to the bride's family. In contrast, young Christian women rarely make these material demands, so some young men become Christians in order to spend less on their weddings, while others use this way to escape from the grip of old customs.

In the countryside quite a few people turn to religion because they cannot get away from troublesome family disputes caused by narrow-mindedness, selfishness, and lack of mutual respect brought on by poverty and ignorance. In some cases where mothers-in-law used to ride roughshod over the daughter-in-law, the situation is now reversed, and the daughter-in-law is worse, angering her mother-in-law by lording it over her when she bears a son. In other cases, the men are brutal, beating their wives. Tragedies result when family contradictions become severe, even bringing on suicides by poison. When confronted by such insoluble situations, some turn to religion to seek relief.

Christianity encourages the rural people to be good persons, control their tempers, and practice filial piety. An example of this is a hymn, composed by members of a church in Anhui Province, called "Ten Exhortations," which reads: "We advise parents-in-law to listen carefully and don't quarrel with your daughter-in-law; don't scrimp on what you give her to eat and wear, for you please the Lord if you love her." It continues, "We urge daughters-in-law to listen carefully and don't quarrel with your parents-in-law, for the Lord will help you to live a long and happy life and have a daughter-in-law just like yourself, a person with a good name." This closely resembles a popular book of the Ming and Qing dynasties that urged people to be good. It is said that this kind of propaganda is very effective; if a woman quarrels with her husband, he will say, "Go and believe in Jesus."

Bureaucratism is the most prevalent of the old ideologies among the ranks of the cadres. Deng Xiaoping said, "The main abuses of the leadership and cadre system of the party and the nation are bureaucratism, overconcentration of power, lifelong tenure for leading cadres with a variety of privileges, and the patriarchal system" (Selected Works of Deng Xiaoping, p. 287). One of the good traditions of the Chinese Communist Party is its close ties with the masses of the people and the mass line. Now, many years after the victory of socialist revolution, most of our cadres carry on this tradition well, but some are tainted with bureaucratism, disregard the people's suffering, and go after personal privileges. Investigations have shown that cadres and units offer no help or concern to people who have difficulties in their life and work. Not knowing where to turn for help, they seek comfort in religion.

In one case, a young woman developed neurasthenia from mental stress and could not continue her studies. She went to work but was twice dismissed by her employers. These setbacks intensified her illness, and she found sympathy and help from members of the church. One of them gave her a book about Helen Keller, which helped her to face life and become a devout Christian.

Another woman, a cadre with a large family, was burdened with long-standing financial problems. When she got no help from her work unit she turned to religion and became a devout Buddhist.

In some places the people have no choice but to offer bribes to greedy cadres. Those who can't afford to pay bribes turn to the gods for help. For example, young men from the villages who want to join the army or get a job, or young fishermen who want to join the crew of an experienced captain skilled in modern technology (which has much to do with productivity and income), have to get the approval from a few cadres who demand gifts first. Because of these irregular practices, these cadres are called "living Buddhas" by the people. Since they can't afford to "burn incense" before these Buddhas, they are forced to turn to clay Buddhas. Because they can't afford to buy gifts for the cadres, the only thing left to do for some Zhoushan fishermen is to pray to the Buddha in their local shrine, hoping their sons can find work on the boat of an experienced captain.

Many cadres and people are unhappy with the continuing influence of such old feudal and bourgeois ideas. They are unwilling to wallow in the mire but are powerless to wash away the dirt, so they preserve their own integrity, hating the world and its ways, by hiding themselves in the world of religion.

One young man said that he was born into the new society, was brought up under the red flag, and thought everything was fine when he first stepped out into society. But the ugly things he saw discouraged and depressed him, and, unable to analyze the root sources of these things, he couldn't cope with them properly but instead took the way of escape into religion.

Hardships Due to Setbacks and Errors in the Work Place

It takes a long time to consolidate and perfect the socialist system. Compared with capitalist and feudal societies, the history of the socialist movement is short, and the history of socialist nations is even shorter, so the laws of development of socialist societies are still being probed. Our country became a socialist society after a democratic revolution that followed a semicolonial and semifeudal society. If we are to establish a socialist country with Chinese characteristics, we have to undertake arduous explorations under the guidance of Marxism in our national context, and errors and setbacks are unavoidable.

"Leftist" policy errors were made since the completion of socialist reform owing to our lack of experience in socialist economic construction, hasty and premature actions, and the erroneous policy of taking class struggle as the key political link. The serious, protracted, and widespread mistakes made during the "Great Proletarian Cultural Revolution" in particular have brought disastrous consequences to the country and the people, making some feel that their life course has been aborted. Some people, despairing of life in the real world, look for spiritual comfort in religion.

During the "Great Proletarian Cultural Revolution," many cadres, intellectuals, and their family members suffered greatly. Nonbelievers became believers, and indifferent believers became zealous. For example, a woman in Fujian who suffered bitterly after her husband died under persecution became a Buddhist. Not only did she become a vegetarian and pray regularly, but she became a backbone member of the Buddhist community, working hard to raise money for repairing temples.

A Christian woman in Shandong Province had become lax in her faith, but when her sick husband was targeted and accused during the "Cultural Revolution" and nearly persecuted to death, she could do nothing else but devoutly pray. The whole family has been firm in their faith since then.

Many other believers who were persecuted in the "Cultural Revolution" solely because of their religious belief did not give up their faith; on the contrary, this aroused an even more ardent religious fervor and devotion. During the ten years of chaos these believers never stopped their religious activities, scattering their meetings and going underground. In some cases unusual methods were used, like the Christians somewhere in Northwest China who went out into the wilderness to hold "wilderness worship meetings." In Guizhou Province Christians held night-long religious services in basements, stationing watchmen and using dogs and chickens in cages to disguise the entrances. In Wenzhou, Zhejiang Province, young people walked several miles at night to gather and worship in the mountains.

According to some people who took part at the time, these secret activities stirred up more religious commitment than overt meetings. Persecution only served to stir up their resolve to defend the faith, influencing other believers to stand firm. One example is a Christian community in Zhejiang Province where three young women had their heads shaved because of their religious faith. They said, "Our heads are shaved, but not our hearts; we have taken one more step toward God."

In some places, when Christians were arrested, other Christians, whether acquainted or not, would visit them and bring them food and other personal necessities. During the ten years of chaos, some people who were not seriously persecuted themselves lost hope for the future and became depressed, which led them to turn to religion.

In Zhejiang Province, where there was a fierce factional struggle with frequent armed fights, one youth who got fed up with all this dreamed of a world without strife and became a monk, because he thought that only Buddhism could make that a reality. In one county in Fujian, more than half of the eight hundred monks and nuns secretly converted during the "Cultural Revolution." Without question, all these examples are directly related to the events of that period.

At the time [in the mid-1960s] when educated [urban] young people were settled in rural areas, children from Christian families were also sent to the countryside or border regions. Before that they had just followed the religious practice of their families without necessarily being actual believers themselves. But the work was heavy and life monotonous on the farms, and there was no one to care for them. When their spirits were low, they found comfort in religion.

One young man from a Christian family sang hymns and read the Bible to raise his spirits while he was in the countryside, showing how easy it is to get a sympathetic response for the passive side of a religious world outlook.

The Influence of Overseas Religious Forces

Religion has its international character. Religious contacts between China and other nations have naturally increased since we began the open-door policy, so our religions have inevitably been affected by religions abroad.

China's religions, while holding to the principle of independence and self-government since the founding of new China, have made contacts with religious circles abroad, carrying on religious activities and academic studies together, strengthening friendship between Chinese and the people of other nations, helping the cause of world peace, and bringing interchange among religions. Some foreign friends, in the tradition of helping others, have offered, without conditions, material assistance to religious enterprises in China, including religious books and supplies. Some monasteries and temples in our coastal regions have links with certain temples in Southeast Asia (such as branch temples) where there are overseas Chinese Buddhist monks and sincere believers. When they return to China for visits, they often contribute money for repairing ancient temples out of affection for both their motherland and their religion. Some large temples have been completely renovated in this way, which helps to maintain our cultural relics while contributing to the survival and spread of Buddhism.

In addition, religious people in other countries have used various ways to spread their religious influence throughout China. For example, in the early period following the "Cultural Revolution," when the Catholic and Protestant churches were just getting going again, they were not prepared to print Bibles, hymnals, and other materials, so foreign Christians and overseas relatives and friends of Chinese Christians sent such publications into China any way they could. Overseas Chinese from Hong Kong, Macao, Taiwan, and other places brought "Bibles" to encourage their relatives in their faith.

Religious influences from outside are particularly evident in the border areas of China, where certain minority nationalities live on both sides of the border. Many of them have relatives who come and go frequently, facilitating religious contacts.

It should be noted that hostile outside forces are using religion for organized sabotage activities against our country.

Religion is no longer an instrument of the reactionary ruling classes in our socialist society, but the international situation is complicated, and there are still some anti-China elements and reactionaries who fled abroad and are engaged in sabotage activities against our country using the disguise of religion. Contacting reactionary elements inside China, they set up bases, send in agents, import religious books and audiotapes, and ensnare people into formal religious activities. Using religious language, they disseminate reactionary political propaganda and undermine the stability, unity, and normal order of society.

In a few places where class struggle has erupted between the enemy using the cover of religion and ourselves (antagonistic contradictions), the widespread influence of religion can be seen. Take the case of "Brother Andrew," an international Christian anti-Communist organization that specializes in slandering socialist countries, saying they persecute religion, and raises money to smuggle religious books. In June 1981 this organization attempted to smuggle a large load of Bibles into China on the coast near Shantou; although this attempt failed when the shipment was intercepted by Chinese militia, they say they will carry on these schemes.

Reactionary Catholic forces abroad are also engaged in secret activities aimed at undermining the independence, self-government, and autonomy of the Chinese Catholic Church and gaining control of Chinese religious organizations and religious affairs. In addition there are people who, under the pretext of "evangelizing China" and "showing concern for the souls of one billion Chinese," carry on a variety of activities in the vain hope of changing China's socialist system. Under the guise of religion, they carry out sabotage and hoodwink a part of the masses, widening their religious influence. This is one of the objective reasons for the existence of religion in the socialist period.

Psychological Factors

Religious belief is a kind of psychological activity that is related to the believer's knowledge, emotion, and will. Psychologically, the objective material world and social reality are primary for the believer. But a person's psychology and will are products of the human brain. As Lenin said, "Mental things, ideology, etc. are the highest material product, functions of the particularly complex material thing called the human brain" (*Complete Works of Lenin*, 14:238). The process of psychological reflection integrates the subjective and objective. Owing to differences in life styles, in the actual practice and levels of education, and in physical makeup, the psychology of individual humans cannot be the same.

In the psychological process by which religious belief is generated, the process of cognition is fundamental. Using his cognition, man takes religious creeds as truth, and his emotions will generate corresponding religious emotions that result in the actual religious decision. These three elements are mutually interrelated and influence each other.

Cognitive Differences

The process of human cognition is complex. Correct cognition should follow the law of "practice–cognition–more practice–better cognition," that is, the objective appearance of the objective world is reflected in the human brain through the five senses, becoming perceptual knowledge. Through analysis and synthesis, the brain sorts out these sensory impressions, forming abstract rational knowledge, that is, ideas and concepts. Any idea or concept has to be tested in practice to find out if it is correct. Human history has proven that it is a long, repeated, and difficult process to arrive at correct cognition. Deviations and errors often happen in the process, because human cognition is usually limited in two ways, as Engels said: "Every ideological image of the earthly system is always limited objectively by historical conditions and subjectively by the physical and spiritual conditions of the person receiving an ideological image" (*Selected Works of Marx and Engels*, 3:76). Man's consciousness is not passive and negative, like a mirror that mechanically reflects objective reality, but it takes the initiative, actively reflecting according to its own conditions.

Cognition is both limited and influenced by the level of one's knowledge, ways of thinking, and state of health. There is the possibility of correctly reflecting objective reality and the possibility, as well, of distorting the reflection, divorcing the subjective from the objective.

Religion is an illusory reflection resulting from the limitations of human cognition and related to the limited cognizance of the object, thus showing the deviations and errors that occur in the cognitive process.

In the primary stage of religion, all natural and social phenomena and natural objects that were not understood were worshipped as deities. As society, science, and culture progressed, and man's knowledge about the objective world and its laws increased, the reflection [of this reality] in religion decreased. For example, smallpox was prevalent in old China, and people could only go to the temples to pray before the "Smallpox Goddess" because they had no medical cure for the disease. Now, with the discovery of the smallpox vaccine, man has overcome this god of plague, so no one bows before the "Smallpox Goddess" any more.

However, the fact that there are still natural phenomena that cannot be understood, even at present levels of scientific progress, shows deviations and errors in methods of cognition; these are the principal sources of religious thinking for some people, in particular the subjective sources for the religious faith of some intellectuals.

For example, present understanding of the universe and the motion of matter marks a great step forward in man's understanding of the universe. Cosmic phenomena that could not be explained in the past, such as the reasons for solar and lunar eclipses, have long been understood. Landing a space vehicle on the moon showed that neither Diana nor a goddess of the moon can be found there. The development of geophysics and geochemistry has also proved that there is neither a devil nor a hell. But microcosmic and macrocosmic mysteries still abound, so a "God of Creation" and a "Fa Xiang" [Buddhist deity] still enjoy a large following. Some Christian intellectuals admit that their religious belief takes the "conformism theory" of nature as its basis.

Some people draw religious conclusions because of [unexplained] questions about the universe and the motion of matter, but that is because they cannot correctly understand the contradiction between that which can and cannot be known, between relative and absolute truth. Engels says, "Human thought is the highest, yet not the highest; its cognitive ability is infinite, yet limited. In terms of its natural character, mission, possibility and the ultimate end of history, it is supreme and limitless; speaking of each individual, it is not supreme and limitless" (Selected Works of Marx and Engels, 3:126). There are contradictions between man's finite cognitive ability and the objective world that is developing infinitely. Man cannot instantly grasp cosmic and ultimate truths, but this is not equivalent to lack of understanding of the material world. People who cannot deal dialectically with questions that are at present unanswerable will probably accept the simple answers offered by religion.

Or, take man's understanding of life. Modern scientists in their explorations have been trying to solve the riddle of life. In "Anti-Dühring," Engels, basing his argument on the level of science of his time, pointed out that life is a high-level form of material existence. Scientific research on the structure of living proteins is making steady progress. In 1965, Chinese scientists succeeded in the artificial manufacture of insulin, and in 1981 they succeeded in turning yeast alanine into ribonucleic acid. These are great contributions to the science of life, but up to now, man still cannot create life in the laboratory, and the riddle of life awaits further exploration.

China has made great progress in health care and public sanitation since entering the socialist period, greatly lengthening the average life span, but people still die according to the laws of nature. The question of life and death is still a universal concern. The dialectic view of life holds that both life and death are forms of matter in motion, with simultaneously both relationship and differentiation between the two, a unity of opposites that negate each other. In the sense of a ceaseless metabolism, life means death. Engels said, "Life is always considered in connection with its inevitable consequence, that is, death, which is always present as a seed in life. . . . Whoever understands this will reject the saying that 'the soul never dies' " (*Selected Works of Marx and Engels*, 3:570).

But most people cannot accept the scientific view of life and death because they are unwilling to accept the fact of death. Some people, for family, social, or sentimental reasons, and to calm their anxiety about death, hold tight to the illusion of immortality of the soul, the "other shore," the extension of life after death. This is why they turn to religion.

For example, an intellectual with a brilliant professional career could not stand the loneliness when his beloved wife died, so he went to a Christian pastor to learn about the church's teachings on immortality of the soul.

Everyone has to deal with another kind of question, that is, the unexpected circumstances of life. Socialism is a superior system in which people expect to find happiness by taking the future into their own hands. But in reality, unexpected things happen to people in this society in matters such as health, marriage, higher education, career, joy and sorrow, and life and death. Because people don't often probe beneath the unruffled surface of life, they are often at a loss in dealing with spiritual suffering caused by sudden adversities. There are still plenty of bitter experiences for the individual in socialist society that can come from setbacks and failures in love, education, employment, or death of a spouse. These things happen out of pure chance as well as from social causes, perplexing some people who then look for answers in the fatalism that religion expounds.

The experiences of human life, such as birth, aging, sickness, and death, follow inexorable laws, but sometimes and in some situations unexpected things happen. In fact, there is a complex causality for the processes of life itself, including both the inevitable and the accidental. As material things develop, things may happen accidentally from external, nonessential causes. To free oneself from fatalistic thinking, one must understand the relationship of the unity of opposites between the inevitable and the accidental. To see everything as either inevitable or accidental can lead to a religious way of thinking.

When Lenin spoke of human cognition as not a straight line but an infinite curve, like a chain of circles or a spiral, he said, "Any segment of this curve can become (or partially become) an independent and complete straight line, and this straight line can lead people (if they only see the trees and not the forest) to the mud pit, to monkism" (*Complete Works of Lenin*, 38:412).

Religion has always had its own set of explanations for questions about life on earth, the universe, and human life that have been passed down to this socialist period. Their common feature is setting the knowable against the unknowable, the inevitable against the accidental, the relative truth against the absolute truth, and to replace the random nature of things with the human sense of purposefulness. This way of linear thinking falls into the categories of idealism and metaphysics. Admittedly, idealistic, metaphysical, and linear ways of thinking are deviations and errors that can easily happen in the process of human cognition. Subjective and partial ideas that often occur in daily life and work spring from the same source. According to the Marxist viewpoint, there is not an impassable demarcation line between truth and error; as Lenin said, "One more little step, seemingly in the same direction, and truth will become error" (*Complete Works of Lenin*, 4:257). He calls religious idealism "a blossom which can bear no fruit." When one is clear on this point, one can understand the phenomenon of people believing in religion because of errors of cognition. Of course persons with errors of cognition are not necessarily religious believers. This is a question of a general dialectical attitude in dealing with unknowable phenomena. Although there will continue to be things that cannot be understood, they will not lead to religious ideas once man has a scientific and dialectical world outlook.

Emotional Needs

Emotional factors are very important in religious psychology. In his books *Essence of Christianity* and *Essence of Religion*, Feuerbach said, "Emotions are the basic instrument of religion," and "The essence of God is manifested in the essence of emotions" (*Selections from the Philosophical Writings of Feuerbach*, 2:34).

Human emotional needs and the engendering of those emotions are closely connected. To maintain his existence and development, man generates needs from certain conditions of external circumstances. Only when external matters are relevant to these specific needs of man can corresponding activities be induced. When his needs are met, man feels happy; if they are not, he feels unhappy. In the socialist period, although psychological functions have their special features, they have a common process. As a highly developed creature, man has a variety of needs. Besides basic physical needs, such as food, clothing, housing, sex, and mobility, man has higher-level spiritual needs. Generally speaking, man has to have the basic materials in order to live. But, since food and clothing alone do not provide a satisfying life, we must intensify the building of a spiritual civilization at the same time as we build a socialist material civilization. The diverse needs of the people can only be satisfied with a rich spiritual life.

Marx said, "Religion is the sigh of the oppressed, the sentiment of a heartless world" (*Selected Works of Marx and Engels*, 1:3). Engels said that those who have lost hope for material emancipation will "seek spiritual emancipation" and "ideological comforting" (ibid., 18:334). These theories illustrate how people turn to religion in the search for satisfaction of spiritual and emotional needs when troubled and oppressed by life experiences. Religious consciousness is an illusion remote from reality. It is not the active illusion of the so-called ideal, but the passive illusion of "daydreams." But the engendering of passive illusion comes, after all, from man's individual desires. As Engels depicts it, religion "deprives man and nature of all their content, and then passes them on to the unreal image of a god on the other shore, while the god on the other shore shows his mercy by returning part of the bounty to man and nature" (*Complete Works of Marx and Engels*, 1:647). It is precisely because the desires of people cannot be fulfilled in the real world that they take the illusory detour [of religion], hoping to bring something back from the god on the other shore. In a socialist society there are still people who, because of contradictions in their social life, bitter life experiences, or the state of their physical and spiritual health, psychologically feel the need of religion. This can be expressed as follows:

1. The search for a spiritual prop. When people feel insecure in their daily lives and lack assurance of ever achieving a happy life, it is quite possible that they will turn to a supernatural divine power on which to rely. Feuerbach has described this psychology, saying, "The premise of religion is the conflict or contradiction between the will and capability, between wish and acquisition, aim and result, phenomenon and reality, and thinking and being" (*Selected Philosophical Writings of Feuerbach*, 2:462). He maintains that "Man's sense of dependence is the foundation of religion" (ibid., p. 436). All religious rites, such as sacrifices, prayers, and so forth, are expressions of man's supplication to and dependence on God.

We discovered in our investigations that there are still people today who pray to God or Buddha because they feel they cannot manage their own fate. For example, notes were placed on temple incense braziers in recent years when some youths had difficulty finding jobs or going on for higher education. The notes would say, "Bless and protect me, and help me to be accepted by a university," or, "Bless and protect me so that I can earn a high mark on the employment examination and get the job that I want." Similar notes have been found in the offering boxes of churches.

People who have suffered blows and setbacks in life are more likely to have a sense of dependence. For example, a certain young villager who lost his mother in childhood fell in love with a fellow student, but after an eight-year love affair failed to win her hand when the girl's parents arranged for her marriage to someone in the city. The painful experience broke his heart. Believing that "the youth in my heart has died," he became a monk.

People with a dependency psychology who fail to achieve their goals will hold onto this psychology to satisfy other feelings. For example, besides the social reasons for sick people to believe in religion, such as poverty and lack of doctors and medicine in some places, there are psychological reasons, that is, the heavy mental burdens of these people. Our investigations showed that most of them suffer from chronic or life-threatening illnesses. The former are anxious to be freed from the bonds of illness, while the latter grasp religion as a thread of hope in the midst of their despair. [This kind of] spiritual dependency can sometimes be effective in curing mental troubles and make people feel better, and psychological relief sometimes strengthens their ability to endure pain. Those who turn to religion because of ill health often say, "If cured, we thank God; if not cured, we go to paradise after dying. Living or dead, we are in the arms of God." As long as people continue to feel they cannot manage their own fate, even if certain goals are achieved, it is possible they will look for a spiritual prop in religion. For example, some poor fisherwomen of the Zhoushan district were religious believers because they were poor. They were ashamed because they could not afford to buy incense. Now they have money and take part in Buddhist ceremonies with enthusiasm.

A sample study of one hundred households in Daishan County showed that the percentage of Buddhists among the richer families whose average income was over 300 yuan per capita in 1983 was 33.9 percent, while only 19.4 percent of those whose income was under 150 yuan were Buddhist believers or worshippers. The reasons for the religious faith of the richer fishermen was their belief that they became rich, first, because of the party's policies and, second, because of the gods' blessing. On the one hand, when they are prosperous they thank the gods, but on the other hand they worry that without the gods' blessing they will lose their wealth. As the reforms take effect in the cities and villages some self-employed farmers, artisans, and peddlers, having earned a lot of money, have become enthusiastic religious believers. This is because the revitalized economy brings them opportunities to become rich, which at the same time offers risks. They still feel it is hard for them to be masters of their own fate. A young man in Shanghai who sells sofas often worships Buddha and gives generously to the temple. When asked why, he said, "I hope that with Buddha's blessing I will prosper each year, my business will grow, that the [government] policy won't change, and that everything will go as I want it to."

2. The search for satisfying fellowship. Man does not exist as an isolated individual, but usually associates with other people. Marx said, "Therefore it is these private and personal relationships, these individual and mutual relation-

ships—which are recreating each day a kind of ongoing relationship" (*Complete Works of Marx and Engels*, 3:515). Small communities formed by people of common convictions, social norms, and moral values bring satisfying social contacts and feelings to members of the communities. Religion is this kind of a community, and the religious conversion of some people is a direct consequence of the attractiveness of such a community.

Religion has a centripetal force, bringing its members together and sometimes resulting in the spontaneous formation of organized activities. Buddhists are organized rather loosely, with believers going as individuals to the temple to burn incense and offer prayers to Buddha. But crowds of people can be seen burning incense in famous temples on sacred mountains on the days of religious festivals. Groups of pilgrims, mainly older women, are led by zealous believers, traveling long distances, making nothing of hardships, helping others in the group and fully manifesting the sharing mentality of a religious community.

Among Catholics and Protestants, who are better organized, the sense of community is even more obvious. When persons are known to be members of the same faith, they will be offered a cordial welcome.

All religions emphasize congregational worship—the Mass for Catholics, church services for Protestants, *Fahui* for Buddhists, *Daochang* for Daoists, *Zuma* (Friday service) and *hadj* (pilgrimage) for Muslims. The architecture, liturgies, and music all help to arouse religious feelings during worship. More important, as believers focus on the particular tenets of their faith, they stimulate each other's religious feelings. Even more important is the mutual religious stimulation that results from congregational worship, using the particular rites and practices of each religion; such religious feelings unite each individual with the congregation, strengthening each one's faith.

People's understanding of religion and life values can spread rather quickly in religious groups, forming a kind of mass psychology that both guides and limits the activities of the individual. For example, the exemplary lives of zealous believers will serve to encourage ordinary believers. When an individual believer's faith wavers, usually others will admonish him and do their best to strengthen his faith. Members of a religious group will join forces to defend their faith when their religious life encounters difficulties. This is one reason why the faith of many believers grew stronger, even under persecution, during the "Cultural Revolution."

Nonbelievers admire this strong sense of community of religious groups, and for this reason they are drawn to become members. When a young Shanghai woman became chronically ill, her fellow students, friends, and even her lover gradually separated themselves from her. Her brothers and sisters avoided her, making such ironical remarks as "It's a waste for her to eat," and she fell into a deep depression. When some religious believers showed concern and compassion for her, she became a Christian, saying, "I am sick, but my brothers and sisters are indifferent to me; only my Christian brothers and sisters help me, both spiritually and physically."

As for those ethnic nationalities where most of the people believe in a single religion, the religious mentality of the group is even more distinct. They are protective of their [ethnic] nationality characteristics and are very sensitive on religious matters, allowing no infringement [of their religious rights].

The Search for Moral Restraints

Morality determines people's actions in society and also affects the inner feelings, consciousness, and character of an individual. One often makes moral choices and evaluations regarding one's own behavior in social life, relying on the constraints of personal convictions in making such choices. Conscience has a strong bearing on one's moral life. As feeling, it has the function of self-control, restraining evil tendencies. It makes man aware of his social responsibilities, feeling satisfied when he makes the choices that seem right, and censuring himself when he makes the wrong choices. Some people with weak self-control feel guilty when they do something wrong, but, unable to extricate themselves, fall into depression and turn to religion for help.

Religious morality can have a restraining function on believers because they believe they must not disobey the religious teachings and principles or God will punish them; whether or not they are punished in this world, they will be judged and tortured in the next world. Believers also hold that religious faith will strengthen their determination to be good, helping them to overcome immoral tendencies. We discovered in our surveys that some young people were tainted with bad habits, even joining gangs of hooligans, due to the decline of social morality and the flood of anarchism during the ten years of chaos. Some of them mistreated their parents, others engaged in stealing and robbing, so that people no longer trusted them, and their hearts were hurting. Some became religious converts, hoping to achieve moral self-restraint through the psychological process of "conversion" ("change of heart" or "repentance"). When unhealthy tendencies appear in society, right-living young people avoid having any part in them, while others turn to the norms and principles of religious morality to "protect themselves with religious faith."

Reasons for the Persistence of Religion

We stated above, under three headings, the reasons why people continue to believe in religion in the socialist period: the traditional influence of religion, the present social conditions that lead to religious belief, and psychological factors. These will continue to function for a long time in the socialist period as causes for religious belief.

Traditional religious influences have a long history in China and will continue for a long time, particularly where they are combined with the culture and customs of [ethnic] nationalities. As we implement the open-door policy, overseas religious influences will inevitably increase, but generally speaking these are limited to providing religious materials that help people understand religion. The reasons for religious belief can be summed up under two headings: objective social reasons and subjective mental or psychological reasons. The process that gives rise to religious belief comes from the mutual interaction of objective and subjective elements; these are interdependent, and neither can be slighted. Of the two, objective social existence plays the decisive role; but under the same social conditions, if an individual's psychological conditions are not suited, he will not come to believe in religion. Among persons who cannot correctly understand nature or deal with social contradictions, only those who have had some religious influence in their social contacts will become religious believers. As long as the social and psychological sources on which religion relies are present, religion will persist.

In today's society the emotional needs and the levels of understanding [general knowledge] of the people cannot be standardized, so these will continue at diverse levels, along with the psychological reasons for religion, for a long time to come.

Speaking of differences in understanding, only a minority of our one billion people have a progressive scientific world outlook at the present stage. The action of human cognition is complicated, as various thoughts exist simultaneously in the human brain, often causing overlapping and mixing of ideas in the process of cognitive integration, even leading to a multiple consciousness when persons take action, so they adopt a materialist viewpoint when dealing with some problems and an idealist viewpoint with others.

Thirty years ago Zhou Enlai said that some Communist Party members adapted well both politically and ideologically to the demands of the socialist economic system, but they were afraid of ghosts at night. This phenomenon will probably continue for a long time. Some scientists hold strictly to a materialistic and scientific point of view while doing scientific research, but they still have an idealistic world outlook, even believing in religion.

People's emotional needs differ. Attitudes toward the joys and sorrows of life are determined by differing world views. Those who have established a communist world view can actively overcome difficulties. While some may not have attained a lofty realm of thought, they do not seek after happiness based on illusion, so they are not drawn toward religious belief. However, there are always some people who, in their search for emotional stability, become religious believers because of complex social conditions and a variety of cognitive reasons. The need for religion comes from a variety of psychological needs among these people of different ages, sex, and personal characteristics.

To emphasize the enduring nature of psychological factors does not imply that religion is an ingrained human instinct. While psychological factors are important in religious belief, the decisive factors affecting human psychology are societal. This is because human nature is the sum total of social relations. The human character is related to the person's physical qualities, but it is formed under the influence of [social] circumstances and education. In the final analysis it is decided by the nature of society. Marx and Engels pointed out: "It is not ideology that decides life, it is life that decides ideology." This method of study is premised on man, "but not the man in an illusion, divorced from the world, but the real man in the process of development, the man that can be observed under specific conditions" (*Selected Works of Marx and Engels*, 1:31). The reason why humans have different understandings of the objective world and different needs, and some have an illusory religious understanding, is that they live in specific social contexts and have different family influences, social positions, education, and practical experiences. The social character of a person is expressed in his class character in a class society. After the classes are abolished, various sources for religious belief still exist. In socialist society, people still feel the need to rely on God because they feel they cannot be masters of their own fate. They feel lonely and seek a community relationship in religion. These psychological factors are, in reality, the reflection of objective society in the subjective human consciousness.

Some of the social sources of religion mentioned earlier in this chapter are changing. In the wake of economic reform, our productive forces are growing and the impoverished state of some regions is gradually changing. While building a material civilization, we also lay stress on building a spiritual civilization, raising the social consciousness of the people, overcoming social malpractices and unhealthy tendencies, and, in the end, improving human relationships. The overall errors and setbacks that arose in the process of social construction have been put right, but we must clearly reckon with the difficult long-run tasks of building a modernized, highly civilized, highly democratic socialist country with its own characteristics in an economically backward nation with such a large population as ours. Painstaking efforts will be needed to raise the levels of material and cultural life of the people. We need to probe and experiment in many ways in order to grasp the laws of building a socialist society, and in this process passive elements and partial errors will possibly appear. As long as various social contradictions still exist in a socialist society, the social soil for religion will remain.

The persistence of religion in socialist society, as mentioned in this chapter, is also due to the fact that the various causes of religion are interrelated in complex ways. These causes do not exist in isolation, but individually and laterally are interconnected, permeating each other and influencing each other in different degrees, both extensively and intensively. As Lenin said, "The action of cause and effect is, in fact, equivalent to the movements of matter and of history, whose internal relationships have been grasped in different degrees, intensively or extensively" (*Complete Works of Lenin*, 38:170).

We cannot simply add and subtract among the host of reasons for religious belief, as if subtracting one cause will eliminate one opportunity for the growth of religion. The actual situation is nothing like this. While there will be no potential religious converts resulting from class oppression after the elimination of classes, it will still be possible for people to turn to religion because of suffering caused by social contradictions. Some people do not suffer from social contradictions, but they become religious believers because of the torments of ill health. People have different specific reasons for their religious belief, but the difficulties they experience are very real to each of them. When they are poor, they entrust their hope for a bumper harvest to God's care, but when their living improves, they still rely on God because they don't think they can take charge of their own fate.

Young people from religious [ethnic] nationalities or from families strongly influenced by religious traditions do not necessarily have a devout religious faith, while youths entirely outside traditional religious influences might, because of psychological needs, approach religion on their own initiative in their search for an ideological way out. The reflection of the intellectual and psychological needs of a person is constrained by objective material conditions; so ideology will change along with the existing material society, but at a much slower pace. It can be concluded from this that man's religious ideas will persist for a long time, even when the social causes on which religion depends are gradually removed.

It can be seen from this analysis that specific conditions determine whether or not an individual believes in religion, that individuals vary greatly, and that this is strongly influenced by chance. But speaking broadly, the social and psychological sources of religion and the functional relationships among them are enduring and are an inevitable function of this historical period; so, considering the present level of our productive forces, the ongoing reform of our productive relationships and the basic prospects for popularizing science and culture, we can expect religion to continue in our nation for a long time to come, which conforms with the laws of historical development. If we do not observe objective laws and use force [in the attempt] to abolish religion, as was done during the ten years of chaos, giving the false impression that religion had perished, we shall deceive ourselves as well as others, and suffer social effects that are contrary to what we want.

Having examined the reasons for the persistence of religion through time, we should also look at the internal objective conditions in society that are not helpful to religion and restrain its growth. On the one hand, religion is an idealistic world outlook that, by its very nature, cannot serve as a means for correct understanding of the world and for bringing about reform. Therefore, its development in a socialist society cannot avoid an innate self-limitation.

On the other hand, our socialist construction is making great strides; as the material living standard of the people rises, they find need for spiritual satisfaction in many areas. The popularization of culture and science and the widespread dissemination of the theories of historical and dialectical materialism will weaken the social foundations of religion at the grass roots and help more people to build a correct world view and outlook on life, thus freeing themselves from the illusion of religion. All varieties of religious believers were diminishing in numbers during the 1950s. The main reasons for this were the great changes and achievements taking place in society, which resulted in religious indifference among many believers who found their satisfactions in the practical world.

The main reasons for the revival of religion in some parts of our country in recent years are the ideological confusion and serious economic setbacks caused by the ten years of chaos. The rapid growth of religion in these regions will probably slow down in the wake of nationwide economic expansion, the normalization of political life, and the restoration of social unity and stability. When seen from the perspective of history and the present state of our nation, the growth and decline of religion will go in cycles, depending on time and place, but generally speaking, its growth will have certain limits and cannot continue indefinitely.

Religion, like everything else, passes through stages of birth, growth, and decay and will eventually die out. Marx said this about the conditions that would lead to the withering away of religion: "Only when the relations of actual daily life become clearly understood, and the relations between man and man and man and nature become most rational in the eyes of the people, can the religious reflection of the real world die out" (*Complete Works of Marx and Engels*, 23:96–97). In "Anti-Dühring," Engels said, "Only when the time comes that man proposes and man also disposes will the final alien forces reflected in present-day religion die out" (ibid., 3:356). This is to say that only after the efforts of several generations, when humanity completely frees itself from all poverty, ignorance, and spiritual emptiness, when a highly developed material and spiritual civilization has been built, and when people can consciously deal with life and the world scientifically with no need to seek sustenance from the illusory world of God, will the religious reflections of the real world finally pass away.

Early in 1951 Zhou Enlai stated clearly that religion would not disappear in the socialist period. At that time some people believed that Catholics would give up their religious faith when they received their shares of land, but Zhou Enlai said, "Don't mention [the time of] land redistribution; there will be religious believers even when we achieve a socialist society" (*Selected Works of Zhou Enlai on the United Front*, p. 201). He also said, "Not only are there religious believers in socialist countries today, but can you say they will all disappear in a Communist society? We cannot say that for certain" (ibid., p. 383). The first of these theories on the long-term persistence of religion has been historically demonstrated, and the latter deserves our serious consideration.

5 | Coordinating Religion with Socialist Society

IT WAS reported in chapter 3 that after the liberation of all China, rumors and discord were spread about by imperialists and reactionaries, causing a number of believers to doubt the policies of the Communist Party and the people's government. Can religion coexist with socialism? Should religious believers work for the building of socialism? On the other hand, some Marxists overemphasized the conflict between Marxist and religious world views, pointing out the negative functions of religion throughout history, and viewing religion as an obstacle to the building of socialism. This is how the relationship between religion and socialism became a matter of concern when viewed from different angles. Both affirmative and negative experiences during the past thirty years demonstrate not only the necessity of harmonizing religion and socialism, but also the possibility of doing it. An important task is to understand and deal correctly with religion in the socialist period, scientifically explicating this phenomenon using basic Marxist principles.

The Bases and Implications for Compatibility

Many religions have appeared throughout history. Some are still alive today, while others have died out; some have changed from a regional or national religion into a world religion, while others are only archeological relics or items mentioned in history books. Why is this? The important factor is whether or not a religion can adapt to the demands of a developing society and can adjust its doctrines, organization, and rituals to the changing society, thereby continuing to play a role in the life of a society.

Let us take Christianity as an example. Engels said, "Christianity, like all great revolutionary movements, was created by the masses" ("Revelation," in

Complete Works of Marx and Engels, 21:11). In the first century A.D., Jewish slaves and paupers nursed a strong class hatred for their Roman rulers and the slavery system. In despair after the failure of numerous uprisings, they adapted to the historical situation and triumphed over other religious sects, taking on certain features of Judaism and gradually evolving. At first the rulers oppressed Christianity, but later they made use of it, making it the state religion of the Roman Empire. "Christianity adapted to the developing feudal system during the Middle Ages, creating a religion with corresponding feudal ranks" ("L. Feuerbach and the End of German Classic Philosophy," in *Selected Works of Marx and Engels*, 4:251). Between the thirteenth and seventeenth centuries, along with the seeds of capitalism that were beginning to grow, the rural, town, and city people rose up, demanding the abolition of the Catholic church's monopoly in the realm of ideology. Their struggles, including the various religious reform movements, were all "repeated attempts to make the old theological world view fit the changing economic conditions and the new way of life of the new classes" ("Juristic Socialism," in *Complete Works of Marx and Engels*, 21:545–46).

Again, consider the Christian belief in "equality." In early times "Christianity knew only one point in which all men were equal: that all were equally born in original sin—which corresponded perfectly to its character as the religion of slaves and the oppressed" ("Anti-Dühring," in *Selected Works of Marx and Engels*, 3:143). But later on, slaveowners, landlords, and bourgeoisie preached the "equality" of paradise, propagating this doctrine to cover up the evils of exploitation and making the exploited willingly endure the sufferings of inequality in real life while looking forward to "equality" in the heavenly kingdom.

In a class society, despite different economic status, political interests and social demands, people of different classes may believe in and join the same religion. However, believers of different class status usually have different viewpoints and attitudes toward the problem of how to adapt their religion to society. Take Chinese Daoism, for example. In the Eastern Han dynasty, Daoism was a popular religion, reflecting the interests and needs of the majority of peasants and lower-level intellectuals, that is, political equality, a fair share in the economy, and a trend toward ideological independence from the Confucian school. Therefore, early Daoism, being naturally suited to the interests of the peasant class and lower-level intellectuals, was used in peasant uprisings. But in the eyes of the ruling class, Daoism should be suppressed as treasonous and heretical. Since the Wei and Jin dynasties, ruling classes have propped up some of the Daoists, gradually combining Daoist beliefs with the concept of the five constant virtues and the Confucian code of ethics, transforming Daoism into a religion that suited the interests of the Chinese feudal ruling classes and could be used for their purposes. The process by which religion undergoes change shows that, in class societies, the problem of adapting religion to society in the final analysis is the problem of adapting religion to class interests.

The Taiping Rebellion, in its initial stage, preached that "all people in the world are brothers,'' and ''all people are one family under heaven, living peacefully together,'' using ideas of political and economic equality under the guise of religion to mobilize the masses to overthrow the Qing dynasty. Currently the world situation is turbulent, with the national liberation struggles of the Third World surging ahead. To adapt to this situation, new religious sects and theological ideologies serving the interests of various nationalities and classes are constantly emerging. History and reality have shown that religion is not immutable and frozen but continually changing as it adapts to the evolutionary changes of society.

Since we entered the socialist period, the social status and mental attitudes of our people have greatly changed in the wake of the abolition of the exploiting class and its system of exploitation. The class sources for religion have perished, and the concepts, organization, rituals, and disciplines of religion have, one after another, changed and continue to change while adapting to the grass-roots changes of society during the past few decades. Religion has made this series of grass-roots changes under socialism because the majority of believers are workers, peasants, and intellectuals, and, like nonbelievers, who constitute the majority of our people, are masters of the country. No matter whether it is the achievements of socialist reform and socialist construction, or the glorious goal of building a highly civilized, highly democratic, fully modern nation, religious believers find this inspiring and attractive. Religious believers under socialism, both for their own interests and for this great social goal, have made appropriate adjustments in religion and consider the realization of the advanced goals of their nation and society to be an integral part of their religious faith. They believe that to love their country, abide by the law, and actively forge ahead are moral norms that result in harmonious relationships between themselves and nonbelievers. This is the basis for harmonizing religion with the basic features of society.

What is meant by compatibility is proper cooperation among various elements. It does not mean asking either side to abandon its own unique features. As Zhou Enlai said, ''There are both religious believers and nonbelievers in China. . . . These two groups of people should live together on friendly terms. . . . Nonbelievers can cooperate with believers. Those who believe in different religions can also cooperate. This will help promote unity and mutual aid among the great families of our [ethnic] nationalities'' (''On Several Problems of Our Nationalities Policy,'' in *Selected Works of Zhou Enlai on the United Front*, p. 387). Harmonizing religions and socialist society should include at least the following:

1. Led by the party, religious believers and nonbelievers should form a broad patriotic united front to struggle for the gradual realization of a modernized agriculture, industry, national defense, and science and technology so as to build a prosperous, highly civilized, highly democratic socialist nation.

2. By holding firmly in a common commitment to patriotism and socialism, religious circles should make certain that their ideas, beliefs, ethics, and behavior fit the demands of the new society. In their daily life, religious believers should love their country, abide by the law, serve the people, and contribute to society.

3. Religious circles should utilize their specialties in the fields of religious research and international relations, enriching socialist culture by carrying on the fine national [religious] cultural heritage, and helping the cause of world peace by enhancing friendship among the peoples of the world.

4. The party, the nation, and the entire society should deal correctly with religious issues in law, policy, and daily life, by respecting and protecting the freedom and rights of citizens in their religious beliefs.

The constitution, not materialism, and neither "abolition" nor promotion of religion, is the criterion for compatibility based on patriotism and socialism. As for world view, it is not strange that two different ideological systems, theism and atheism, idealism and materialism, can coexist in a socialist society; these are not peculiar to socialist society, nor are they bound to end during the socialist period. Although these differences are related to religion, in the history of knowledge, they go far beyond the realm of religion. These contradictions will still exist when present religious forms come to their natural end. As for the rich contents of religion, the idealist world view of religion is only one element. There are other elements, such as believers, rituals, and religious organizations, which, in comparison with world view, are more closely and directly linked with social life.

As for the thinking of individual believers, the world view of the majority is complex and pluralistic. There may be idealistic components in the world view and outlook on life of some beliefs; the world view, political attitudes, and social viewpoints of people are usually filled with complex contradictions. Examples can often be seen in real life where people with different political attitudes have the same religious faith, and people of different religious belief have the same political attitudes. Therefore, in the socialist period "it is impossible to ask all the people to have the Marxist consciousness of a Communist Party member, or to demand that all people have the same world view and outlook on life" ("The New Development of the People's Democratic United Front in China," in ibid., p. 445). In a great country with one billion people it is neither possible nor necessary to require that all people have an identical world view; it is even more harmful to stir up disputes between theism and atheism.

The theoretical basis that directs our socialist modernization and construction today is Marxism and dialectical and historical materialism. The core force for leading our cause is the Chinese Communist Party, which is a Marxist political party whose members are materialists and atheists. When we discuss whether or how religion can coordinate with a socialist society, of course we do not mean that the two different ideological systems or the two different world views, idealism and materialism, can accommodate to each other, nor do we mean that, as some people abroad advocate, religion should be used to supplement or replace Marxism. As Zhou Enlai said, "We only hope that patriotic religious circles will love our motherland, willingly serve the people, and study hard" (ibid.). That is to say, nonbelievers and believers can cooperate and work together for socialist construction.

Conditions for Compatibility and Its Ways of Expression

Compatibility involves mutual relationships. The association of religion with socialist society involves both ways in which religion accommodates to socialist society and how the state and society deal with religion.

Although traditional characteristics of religion's role in Chinese society carry over into the socialist period and current relationships, even more significant are the differences between the old society and the new epoch. On the one hand, religious believers are still a minority among China's people, and they are not in a leadership position; on the other hand, the leaders of our socialist society are the progressive class and the party. With the help of dialectical and historical materialism, people have objective knowledge of the growing possibilities and of the necessity for harmonizing religion with socialist society and can consciously support and work to create those conditions.

There are conditions for compatibility. We have found, from the practice of the past thirty-odd years, that there are two basic conditions for compatibility between religion and socialist society.

1. The basic condition on the side of religion is that believers should love our country, abide by the laws, and work actively with all the people to build a socialist material and spiritual civilization.

In the final analysis, harmonizing religion with socialist society is harmonizing religious believers with socialist society. As stated above, the majority of believers were skeptical because they were not familiar with the party and socialism after the founding of new China. But the victory of the people's revolution and the accomplishment of socialist reform caused profound changes in the social system. Religious believers, along with people from all walks of life, were liberated, freed from exploitation and oppression. The reality of religious freedom exposed the falsehood of reactionary rumors, and social reform changed their escapist and skeptical attitude which came from exploitation and suffering. They support the new society and the policies that benefit all the Chinese people.

Since the Third Plenum of the Eleventh Party Congress the emphasis has been shifted to building socialist modernization. Establishing a socialist society with Chinese characteristics reflects the wishes of all Chinese people, as well as having basic benefits for religious believers. The concern of believers for their practical life is the reason for their basic attitude of supporting socialism. If some religious ideas get in the way of their search for happiness, they voluntarily make adjustments. Some religious people in rural areas used to attend worship services regularly, no matter what season of the year; nor would they take medicine when ill, go to the cinema, or listen to radio broadcasts. They thought this was proper behavior for pious believers. Following the development of the rural economy and consequent improvement in the people's welfare, many of these people have changed their views. For example, religious believers bought radios in order to hear the weather forecasts; they temporarily stopped going to church during the busy seasons to avoid interfering with farm work; and some of them began taking medicine as soon as they became ill.

Believers always have their own explanation of how they understand the happy life brought by socialist society, saying they pursue the will of "God" in their search for a happy life on earth. For example, in recent years, following the overall implementation of the party's policy on religion, when the famous mountains and temples of Buddhism and Daoism were reopened and repaired they were flooded with tourists and pilgrims. Many stories about omens and auguries were passed around among the believers, spreading a message of national prosperity and peace that conformed both to the people's and to God's will. Some explanations are linked to theological ideas that trace back to the early periods of these religions; they find grounds in their scriptures, original beliefs, and doctrines that are consistent with and justify their struggle for socialist society. Engels said, "Both Christianity and workers' socialism preach that emancipation from slavery and poverty will come in the future; Christianity seeks emancipation in paradise, in life on the other shore after death, while Socialism seeks emancipation in social reform here on earth" ("On the Early History of Christianity," in *Complete Works of Marx and Engels*, 22:525). This teaches us that the birth of Christianity reflected the wishes of the oppressed for liberation. In the old society, the motivation of many workers who turned to religion was exactly that, while today socialist society opens a brilliant future for creating real happiness in the present life, thereby realizing the wishes of their ancestors. This real happiness has set a solid foundation for coordinating religion with socialist society. Because of this, despite the fact that imperialists and domestic reactionaries used the conflict between theism and atheism to stir up disputes and sabotage during the past thirty-odd years, the convergence of the political and economic interests of the broad masses of believers with those of socialist society have bankrupted this kind of plotting and sabotage.

2. The basic condition for the party and government is resolutely to carry out the policy of freedom of religious belief.

The party and state have adhered to the scientific theory of Marxism, Leninism, and Mao Zedong thought since the founding of new China, adapting it to the practical situation of our country, and formulating and carrying out a series of policies and directions concerning religion.

These guiding principles and policies include making sure that religious belief is an ideological problem among the people [not between the people and enemies]; putting the policy on religion into practice and protecting the right and freedom of people to believe in religion; resolutely abjuring ideas and actions that erroneously hope to abolish religion by administrative decree or other forceful measures; clearing away imperialist and other reactionary influences inside religion; supporting the anti-imperialist and patriotic actions of Catholics and Protestants who run their churches independently; and supporting the democratic reforms of Buddhism and Daoism that abolish the feudal exploiting system.

"Leftist" errors of the party in its religious work increased after 1957, particularly during the "Great Proletarian Cultural Revolution" when the counterrevolutionary clique of Jiang Qing and Lin Biao completely stifled the correct policy of the party on religious matters, thus denying, both theoretically and in practice, the efforts of religious circles to adapt to socialist society. Religious circles were threatened with extermination, and contradictions between religion and socialist society were artificially aggravated.

Since the Third Plenum of the Eleventh Party Congress, the party's Central Committee has corrected the extreme Leftist line, reaffirming and developing the correct policy on religious questions, and stressing that at the present stage the basic interests of believers and nonbelievers are politically and economically identical, and the differences in ideological belief are secondary. The aim in implementing the policy of religious freedom is to unite the people (believers and nonbelievers) of all nationalities throughout the country for building a strong and modern socialist nation. As the policies of the party and state on religion have been implemented, the broad masses of believers have rallied around the party even more closely in the struggle for the four modernizations.

To study the bases or conditions for coordination is not just a theoretical question but a practical one, related to the implementing of the policy of freedom of religious belief so that believers will have full play to make their contributions to society.

Investigations of the actual situation in certain places show that when religion is in harmony with socialist society it can lead believers to play their role in helping society. This role can be summarized as follows:

a. Workers, peasants, and intellectuals who believe in religion work hard to develop industrial and agricultural production, raise the scientific and technological level, and open up new prospects for building socialist modernization.

There is a village where Catholics live together, forming 70 percent of the village's population. In the reform of the rural economy, they brought into full play all their resources to improve production. In the past four years, average per capita income increased fivefold. One Catholic taught other farmers what he had learned in planting chives and helped nearly two hundred households to become specialized chive farmers, bringing in more than 300,000 yuan for the village. Believers and nonbelievers help each other in this village, utilizing their talents and making progress together in the building of the two civilizations.

In certain towns and villages of a Zhejiang county where many Protestant Christians reside, statistics show that their production does not lag behind that of other villages. For example, the crop yields per mu of a certain production brigade composed of Christians is the third from the top in the whole village, and the average income per capita is in first place. In one township Protestant Christians make up 17.5 percent of the population, and in 1983 their per capita income was listed as first among nine townships. One village of this township, where sixty out of seventy-five families are Christian, was first in the sale of pigs, with the second highest per capita income in the township. In 1983, when there was a crackdown on criminal activities in this county, not one Christian was arrested or investigated in the nine towns with a high proportion of Christians. Local cadres said that Christians have good relations with their neighbors and readily take part in public works such as repairing the sea dikes. From this it can be seen that religious belief does not lead to social instability or lagging production. This is because the religious people not only pray to the gods for bumper harvests and peace, but also understand that they must rely on the correct policy and leadership of the party and on their own grasp of scientific technology to maintain social order. In their eyes, praying to the gods for help does not exclude reliance on the party, the government, and their own efforts.

Some overseas Chinese intellectuals, industrialists, and family members who return to China are religious believers. Their contributions of inventions, investments, endowments, imported techniques, and so forth have helped speed up the four modernizations by opening to the outside and stimulating the inside and are a force that cannot be overlooked.

In recent years, religious believers in many places have organized "conferences for exchanging experiences in serving the four modernizations," "conferences for commending people for loving both religion and the nation," and "conferences for exchanging experiences in loving both religion and the nation," which raised the banner of loving both religion and the nation and encouraged religious believers to serve the four modernizations. According to incomplete statistics for the year 1985, 350 Shanghai Catholics were selected as advanced model persons at different levels, and 650 Shanghai Protestants were selected for various progressive awards. Physicians, engineers, teachers, specialists, workers, shop assistants, and housewives from national, municipal, district, factory, and local business levels were awarded such glorious titles as model workers, advanced workers, "three-eight" standard-bearers, and "five-good" families.

Religious believers, like nonbelievers, receive affirmation and encouragement for meritorious deeds to assure harmonious relationships between socialist society and religious believers, and to stimulate them to work even harder for the four modernizations. One such person, a telecommunications engineer, was harshly treated during the ten years of chaos. After the party's policy on intellectuals was restored, he was allowed to resume his work post and in a short time invented a series of advanced techniques that pushed our railway communications into the top ranks of the world.

Another religious person, a doctor, while doing advanced studies abroad devoted himself to treating an overseas Chinese suffering from a chronic disease. By using both Western and Chinese treatment he prolonged the patient's life and won critical acclaim. Upon his return to China, he presented a reward of 30,000 yuan to his hospital. Another religious believer, a gynecologist, was the first doctor to cure dismenorrhoea, helping relieve many young women from suffering and mental anguish. Still another believer, a woman engineer in an electric light bulb factory, succeeded in making an advanced electrode that is rare in the world. These are some examples of outstanding achievements by religious believers.

Many facts show that the patriotic religious believers, bursting with socialist zeal under the banner of loving one's religion and one's nation, can join with the broad masses of nonbelievers to form a mighty current. Religious life in practice has also shown that "love of country" and "love of religion" can unite, and that religion can be in harmony with socialism, stimulating religious believers to take part in building the motherland, socialism, and a better paradise on earth.

b. Certain religious beliefs can serve to mobilize believers to take part in building the four modernizations.

Complex ideological elements have emerged during the long history of religion. Religious ideologies usually contain both false theories supporting the systems of exploitation and elements reflecting the wishes and demands of the oppressed people. What religion preaches and what it avoids both reflect the unique features of its particular time and society. Since Liberation, the historical reforms of our social system and the tremendous changes that have occurred in religious circles have been inevitably reflected in the realm of religious ideologies. Marx and Engels said, "In the wake of each deep reform of the social system, people's viewpoints and concepts will change; which is to say that the religious concepts of man will also change" (*Complete Works of Marx and Engels*, 7:240). The "viewpoints and concepts of men" mentioned here of course include nonbelievers' views of religion as well as the religious ideologies of believers.

Except for explaining the new atmosphere in new China and refuting the false theories of imperialists and domestic reactionaries aimed at sabotage and destruction, the changes in the ideology of religious believers over the past thirty-odd years serve mainly to help religious believers understand the convergence of "loving one's country and loving one's religion" so they can plunge actively into the new life under socialism. The convergence of certain religious beliefs with patriotic consciousness is a significant development. Of course, those who played the most important roles were patriotic religious leaders who, pushed by the enthusiasm of the broad masses of believers to support the new society, realized that the original explanations of certain religious beliefs were not suited for the new situation, so they launched the [movement to] "purify the faith," probing anew into the scriptures and creeds, gradually eliminating those explanations of beliefs and doctrines that didn't fit with socialist society, and coming up with religious ideas that did fit the spirit of the times.

The policy on religion has been fully implemented over time since the Third Plenum of the Eleventh Party Congress, and the idea of "loving both one's nation and one's religion" has come into full play as the new situation created by the building of material civilization has encouraged patriotic zeal among religious circles.

The year 1983 marked the thirtieth anniversary of the founding of the China Buddhist Association. In his report, "Thirty Years of the China Buddhist Association," Chairman Zhao Puchu called on Buddhists to establish the idea of Buddhism on earth. "We advocate the idea of an earthly Buddhism that observes the five commandments, the ten goods for self-purification, and cultivation of the four merits and six good deeds to benefit others," he said, and should "consciously take as our responsibility the realization of a clean earth by contributing our light and warmth for the building of this majestic land with joyful spirit through the lofty cause of socialist modernization." "Majestic land with joyful spirit" means the broad masses of Buddhists actively taking part in the construction of the Four Modernizations and making every effort to serve the people.

Christian theological thinking has been vigorously revived in recent years. Bishop Ding Guangxun, chairman of the China Christian Council, moved theological theory a step forward, summing up the experience of Chinese Christians in running their church independently in his article, "Witnessing for Christ in China," which was published in the 1984 issue of *Journal of the Jinling Union Theological Seminary*. He said that "Chinese Christians must first be in close touch with the people if the Chinese church is to be a church of their own," and "universality is realized through nationalism." He also expounded the idea of "loving both one's country and one's religion" from a theological point of view, holding that "transcendence or life of the spirit does not unconditionally deny good things here on earth, but gives support for our participation in history."

In 1983, Catholic leaders set up the task of "developing theological studies." Patriotic theologians said that theology "must not proceed from church pronouncements only," but, using the Bible as the standard, should move forward in explicating and articulating the faith, "creating a Chinese Catholic theology that fits China's situation and the interests of the broad masses of the people." They also developed new, concrete standards for moral theology based on patriotism, saying: "The interests of the people set the standards for moral theology, for our behavior, and for that of the church."

Because of the oppression and exploitation suffered by Muslims as national minorities throughout [China's] history, they emphasize the difference between believers and nonbelievers in their religious propaganda, encouraging Muslims to close ranks in order to deal with persecution from other nationalities and nonbelievers. In today's socialist society, where all nationalities live together in peace in the big family of "Zhonghua" [China], the imams, in their preaching, encourage Muslims to do their part to make unity among the nationalities succeed, stressing that "loving one's country is part of the holy teaching," and that they should work for the building of the socialist four modernizations.

The common feature of all these changes in religious thinking is the merging of "loving one's nation" with "loving one's religion," and the interests of "this life" with the "future life." Thus these religious ideas are very effective in activating religious believers. Some of them say, "Religious faith now means that we have both prospects in this world and hope in the future world; we work hard in this life, and go to paradise after we die." Naturally, by advocating "loving both one's nation and one's religion," religious circles have weakened, to some degree, the negative influences of old religious ideas.

c. Certain religious moral teachings will lead believers to forsake evil for good, thereby helping social stability and unity.

Religious morality is a religious form of human moral norms, a social morality under the cloak of religion. The content and forms of religious morality were not fixed and unvarying throughout the history of religion. To suit different social needs, the concrete contents differed at different times. When religion was used by the ruling class in the old society, its negative functions predominated. In socialist society, since religion no longer is attached to a reactionary ruling class and is no longer the moral justification for a ruling class, its negative functions have been eliminated. Today many religious moral teachings, such as do not steal, do not commit adultery, do not covet, and do not lie, keep believers in bounds and provide real help in maintaining social stability and order. This is another way that religion and socialist society can work together.

All religions claim that they pursue that which is good, believing that "doing good" is a necessary condition for entering paradise. Goodness has class characteristics in a class society. The goodness advocated by religious ethics is also subordinate to class interests. Religious morality in the socialist period still encourages believers to be good, and religious people are at the same time doing good for society. But the goodness of today's religious morality is different from that of the past, in both its nature and its content. Good and evil, as seen in religious morality today, generally coincide with the people's views of morality. The results of field surveys show that many believers converted to religion because they were discontented with the moral status of society after the ten years of chaos and came to appreciate religious morality. During those ten years, very few religious believers took part in beating, smashing, and looting. Some believers held firmly to the commandment, "do not bear false witness against others," preferring to suffer torture rather than to bear false witness against other people. The customary norms for behavior between believers and their families and neighbors, and in dealing with contradictions between mother-in-law and daughter-in-law, husband and wife, brothers, sisters and in-laws, are humility, forgiveness, universal love, equality, and so forth.

The results of one investigation show that 93 percent of the adults living in two villages in southern Xinjiang are Muslims. Almost none of the men in the village drink alcoholic beverages, 70 percent do not smoke, and there has never been trouble caused by drunkenness. Criminal cases in these two villages quite obviously decreased after the policy on religion was reinstated.

In the autonomous county of Tashkul Gandajik in southwestern Xinjiang

Province there have never been major crimes such as murder, arson, rape, and robbery, and very few cases of pilfering. With no one in jail, the jailers had to find other work to do. It is common practice not to pocket money or other items found on the street. Local people believe that this is related to the disciplines of Islamic teaching. It can be seen that religious morality is effective in improving social morality in places where the majority of residents are religious believers.

Socialist society is a new society born out of the old society. The morality of socialist society is an amalgam, a multilevel structure. Communist morality forms the top level, the norm for the advanced persons. There are norms at other levels, religious morality, which sets the behavioral norms of religious believers, being one of them. Although the moral teachings of religious believers differ from Communist morality, they do teach people not to benefit themselves at the expense of others or the general public. Therefore, looking at actual social life, the religious morality that leads believers to contribute to society should be affirmed without question. As Zhou Enlai once said, "Some religious beliefs play positive roles" (*Selected Works of Zhou Enlai on the United Front*, p. 318).

d. Members of religious circles take part in public welfare, protect religious cultural relics, and carry on academic religious research, thereby contributing to economic and cultural progress in socialist society.

Since the progress of socialist construction, professional religious personnel have changed their old habits of depending solely on religious functions or religious properties for their living, plunging fully into the building of the socialist four modernizations.

Most Buddhist and Daoist temples and monasteries have begun productive-labor projects. Some temples located deep in the mountains are engaged mainly in diversified projects, such as farming, forestry, and cultivation of tea and herbs. Fifty Buddhist temples in Fujian Province had an income of nearly 530,000 yuan from agriculture and sideline production in 1983, and the average per capita annual income of monks and nuns was 450 yuan. The Changdao Daoist Temple in Sichuan Province makes "Cave Milk Wine" out of the *yangtao* fruit, a local specialty, using a secret Daoist prescription. The wine is well-known in Sichuan. Changdao Temple also has a tea factory producing "Cave Tribute Tea," and two other factories serving tourists and society in general, one making beverages and the other pickles. Monks provide other services for tourists and pilgrims who flock to temples located in spots known for their scenery and antiquity. For some of these, like Beijing's Yonghe Temple, Hangzhou's Lingyin Temple, and Shanghai's Yufo and Longhua Temples (all Buddhist), and the Daoist temples Daoyuan of Maoshan, Wuliang Guan of Qianshan, and Guangzhou's Sanyuangong, the income is sufficient to meet the operating expenses of the temples and the personal needs of the monks, with money left over for building repairs and maintenance. Other temples, with no farmland or forests and only a few tourists and pilgrims, are forced to rely on handicrafts such as sewing, weaving, making religious objects, and so forth.

There is a saying, "Famous mountains under heaven are mainly occupied by monks," and, indeed, the monks have contributed to the greening of our country. Through the years, the monks of the Fuyuan Temple in Zerong County, Fujian, have planted more than 1,000 mu of trees, forming a green sea around the temple. In the same province, monks of the Jinbei Temple, Ningde County, have planted 130,000 trees in recent years. Their income from cultivating tea plantations was 16,000 yuan in 1981 and 30,000 in 1983. Monks of the Guoqing Temple, Tiantai, Zhejiang Province, have even organized a professional staff for afforestation. There are reports of a Daoist monk in Yunnan Province who has lived in remote areas for several decades who has planted more than half a million precious Chinese fir trees. To collect species he has to climb dangerous cliffs and trees. In recent years our country has called on the people to plant trees. When he heard that precious lumber deep in the mountains and forests was being stolen, he set off on his own into the dense forests to protect them, despite being over seventy, carrying simple cooking utensils and bedding. Although the old Daoist did this because of his religious morality, we should affirm what he has done, because it is needed for the socialist building of the four modernizations, even though most people cannot do it.

Since all of China's religions have long histories, there are religious relics and antiquities in almost every temple and church. For example, there are the stone images in Buddhist caves, wall paintings in Daoist temples, and the classical scriptures of Buddhism and Daoism that are found all over the country and have become rare national treasures. For a long time religious relics were cared for by religious circles. Since Liberation, our National Commission for Preservation of Antiquities has carefully safeguarded religious relics. During the ten years of chaos some relics were saved by monks who risked death. Not only are these religious relics part of our national cultural heritage, they still enrich people's spiritual lives and are a factor in carrying out patriotic education.

All religions are actively sorting out historical data, collecting books, publishing religious magazines, and contributing to religious research. The library of the Chinese Buddhist Association contains up to 120,000 Buddhist scriptures. The Chinese Daoist Association has set up a research group to sort through tactics for cultivating the inner person and to carry forward Daoist ways of keeping fit and lengthening life. They have videotaped Daoist ceremonies. Chen Yinning, the former chairman of the Chinese Daoist Association, has said, "*Qigong* (deep breathing) cures illnesses and *donggong* (action) strengthens the body. *Jinggong* (quietness) cultivates character, and medicine lengthens life." Others, such as *neidan* and *waidan* and the philosophy of Laozi and Zhuangzi all use Daoist learning, on which the spirit of Daoism is based. He also said, "As long as Daoist learning survives, the Daoist spirit will have sustenance."

All religions have revived or initiated their own publications since the policy of religion was implemented following the Third Plenum of the Eleventh Party Congress. Besides expounding on religious doctrines and unifying believers, these publications have done a great deal of work collecting and sorting out information on our religious cultural heritage.

e. Contacts between religious circles here and abroad are of vital importance for enhancing friendship with peoples of different nations and for maintaining world peace.

Religion, for people of faith, is the tie that binds them together. Religion is also a worldwide phenomenon, and for over thirty years people in religious circles have made positive contributions in widening our nation's contacts with countries abroad, advancing friendship and understanding between our people and those of other nations, opposing wars of aggression, and advocating world peace.

Soon after the founding of new China, Chinese religious circles took part in the international peace movement, joining with many internationally well-known people and increasing understanding and friendship between us and many nations. In recent years, our religious circles have become even more active in international exchanges. Christian circles have received in succession the archbishops of the state religion of Great Britain (the Anglican Church) and the Swedish state religion (the Lutheran Church), Christian leaders from Asian countries, and delegations from the United Church of Canada and the National Council of Churches of the United States. Christian delegations were also sent from China to more than ten countries in Europe, Asia, North America, Africa, and Oceania to attend a number of international conferences where they introduced the present situation of Chinese Christians and discussed the changes and developments in Chinese Christian theology. After his arrival in China, Archbishop Runcie of Great Britain praised the Chinese Christian "Three-Self Patriotic Movement" at a public meeting, saying that it conforms with the Bible and with China's present situation. These exchanges also extended the international influence of China and promoted friendship between the Chinese people and various peoples of the world.

Our Catholic circles have received large groups of Catholic clergy and laypersons from abroad, including some cardinals, bishops, and archbishops, thus promoting friendship between Chinese Catholics and Catholic circles abroad, and helping to isolate the few elements in international Catholic circles who insist on opposing China.

For a long time, frequent and friendly exchanges between Chinese and Japanese Buddhist circles have made great contributions to friendship between the peoples of our countries and to normalization of state relations. In the spring of 1980, when the statue of the Great Master Jianzhen, who had sailed east, was returned to China for a visit, friendly contacts between Buddhists in China and Japan reached a new height. Chinese Buddhist leaders hosted persons representing various Japanese Buddhist sects, held memorial services for the founders of various sects, and organized dedication ceremonies for figures of Buddha. Chinese Buddhist circles have strengthened their relations with Buddhists in Southeast Asia, Europe, and America, and with overseas Chinese Buddhists.

Islamic circles have strengthened contacts with Islamic countries of Asia and Africa in recent years by sending and receiving delegations. These exchanges have done more for promoting friendship and mutual understanding with these countries, whether or not we have diplomatic relations with them, than anything else. Pilgrimage to Mecca is one of the Five Duties of Islam. According to the Qur'an, "All Muslims are brothers." In addition to performing religious duties while on pilgrimage, our Muslims have promoted friendship with Muslims of various countries, telling them about our policy of freedom of religious belief. Many foreign Muslim leaders said, "We are glad to know that in recent years religious life has been restored inside China and that Islam thrives there again."

There are more than two billion religious believers in the world. They often evaluate the stability and prosperity of a country on the basis of its religious situation. The situation of religion and the people of faith in China has always drawn the attention of certain people abroad. By coming to understand the life and work of our religious people, many of them came to believe our policy of religious freedom and to promote trust and friendship toward our country, thereby forcefully attacking and isolating certain anti-China forces who had tried to use religion for their conspiracies.

In addition, we need a peaceful international environment to carry on [national] construction with all our hearts and wills. People of all nations also want peace. Most religious creeds oppose war and advocate peace. "Peace" is the common language of hundreds of millions of believers all over the world. In recent years, our religious circles have taken an active part in the international peace movement. Buddhist, Christian, and Islamic circles have attended the third and fourth sessions of the World Conference on Religion and Peace, which were held, respectively, in the United States and Kenya, and all of our religions were represented at the Asian Conference on Religion and Peace. Zhao Puchu, chairman of the China Buddhist Association, won the Niwano Peace Prize of Japan in 1985. This international recognition shows the contributions our religious circles have made to the world peace movement.

Never Stop Resisting Discord

To bring religion into harmony with socialist society is an ongoing process. Since the beginning of new China, there have been repeated incidents of discord. This is because socialist society is itself a developing society with economic and political changes constantly posing new problems. Changes in religion, moreover, have always lagged behind society's economic and political development. Therefore, there will always be elements in religion in socialist society that do not fit this society. There is a process for understanding and dealing with changes in religion and adapting it to socialist society. Just as there is a basis for harmonizing [religion with socialist society], there are also reasons why incidents of discord occur. By studying such incidents we can learn more about the laws of harmony. At present there are two main manifestations of discord:

1. Certain traditional religious ideas, systems of discipline, and religious functions can, under certain conditions, play a negative role in society.

All religious ideas, rituals, and disciplines are a heritage from the past with long histories of development. Some elements of this heritage have been discarded, and some new things have been added after entering the socialist society. But it is impossible to come up with entirely new understandings of these religious ideas, disciplines, and rituals. Even those elements that have been interpreted in a new way cannot be deeply absorbed by every believer because of limitations in transmission due to shortage of manpower and communication problems. So certain negative aspects of religious traditions will continue to influence some believers. For example, certain religious ideas that, in essence, are reflections of the sighs of the people protesting against the sufferings of the old world at the same time weakened and benumbed their social feelings, acting as a kind of narcotic. In fact, these negative and pessimistic ideas were for a long time the cause of many disasters.

After Liberation, encouraged by the new religious ideas of "loving one's country and loving one's religion," and joining faith with [daily] life, many believers plunged into the building of a happy life. But the traditional religious notions could not all disappear. Moreover, a few religious people with an axe to grind took advantage of the people's anxiety and social turbulence to propagate pessimistic ideas, trumpeting that "in the year 2000 Jesus will return," and calling on the religious believers to "wait for the Lord's coming," with the result that some believers quit working and lived in idleness, directly affecting both their personal lives and socialist construction.

Some young workers did nothing but read scriptures and worship Buddha after converting, neglecting required political and cultural studies. There were even young women who, hearing that by fasting and prayers one could enter paradise, prayed all day without eating or drinking and, ignoring the advice of others, finally died of starvation.

Believers of all religions usually determine how they will relate to other persons on the basis of their religious faith. In a society where class contradictions and antagonisms exist, enemies and comrades will reverse their relationships when religion is taken as the criterion for separating right from wrong. Although these traditional notions have been resisted by patriotic religious people since the victory of China's revolution, their negative influence is still present to a certain extent, and even now some bad people are spreading these false theories, mixing right and wrong and good and evil.

Moreover, some religious people with conservative ideas and low cultural level often pray to the gods instead of going to a doctor when they fall ill, because they don't understand science and believe in miracles. For some new believers, whose reason for turning to religion is to cure illness, the frequent result is not only death caused by delay in seeing a doctor, but the use of heterodox stories by people with ulterior motives who deceive the believers. To solve this problem at the local level means raising the levels of material and cultural life, the steady improvement of medical care and safeguarding public health, and continuous education in scientific knowledge. In some regions people go to the doctor when they fall ill because monks and nuns have posted this notice in the temples: "Incense ashes cannot take the place of medicine." This is quite correct. But it will probably take a long time to change the old habits of praying for healing, because "miracles are the use of supernatural methods by humans to achieve what they want" (Feuerbach). As long as man is under the control of nature, with his aspirations objectively restricted, he will place his hopes in divine miracles.

In addition, some believers spend too much time in religious activities, interfering with social order, economic production, and daily life. Others, under the influence of religious fanaticism and distorted reading of the scriptures, have even "killed a son as a sacrifice," violating criminal law. Religious groups in some places, deeply influenced by tradition and strong feudal ideas, force young people to recite scriptures, interfere with freedom of marriage in the name of religion, and oppose birth control. Of course, these things are not found in all religions, and the causes are rather complicated. What is more, all these have met with opposition and resistance from most patriotic and law-abiding people of faith. Citizens have the legal right to their religious faith, and normal religious activities are protected by the laws of our country. But if religious activities harm the physical or mental health of other people, impede social order, or interfere with public justice and education, they go beyond the law and should be dealt with according to the law.

2. Reactionary forces at home and abroad have tried every means to control and make use of religion in China to engage in illegal activities, to oppose socialism, and to sabotage social order.

Religion has historically been a spiritual instrument used and controlled by the reactionary ruling classes. After Liberation, the system of exploitation in China was wiped out; the exploiting classes no longer exist, and class confrontation on a large scale no longer occurs. But class struggle does still exist in certain ways, and the struggle cannot but be reflected in religion. For example, since the Third Plenum of the Eleventh Party Congress our religious policy has been reaffirmed. Once again the people have democratic rights and freedom of religious belief, and all normal religious activities have been revived. However, foreign imperialists and other anti-China forces and religious groups antagonistic to China are making use of our open-door policy, carrying out despicable political infiltration under the guise of religious evangelism. Some have even colluded with individual reactionary believers or criminals to carry out espionage and other reactionary activities. Beginning in 1978, the "Yellers" [a Christian sect] penetrated into the provinces of Zhejiang and Fujian, spreading inland into

Jiangxi and Henan provinces, buying over some people and roping in others, overtly spreading anti-Communist rumors, deliberately attacking the party's leadership and the socialist system, hurling abuses on the Christian Three-Self Patriotic Movement, and even organizing people to make trouble, seriously wrecking social stability and unity. Because of this, the relevant government agencies dealt with this severely in 1984. The reason these things happen is that the international anti-China forces are not willing to give up. Nevertheless, their conspiracies will come to nothing in the face of the heightened consciousness of the broad masses of people, including religious believers.

A few of the missionaries and mission groups who left our country in the early 1950s tried to regain control of our churches by various means, ignoring the standpoint of Chinese believers who insisted that the church be run independently. In addition, some criminal elements took advantage of the lack of patriotic religious leadership in some regions, or the hiatus prior to the resumption of normal religious activities under the patriotic religious organizations, to make use of religion to embezzle money, seduce women, and ruin people's health. Their activities encroached on the people's interests, bringing direct harm to socialism. The occurrence of these illegal activities was related to the present economic and cultural backwardness of our people, and also to the fact that local patriotic religious organizations and circles had not yet resumed normal activities and so could not effectively resist them.

The discordant happenings mentioned above involve, in essence, two kinds of contradictions that have to be tackled in different ways. We have to enforce education on patriotism and support religious patriots in order to help believers to overcome those discordant factors caused by inner contradictions resulting from traditional religious ideas. As for those enemies both inside and outside our country who use religion for reactionary activities, we have to, on the one hand, educate believers and nonbelievers in order to raise their powers of discernment and vigilance so as to resist them consciously; on the other hand, basing our actions on facts and taking the law as the criterion, we should attack these reactionary activities. As for those who engage in illegal activities in the disguise of religion, we have to unmask them and enforce the law if they violate it. Finally, we have to conduct patient education with those believers who have been misled, arousing their patriotic consciousness and sense of national dignity, and leading the people of faith firmly to take the road of loving their country, abiding by the law, and running the churches independently.

"Compatibility," as mentioned above, is two-sided. Compatibility of religion with socialist society requires that religion adapt to the ongoing development of society; it also requires that society respect objective reality and deal with religion correctly. Discord is also two-sided. Discord will occur if the cadres responsible for dealing with religion do not acknowledge the existence of religion and fail to implement the policy of freedom of religious belief. For example, if they do not act according to the constitution and use administrative decrees and other forceful measures to interfere with the people's religious faith and normal practice, they not only wound their religious feelings, but also set back their commitment to participate actively in building the four modernizations. On the other hand, if we do not attack those illegal activities carried on under the cover of religion, the building of the four modernizations will also suffer.

Compatibility [of religion and society] takes place over a long period of time, as can be seen by the changes in religion since the founding of new China. Whether or not the religious communities and their religious beliefs can adapt to socialist society really depends on the joint efforts of the leaders and the people of faith.

Whether it is [traditional] religious beliefs, religious groups, or the believers themselves, their ability to adapt to socialist society really depends on the joint efforts of religious leaders and the people of faith. In the end, it will be decided by the conditions of development of socialist society. If the society is not stable, life will be difficult and there will be a lopsided growth of religion with concurrent negative influences. As our economy grows daily, the standard of living of our people rises continuously, and since this is what the people want, harmony [compatibility] is inevitable. Meanwhile, we should recognize that religion is a kind of ideology with a relatively independent historical development, and adapting things handed down through tradition with the continuing reform of society cannot be done once and for all. Therefore, overcoming discord will require a long period of time.

6 | The Policy of Freedom of Religious Belief

RELIGION will exist for a long time in the socialist period. One important condition for bringing harmony between religion and socialist society is for the party and state to adopt correct policies and guidelines, respecting and protecting religious freedom, and carrying out patriotic and united front work with persons in religious circles.

Theoretical Basis and Content of the Religious Policy

The basic policy of the Chinese Communist Party on the religious question is to respect and protect the people's freedom of religious belief.

Citizens of the People's Republic enjoy freedom of religious belief. This right is protected by the constitution and the law. The policy adopted by socialist China for dealing with the religious question has a deep theoretical basis and is founded on a rich historical experience.

Religious freedom was propounded by the bourgeois class in the early capitalist period in opposition to the feudal system. It was a revolutionary slogan for those historical times. But the bourgeois class did not and could not thoroughly accomplish [the goals] of this slogan. After attaining power, it still supported and made use of religion insofar as it suited them, and discriminated against other religions and nonbelievers. The historical responsibility of thoroughly implementing freedom of religious belief and using it to benefit social progress has fallen on the shoulders of the proletarian class.

Historical materialism believes that religion, as an illusion reflected in man's mind, is the external force that governs the daily life of people. In class society the social suffering created by class oppression and the system of exploitation is the major source for religion. The ruling classes throughout history have made use of religion as a tool to benumb the will for struggle of the people. Religious ideas "are all close or distant branches of the economic relations that control a specific society" (Engels, English edition of "Socialism, Utopian and Scientific," in *Selected Works of Marx and Engels*, 3:402). In a capitalist society, the duty of the proletarian political party is not to fight these twigs and branches that are offshoots of economic relations, but to unite with the broad masses of working people to overthrow the system of exploitation that produces these twigs and branches. Therefore, a slogan of the proletarian revolution is to support freedom of religious belief and to oppose the use and control of religion by capitalist nations. The main duty of the proletarian political party after the overthrow of the exploiting system and establishment of a socialist system is to unite religious believers with nonbelievers for the struggle to build socialism and to bring about Communism, the highest goal. One of the necessary conditions for this is to practice the policy of freedom of religious belief.

Revolutionary leaders such as Marx, Engels, and Lenin always advocated freedom of religious belief and equality among all religions, firmly opposing the use of religion by any ruling power. In Germany and Russia then, certain religions were in a ruling position and were used by the ruling class as tools to control the people's spirit. Under those historical conditions, Marx and Lenin took freedom of religious belief to be a political right in the people's struggle for social democracy and included it among the guiding principles for the political party of the working class.

In his *Critique of the Gotha Program*, published in 1875, Marx opposed the use of administrative measures to handle the problems of German Christianity. He approved of "freedom of belief" and explained the meaning of this slogan as "everyone should have the possibility of meeting his religious needs, just as with physical needs, without interference by the police" (*Selected Works of Marx and Engels*, 3:23–24). In 1891, the German Social Democratic Party, with the aim of opposing the use and control of religion by the bourgeois state, adopted the Erfurt Program, "proclaiming that religion is a personal affair."

The Orthodox church was the state religion in Russia, and the czarist government used it as an imperial tool to rule all Russian nationalities and persecute other religions and nonbelievers. Because of this, Lenin, in his "Draft Program of the Social Democratic Party and Explanation," written in 1895–96, issued the political demand for "freedom of religious belief." The fifth article, the "Program of the Russian Democratic Party," adopted by the Second Congress of the Russian Social Democratic Workers' Party in 1903, called for "overthrow of the czarist dictatorship system, and establishment of a democratic republic, and constitutional guarantees for unrestricted freedom of speech, publication, assembly, strike, and association." The seventh article called for "abolishing of the social estate system, and equality of all citizens regardless of sex, religious faith, nationality and race"; and the thirteenth article, for "separation of religion and state and religion and schools." In "To Paupers in Villages," Lenin, speaking directly to the ruling position of the Orthodox church, expounded on the meaning of freedom of religious belief. He said, "Everyone should enjoy complete freedom to believe in and to preach whatever religion he wishes, and to change his religious belief. No state official can interfere in the individual's religious belief; this is a matter of personal belief, and no one can interfere. No church or religion should be in a 'dominant position.' All churches and religions should be equal before the law." Lenin took freedom of religious belief as one of the basic political rights of the people, calling on "members of the Social Democratic Party to struggle for this" (Selected Works of Lenin, 1:425–26).

Why do Marxists, who are thoroughly atheistic, advocate freedom of religious belief? How can we correctly handle the divergence of world view between theism and atheism? Is there anything in common between people of different world views? Lenin provided answers to these questions. In his "Socialism and Religion," published in 1905 during the first high tide of the Russian bourgeois revolution, he made this well-known statement: "In our view, the unanimity of the oppressed classes in the revolutionary struggles for the establishment of an earthly paradise is more important than the unanimity of the proletariat about the idea of [a heavenly] paradise" (Complete Works of Lenin, 10:65). That is to say, despite having different religious beliefs, the people are unanimous in demanding liberation and happiness. Later, in "On the Attitudes of the Workers' Political Party toward Religion," Lenin severely criticized certain party comrades for "making religious, rather than political discrimination their first priority" (Selected Works of Lenin, 2:376). In January 1918, after the victory of the October Revolution, Lenin signed the decree, "On the separation of church from state, and church from schools," which stipulated: "the right of every citizen to believe or not believe in any religion, and abolishing of all regulations depriving people of their rights because of religious belief" (item 3); "the guarantee of the right to hold religious services which do not violate social order or restrict the rights of Soviet citizens" (item 5); and, "the separation of schools from the churches" (item 9). Later, to implement these decrees, some concrete regulations were adopted. Freedom of religious belief was also stipulated in the "Constitution of the Union of Soviet Socialist Republics (Basic Law)."

To sum up what is written in Marxist classics on the theory and practice of religion: they considered religion as a historical category, that is, that religion emerges and develops under specific conditions and will surely perish in the course of historical development when the conditions are ripe. The Communist Party is struggling for the realization of the highest ideals of Communism. After humanity enters into the Communist society, that is, the "kingdom of freedom" that understands and reforms the world, not only religion will perish, but also class, state, and political parties, including the working class and Communist parties, for this is the inevitable law of historical development. However, before the historical conditions for withering away ripen, we must protect religion and let it develop according to its own laws. The reason for Marxist nonbelievers to want to protect freedom of religious belief is this: Marxism's basic standpoint is to treat all cases from practice, to respect objective laws, and to work in accordance with those laws.

During the period of the New Democratic Revolution, the Chinese Communist Party observed the basic viewpoint of Marxism and Leninism on religion, combining the features of our religious history with the practical situation, and step by step setting up a correct and complete basic party policy on religion. Mao Zedong has said that while he was growing up in the countryside he had a deep faith in the gods. When his mother fell ill, he went and prayed before the Buddhist gods. After he became a Communist, Mao Zedong's attitude was serious and meticulous on the question of doing away with superstition. Even during the high tide of the stormy peasant movement, he still exhorted the people, saying that doing away with superstition would "naturally follow the victory of political and economic struggles." "It is the peasants who made the idols, and when the time comes they will cast the idols aside with their own hands; there is no need for anyone else to do it for them prematurely. The Communist Party's propaganda policy in such matters should be, 'Draw the bow without shooting, just indicate the motions' " ("Report on an Investigation of the Peasant Movement in Hunan Province," in Selected Works of Mao Zedong, pp. 34–35). In the years 1923–26, all the resolutions passed by Communist Party conferences emphasized the need for careful attitudes in dealing with religion, exhorting party members not to create conflicts deliberately with religious believers. To unite all patriotic forces, there should be no discrimination among parties, sects, religions, and classes in revolutionary activities. The CCP took the road of armed struggle after 1927, setting up the Central Soviet in Jiangxi Province. The fourth article of "Outline of the Chinese Soviet Constitution" adopted by the First National Representatives Conference of the Chinese Soviets on November 7, 1931, stipulated that "the workers, peasants, Red Army soldiers, and working people and their family members, regardless of sex, race, and religion, are all equal before the Soviet law, all are citizens of the Soviet Republic." Article 13 stipulated that "the aim of the Chinese Soviet regime is to see that workers, peasants, and working people have real freedom of religious belief. The policy of separating state and religion will absolutely be carried out." At that time, in the revolutionary base areas, religious belief was already protected by laws. It is well known throughout the world that the Red Army strictly observed the policies on nationalities and religion during the 25,000-li Long March.

In the Soviet areas, foreign missionaries were dealt with in different ways. Proof of that is seen in the case of the French missionary Alfred Bossardt, who lived eighteen months with the Red Army on the Long March during the years 1934–35 ("Another Foreigner on the Long March," Renmin ribao, October 24, 1984).

During the War of Resistance, the Northwest Working Committee of the Central Committee of the CCP drew up, in April and July 1940, the "Program on Hui Nationality Problems" and the "Program on Mongolian Nationality Problems During the War of Resistance," which were approved by the Central

Committee. In both programs, the following clauses were included: "Respect the Hui people's freedom of religious belief" and "Respect the customs, religion, language, and written language of the Mongolian nationality, protect the Lamaist temples, encourage young lamas to take part in productive labor, and oppose and ban any words and actions that slander or denigrate the Mongolian nationality." Article 6 of the Administrative Program of the Shaan-Gan-Ning Border Area, approved by the Politburo of the CCP in May 1941, "guaranteed the human rights, political rights, property rights, and freedom of speech, assembly, association, belief, residence, and migration of all (landlords, capitalists, peasants, workers, etc.) who were resisting the Japanese invasion."

Mao Zedong issued "On Coalition Government" at the Seventh People's Congress in April 1945. This report, with guidelines on the New Democratic Revolution, explicated the policy on religious freedom, listing freedom of religious belief as one of the basic rights of the people. He said, "The most important people's freedoms are freedom of speech, publication, assembly, association, thought, belief, and person. In China they are fully realized only in the liberated areas" (*Selected Works of Mao Zedong*, p. 1071). He also wrote, "The languages, writing, customs, habits, and religious beliefs of the minority nationalities should be respected" (ibid., p. 1085), and "According to the principle of freedom of religious belief, various religions should be permitted in the liberated areas of China, whether Protestant or Catholic Christianity, Islam, Buddhism, or other religions, as long as the believers obey the laws of the people's government, the people's government will protect them. Freedom of belief applies to both believers and nonbelievers, and no one is allowed to use force or discriminate against them" (ibid., p. 1093).

During the wars of Resistance and Liberation, there was sharp and complex national and class struggle inside the liberated areas. The government, while protecting the freedom of religious belief and normal religious activities, would resolutely crack down on hidden foes and reactionary armed forces making use of religion. The government in the liberated areas dealt severely with a case of international espionage among the Catholics in Xian County, wiping out the armed forces disguised as Catholics who attacked the liberated areas with the "North China Battlefield Supervision Service Unit of the Central Military Committee," the "Southern Hebei Communist Suppression Military Unit," and the "Gongjiao Baoguo [Catholic National Defense] Corps."

Mao Zedong, while making and implementing the policy on freedom of religious belief, explicitly explained how Communists must draw a clear line between politics and world view when in contact with the masses of the people. He said, "Communists may form a united front against imperialism and feudalism with some idealists and even religious believers politically, while never agreeing with them on idealism or religious beliefs" ("On New Democracy," in *Selected Works of Mao Zedong*, p. 700). That is to say, if we were to give up a Marxist world outlook and agree to idealism because we want political unity with reli-

gious patriots, we would lose the progressive nature of a proletarian revolutionary fighter, and commit "rightist" errors. If we exclude religious people from
the united front because of different world views, we hinder the achievement of
the party's general aims and commit the "Leftist" error of closed-doorism.
Marxists and Communists have to hold to their scientific world view while
joining politically with all anti-imperialist and anti-feudalist forces.

The protracted revolutionary struggle of all nationalities in China, led by the
Communist Party, has proved that setting up a united front that includes religious
believers has been one of the three great magic weapons that has won the
victory. In old China, the broad masses of believers could not gain real democratic freedoms, including religious freedom, because under the reactionary rule
of the Guomindang, religion was used by the feudal and reactionary forces to
oppress and exploit the people. Therefore, enabling believers to enjoy genuine
religious freedom would attract them to participate in the struggle against reactionary rule. Thus, the implementing of the religious policy in our nation was
naturally imbued with the function and meaning of anti-imperialism and antifeudalism. Because our party sincerely carried out the policy of freedom of
religious belief, and conscientiously protected this basic right of all citizens,
many believers took part in the revolutionary struggles led by the party. Early
after the founding of new China, reactionaries abroad and at home attempted to
sow discord between religious believers and the people's government to cover
up their activities of sabotage and subversion against the people's regime. The
CCP and the people's government, while exposing and cracking down on this
sabotage, continued to practice the policy of freedom of religious belief so that
people could enjoy real religious freedom, and at the same time gave them
patriotic education. With heightened patriotic consciousness, the broad masses of the
people took active part in the land reform, suppressing counterrevolutionaries, and
Resist America, Aid Korea movements, defending the growth of the new regime. In
the profound reforms of the social and economic systems, the people's government,
relying on the efforts of religious circles themselves, and with the support of various
social circles, cleared away imperial and feudal influences inside the religions, abolished feudal systems of oppression and exploitation, further implemented the
policy of freedom of religious belief, and enabled religious believers to work,
with peace of mind, for the cause of social construction and social reform.

At present, our nation has entered a new period of history in which the basic
duty, from now on, is to unite with all our nationalities in concentrated efforts for
modernized socialist construction to build our nation into a socialist nation with
high levels of prosperity, civilization, and democracy. "Socialist modernization
is currently our political priority" ("Hold Firmly to the Four Basic Principles,"
in Selected Works of Deng Xiaoping, p. 149). All our work and all our policy
making must center on this task, as it should on religious questions. As the
Central Committee of the CCP pointed out in 1982 in "On the Basic Viewpoint
and Policy Regarding the Religious Question in the Socialist Period in Our

Country" [Document 19], "In summary, our grass-roots starting point and standpoint in carrying out the policy of freedom of religious belief and handling all religious questions is to unite all religious believers and nonbelievers, to concentrate their will and efforts for the common goal of establishing a modernized, strong, socialist nation. Any words or actions deviating from this basis are wrong and should be resolutely resisted and opposed by the party and the people" (*Selected Writings on the United Front in the New Period*, p. 203).

Respecting and protecting the policy of freedom of religious belief is a long-term policy. There has always been a unified explanation of freedom of religious belief: that is, each citizen has the right to believe in religion and also has freedom not to believe in religion; he has freedom to believe in this religion or that religion; within the same religion he has freedom to believe in any sect; and he has freedom to change from nonbelief to belief, and from belief to nonbelief.

Neither the state nor any organization or individual can forcefully interfere with people's free choice in matters of belief. The state will conscientiously protect people's freedom to believe or not to believe in religion. The state power of a socialist country should not be used either to promote or to ban religion. In the Han areas of our country, where the majority of the people do not believe in religion, we should take care to ensure freedom of religious belief; in areas occupied by [ethnic] minorities, where the majority of the people believe in religion, we should take care to ensure the freedom [of the minority of the people] not to believe in religion.

Freedom of religious belief is not only a policy principle, it also includes concrete contents and stipulations based on this principle. Besides the constitution, there currently are other legal regulations regarding religion. For example, Article 147 of the "Criminal Code of the PRC" stipulates that state cadres who illegally deprive citizens of their legitimate right to freedom of religious belief or encroach upon the customs of minority nationalities may be sentenced, in serious cases, for up to two years in prison or detention.

To put the policy of freedom of religious belief into practice we first have to ensure the rights of religious clergy to fulfill their religious functions under the leadership of the various religious organizations. They must have been educated in religious schools and temples and must be knowledgeable about religion. At present, there are about 59,000 such persons among the various religions of our nation. Since they direct the religious life of the faithful and are closely connected to tens of millions of believers, they exercise an important influence on their spiritual life. Therefore, we educate them politically and unite with them to support socialism so they may lead the religious believers to love their country and obey the laws, to support the unity and solidarity of the motherland, and to adapt themselves consciously to the demands of the socialist society.

Second, an important material condition for normal religious activities is to make reasonable arrangements for places for normal religious activities. At present, there are about 30,000 such places in China. As the numbers of believers change, the number of places for worship may change as well so as to guarantee normal religious functions. "All normal religious services that are carried out in religious places, or in the homes of religious believers according to religious customs, such as worshipping Buddha, reading scriptures, burning incense, worship services, prayers, expounding the scriptures, preaching, Mass, baptism and memorial services, etc., are to be handled by religious organizations and believers under protection of the law, and no one is allowed to interfere" (CCP Central Committee, "On the Basic Viewpoint and Policy Regarding Religious Questions During Our Socialist Period," in *Selected Writings on the United Front in the New Period*, p. 206).

According to government regulations, the properties of all religious organizations should not be encroached on, for they belong to the respective religious organizations and are protected by the law. Each religious organization is the legal entity responsible for safeguarding these properties.

Third, each religion has its own national and local organizations. It is their responsibility to help the party and government implement and administer the policy of freedom of religious belief, to help believers and religious personnel raise their patriotic socialist consciousness, to represent the legal interests of religious circles, to arrange for normal religious activities, and to take care of routine religious work. At present there are eight national religious organizations: the Chinese Buddhist Association; the Chinese Daoist Association; the Chinese Islamic Association (which is both a religious organization and a mass organization of Muslim believers); the Chinese Catholic Patriotic Association; the Chinese Protestant Three-Self Patriotic Movement Committee (which is a mass organization set up soon after the founding of new China with a broad mass basis, based on eliminating domestic imperialist and reactionary influences, and has played and will play a very important role in implementing the policy of a "three-self" and independent church); the Chinese Catholic Church Affairs Commission, the Chinese Catholic Bishops' Conference, and the [Protestant] China Christian Council (which is a religious affairs organization). In addition, there are a number of religious social organizations, such as the Christian YMCA and YWCA, on both national and local levels.

All religious organizations represent the rights and interests of religious circles. Their representatives and committee members in the National People's Congress and the CPPCC at all levels may criticize any action that is contrary to the policy on religion and, through negotiation or legal procedures, may gain an equitable solution.

Fourth, all religions enjoy the right to edit, publish, and sell religious books and magazines, ancient books, religious pictures and figures, and other articles used for religious purposes. Currently, all religions have national periodicals, such as *Fa Yin* (Buddhist), *The Journal of the Daoist Association* (Daoism), *China Muslim* (Islam), *The Catholic Church in China* (Catholic), and *Heavenly Wind* (Protestant Christian). Recently, the Chinese Buddhist Association put in order the *Fangshan Yunju Temple Scripture*, edited, in succession, the "Buddhism in China'' series, and translated from Tibetan the famous Yin Ming book, *Shiliang* and the last six volumes of *Jiesheng mijingshu*. The Chinese Islamic Association printed an Arabic version of the Qu'ran and other religious books. The Chinese Catholic Church Affairs Commission printed the New Testament (*Xinjing quanshu*) and a catechism (*Questions and Answers on Important Doctrines*). The Protestants published the Bible and a new hymnal (400 hymns in all, of which 102 were composed or written by Chinese Christians, using Chinese style and tunes). As for [other] religious classics, government publication agencies organized the scholarly community to revise, rework, and publish them. A Chinese translation of the Qu'ran and a revised *Taipingjing* have already been published, and the *China Tibetan Scriptures* (*Zhonghua Dazangjing*) and others are to be published one after another. The state has allocated large sums of money to repair religious buildings valued as cultural antiquities. Religious circles have also made great efforts to safeguard religious cultural relics.

Fifth, the various religions have opened or reopened religious schools and colleges at different levels to train a young generation of patriotic clergy. At present all five religions have opened such schools at the national level, such as the Chinese Buddhist College, the Daoist Academy, the Chinese Islamic College, the Chinese Catholic Theological Seminary, and the Nanjing Union [Protestant] Theological Seminary. A good many religious schools and academies have been opened in various provinces and municipalities, according to local needs. It is of decisive importance for the future of the various religions to open religious schools and institutes, to cultivate a cohort of young clergy who are politically patriotic, support the leadership of the CCP and the socialist system, and are well informed about religion. Religious groups are running these schools and institutes well under the leadership of relevant government units.

Finally, the citizens' right to believe in religion and propagate theism, as well as not to believe in religion and propagate atheism, is the right of freedom of religious belief granted by the constitution. However, no one should indiscriminately propagate theism or atheism, or, still less, start an argument about either one. One important propaganda task of the CCP is to use Marxist philosophy to educate the masses of the people about dialectical and historical materialism (atheism) and a scientific world view, and to increase dissemination of scientific and cultural knowledge about natural phenomena, social evolution, human birth, aging, illness and death, and good or bad luck. But we have to be very careful in tackling religious questions not to run counter to present policy and to injure the feelings of religious believers.

All freedoms are relative, limited by objective circumstances, and can be implemented only within certain parameters. Freedom and discipline, rights and duties, all are categories with dialectical relationships. ''All citizens enjoy the rights set forth in the constitution and the law, but they also must fulfill the obligations set forth in the constitution and the law'' (Constitution of the PRC, Article 23). Freedom of religious belief, like other democratic rights, has clear-cut contents and definite limits. Religious believers, like other people among the masses, must fulfill the duties of citizens while enjoying freedom of religious belief. No political party (including the Communist Party in power), and no people's organization (including religious organizations), nor any individual has the right to go outside the constitution and the law. All are equal before the law. Therefore we have to know well the limits of civil rights as applied to freedom of religious belief and hold a dialectical view on the relationship between discipline and freedom. This is quite important for the masses of believers, for the handling of religious questions by the religious affairs departments, and for coordinating religion with socialist society.

First, religious believers, like the people of all [ethnic] nationalities, must support the leadership of the Communist Party, support the socialist system, love their country, maintain the unity of the nation and solidarity of the nationalities, take part in the building of the four modernizations along with all other people, keep up good religious traditions, and do good deeds for socialism. All religious organizations should accept the leadership of the government, run religious affairs independently, and never allow any foreign forces to regain influence or interfere in our religious affairs. The four basic principles form the political basis for the solidarity of the people from all [ethnic] nationalities in our country. Holding tightly to the four basic principles does not mean that religious believers have to give up their religious faith.

Taiwan, Hong Kong, and Macao are sacred territories of our country. The glorious duty of the Chinese people is to accomplish the great task of unifying the motherland. When Taiwan returns to China, and when Hong Kong is taken back in 1997, the central government will design and put into effect laws for a system, to be legalized by the National People's Congress, suited to these two areas based on the principle of one country, two systems.

Next, while carrying out the religious policy, we have to distinguish normal religious activities from illegal, criminal, and counterrevolutionary activities using the disguise of religion. The exploiting classes and system have been abolished, so that the contradictions reflected in the religious realm are mainly contradictions among the people. They can be solved reasonably within the scope of the constitution and the law. But class struggle will still exist to a certain degree for a long time. Our enemies, both at home and abroad, will make use of difficulties encountered in our march forward to engage in sabotage. This new form of class struggle will inevitably be reflected in the realm of religion. When antagonistic forces, both at home and abroad, use religion to oppose the socialist system, it is no longer a matter of religious belief, and they must be exposed. There are also a few scoundrels in society who make use of religion to swindle and bluff, cheating people of their money and harming both life and property. We must legally ban these criminal activities.

Third, to carry out the policy of freedom of religious belief, we must distinguish normal religious activities from ideas about spirits and gods, the worship customs surrounding them, and illegal superstitious activities. There are quite a few people in our country who do not believe in a specific religion, but in gods and spirits, worshipping these gods and spirits, and the ancestors, according to traditional customs. This is related to the underdevelopment of science and culture under the semicolonial and semifeudal social conditions of our country after entering modern society. We must solve this problem by using education to popularize scientific cultural knowledge and break away from superstition. Meanwhile, these superstitious activities that do not belong with religion have permeated into various religions. There are also a number of professional superstitious practitioners in society who spread superstition, cheat the people, make money by unfair means, and harm people, violating marriages, and jeopardizing public order. Since the founding of new China, the government has banned superstitious practitioners and punished those who jeopardized public order. Article 165 of ''The Criminal Code of the PRC'' stipulates that ''sorcerers and witches who spread rumors and cheat people of money are to be sentenced for up to two years in prison, or detained in custody or placed under public surveillance, with imprisonment from two to seven years for serious cases.'' As for general superstitious practices that have passed down through history into religious activities, such as fortunetelling, casting lots, and so forth, it is up to the various religious organizations, based on traditional rules and teachings, to clean this up. As for believers who take up such activities at places of worship, clergy should give them religious instruction and guidance.

In dealing with these superstitious activities, as long as religious leaders know and consistently follow policy, strictly distinguishing between normal religious activities and general superstitions, propaganda for eliminating superstition will win the support of religious circles. We must not overextend while disseminating scientific information and opposing superstitious practices, to include normal religious activities among superstitious practices in general, but must preserve the livelihood of religious professionals while banning illegal superstitious activities. We must give patient education to superstitious people, using scientific information and examples of how superstitious practitioners cheat people. We must punish criminal offenders according to the law. As for the counterrevolutionary activities of the reactionary sects, Article 99 of the Criminal Code of the PRC stipulates that ''those who organize and use feudal superstitions and sects to engage in counterrevolutionary activities are to be sentenced to a minimum of five years in prison; lighter cases may be sentenced to under five years in prison, custody, or public surveillance and deprivation of political rights.'' In this way a stable social order and normal religious activities will be ensured.

A Review of the Actual Implementation of the Policy on Religion

The religious work of the party and government and the implementing of the policy on religion have followed a twisting course since the founding of new

China. During the seventeen years from the founding of new China to the "Cultural Revolution," although there has been interference from the "Left" as well as some bad mistakes, the party and the government, under the correct guidance of the party's Central Committee, have, generally speaking, accomplished a great deal in religious work and in implementing the policy on religion. During the "Cultural Revolution" the rights of citizens protected by the constitution were violated and the policy of freedom of religious belief was willfully trampled. Since the smashing of Jiang Qing's counterrevolutionary clique, and particularly since the Third Plenum of the Eleventh Party Congress, the correct policy of the party on religious questions has been gradually restored. Following is a review of how the party and government have administered the policy on religion in four different periods.

The first period was from 1949 to 1957. In the early days, the party and government paid great attention to carry out properly the religious policy and wrote that policy into the constitution. Article 5 of the first section of the General Outline of the Common Program of the Chinese People's Political Consultative Conference, adopted by the First Plenum of the CPPCC in September 1949, stipulates that "citizens of the PRC enjoy the freedom of thought, speech, publication, assembly, association, correspondence, person, residence, mobility, religious belief, and demonstration." In September 1954, the First People's Congress adopted the first constitution of our country. Article 8 declares that "citizens of the PRC enjoy freedom of religious belief." To ensure the implementation of the policy of freedom of religious belief, the government, since 1951, has set up offices of the Religious Affairs Bureau at every level. The principal leaders of the party and government have received religious leaders many times, showing concern for the situation of the religions during the land reform movement, the Resist America, Aid Korea Movement, and the movements for democratic reform. In 1952, while receiving a Tibetan Goodwill Delegation, Mao Zedong said, "The Communist Party has adopted the policy of protecting religion. Whether you believe in religion or not, and whether you believe in this religion or that religion, you all will be respected. The party respects religious belief. This policy, as presently adopted, will continue in the future" (*Renmin ribao*, November 22, 1952). On the issue of the struggle of Christianity against imperialism, Zhou Enlai held four successive talks with Christian patriots, such as Wu Yaozong, carrying on discussions with them late in the night and offering instruction and support for the three-self road followed by the Christians.

Other state leaders, such as Zhu De, also talked with religious leaders, encouraging them to unite with the people and to take an active part in the political life of the nation. At that time the party and government worked hard to implement the policy of freedom of religious belief, giving respect and protection for that freedom, supporting all religions in exposing and denouncing imperialism and feudalism for making use of religion, in banning reactionary secret societies, eliminating counterrevolutionaries who hid themselves inside religious organizations and communities, and making strict policy distinctions between regular religious organizations and activities and reactionaries who used the disguise of religion, and thus protecting genuine religious freedom. Due to the party's and government's persistence in uniting with and educating religious people, the patriotic initiative of religious leaders and the broad masses of believers was brought into play. The party and government enjoyed high prestige among religious circles, who then actively took part in the tasks of defending the motherland, in stabilizing social order, and in advancing economic construction. Religious circles, either consciously or unconsciously, explored in many ways the problem of adapting religion to the new socialist society, including the Protestant Three-Self Patriotic Movement, the Catholic experience of opposing imperialism and running the church independently, and the antifeudalism struggles of the other religions; all had far-reaching historical significance. During that period of time the religious work of the party and government was highly successful, accumulating valuable experience.

The second period was from 1958 to 1966. During that period, due to the continuing, deepened implementation of the religious policy, all religions achieved new successes in freeing themselves from the control of imperialism and feudalism and holding firm to the patriotic road. For example, Chinese Catholics themselves elected and ordained Chinese bishops and made important progress on the road of running their church independently. Islam and Tibetan Buddhism gradually carried out democratic reforms of their internal systems, abolishing feudal privileges, oppression, and the system of exploitation in the form of religion, and leading religion to adapt to the new social system. Religious circles, under the leadership of the party and government, continued studying patriotism and socialism, while some of them, plunging directly into the building of the nation, took part in physical labor to the extent of their abilities.

However, at the same time serious mistakes were made in the party's work with regard to policy direction, causing zig-zag diversions in the nation's political and economic situation. "Leftist" errors of the party in its administration of the policy on religion increased, resulting in many faults, such as the broadening of the Anti-Rightist Movement; the excessive emphasis, in some places, on abolishing the system of feudal exploitation in the form of religion, due to the wrong interpretation of policy; certain comrades erroneously held that religion had lost its basis for existence in the socialist society and tried to wipe out religion by administrative decrees; the seizing of church or temple properties by the government during the "Great Leap Forward" and people's commune movements, suspending religious activities; and, in a few places, "advising" believers to back out from religion.

After 1960, the Central Committee of the Chinese Communist Party, in summing up its experience and lessons learned, redressed its "Leftist" errors and modified the way religion was treated. Nevertheless, shortly thereafter, at the

Tenth Plenum of the Eighth Party Congress in September 1962, Mao Zedong broadened and made more absolute the class struggle that still existed to a certain degree in socialist society. He declared that the bourgeois class would try to make a comeback in the course of socialist history. He also held that the bourgeois class was the source of revisionism. Regarding the question of religion, he did not correctly estimate the basic changes that had taken place in religious circles after they had abolished the imperialist and reactionary influences. Some comrades erroneously held that serious antagonistic contradictions still existed in religion, believing that religious belief was the ideology of the exploiting class, exaggerating the nature of religious belief, which is only of secondary importance, and placing it in the ideological category of class struggle. Thus, they first denounced the so-called capitulationist and revisionist lines in the work of the United Front, Nationalities, and Religion departments. In 1964 they criticized Li Weihan, then the head of the United Front Department, who was in charge of religious work. In 1965, during the "Four Cleans" movement, some local cadres persuaded believers to withdraw from religion and turn in their religious items. In that same year, some ambitious careerists in important positions even said that "Catholics are the landlord party," "Protestants are a special imperialist brigade," and "the task of the Communists is to exterminate religions." These extreme "Leftist" slogans further advanced the erroneous "Leftist" tendencies in religious work. Religious activities in some places were forced to go underground, and believers began to have doubts about the policy on religion, with the result that the unity and trust between the party and believers, which had been built on anti-imperialist patriotism, was in danger of destruction.

The third period was the ten years of chaos. The counterrevolutionary clique of Jiang Qing and Lin Biao used the "Leftist" errors to trample wantonly on the policy of freedom of religious belief and the scientific Marxist theories on religious questions. They totally denied the correct religious policy of the party since the founding of new China and the achievements of the [party's] religious work in the previous seventeen years. They completely stopped the religious work of the party and government. All religious offices, from the central to local levels, were closed, and the religious activities of every religious organization, whether at national or local level, were forced to stop. In this calamity, churches were attacked, temples torn down, scriptures burned, Buddhist figures destroyed, religious artifacts burned, and all normal religious activities, such as scripture chanting, worship services, and Masses, banned. Both religious properties and cultural relics were severely damaged or destroyed. In the name of "making a clean sweep of all monsters and demons," religious circles were recklessly criticized and paraded through the streets, Christians were treated as class enemies, a great many unjust and erroneous cases were fabricated, and some people were persecuted to death.

In the national minorities regions, certain customs were taken as targets for "smashing the four olds." The counterrevolutionary clique of Lin Biao and

Jiang Qing stirred up disputes and hostility between believers and nonbelievers, between one nationality and another, destroying national unity. Under the extremely chaotic conditions of the "Great Proletarian Cultural Revolution," a few people fished in troubled waters, using religion to engage in activities that upset social order, swindling people of their money, and endangering life and property, thus adding to the complexity of religious problems. Of course the goal of the counterrevolutionary clique of Lin Biao and Jiang Qing was to usurp the supreme power of the party and the nation. Religious circles and party and government cadres were only a small part of those persecuted under the ultra-Leftist line. Religious circles, like righteous people across the nation, were opposed to the perverse acts of the counterrevolutionary clique. Most of those in religious circles who suffered serious testing still believed in the party, the government, and the socialist system. Facts have proved that they are patriotic, and that the work in implementing the religious policy since the founding of new China was effective.

The fourth period is from 1976 to the present. Since the fall of the Jiang Qing counterrevolutionary clique, and particularly since the Third Plenum of the Eleventh Party Congress, the party's Central Committee has made an overall summation of the religion question, including both positive and negative historical experiences, and by ideological guidance has accomplished the historical task of bringing order out of chaos. In February 1979, the label of "taking the capitulationist line" was removed from the United Front, Nationalities, and Religion departments by official action of the party's Central Committee. The Central Committee issued many important documents reinstating the policy of freedom of religious belief, restoring United Front and Religious Affairs Bureau offices at national and local levels, and putting into practice the policy of freedom of religious belief. Most important was the authorization in 1982 of the document "The Basic View and Policy on the Problem of Religion in the Socialist Period" [Document 19] by the Central Committee of the CCP, and the adoption by the National People's Congress of the revised constitution of the People's Republic of China. Article 36 of the constitution stipulates that "All citizens of the PRC enjoy freedom of religious belief. No organ of the state, mass organization, or person is allowed to force any citizen to believe or not believe in religion. It is not allowed to discriminate against any citizen who believes or does not believe in religion. The state protects legitimate religious activities. No person is allowed to use religion to conduct counterrevolutionary activities or activities disrupting social order, harming people's health, or obstructing the educational system of the nation. Religious bodies and religious affairs are not subject to control by foreign forces."

In recent years great changes have taken place among many cadres in their understanding of religious policy and problems. In the past, in their "Leftist" dogmatism, they followed Marxist classical writers, rather than the actual practice of religion in our socialist period, holding that religion had lost its basis for existence in the socialist society and attempting to force its extermination prematurely, using administrative means. This was contrary to the basic laws of religious development. Now they have come to a comparatively deep understanding of the objective laws regarding the birth, growth, and withering away of religion, and of the five characteristics of religion in our country—its mass, complex, [ethnic] nationalities, international, and protracted natures. They have come to know that the basic starting point and ultimate goal for dealing with religious questions is to unite all religious believers and nonbelievers, and to focus their will and strength on the common goal of building a strong socialist nation. Due to this correct understanding, our religious work has gradually turned onto the road of promoting social stability and unity, building the four modernizations, and safeguarding world peace. In recent years we have achieved conspicuous success in bringing order out of chaos and implementing the policy on religion. For example, the false and erroneous cases among religious circles during the "Cultural Revolution" and the Anti-Rightist Movement have been investigated and corrected, and the persons rehabilitated. Various patriotic religious organizations at different levels have been gradually revived and are playing an active role. A number of religious academies and institutes have been revived or newly set up to train young professional clergy. Religious meeting places have been renovated and reopened, making religious life available to the broad masses of believers. International religious exchanges have been gradually restored, promoting friendship between the Chinese people and other peoples, and safeguarding world peace. At the same time, those who made use of religion to engage in illegal criminal and counterrevolutionary activities have been punished according to the law.

While affirming the success of our work, we should be aware of the many problems that still exist. The basic cause for these problems is that the influence of "Leftist" ideology has not been completely exterminated. Some say that it is hard to implement policy, and even harder to implement religious policy. These words make sense. The current "Leftist" ideological influences are mainly manifested in the fact that some comrades do not have a comprehensive understanding of the basic view and policy of the party regarding religion in the socialist period in China. They still hold that "religion can only be exterminated, and not allowed to develop; religious freedom means the growth of religion." To implement this policy is to "burn joss sticks to invite ghosts." Guided by this ideology, it would be quite natural consciously or unconsciously to regard religion, religious activities and religious believers as "superstitious and backward," or to be concerned when they see that in some places the number of believers has increased. Thus they always try to restrict, take over, or interfere with internal religious matters, even harming the legal rights of religionists. All this dampens the patriotic initiative of religious leaders and believers.

There are a number of comrades working in the departments of propaganda and education who do not seriously study the essence of the important documents about religious questions and, even more, do not fully implement the policy in their work. For example, in some student textbooks and other books, religious knowledge is still somehow linked to "taking class struggle as the key link." Some press agencies publish news reports that are helpful for implementing the policy, but the journalists and editors of some newspapers often contradict historical facts or denigrate the image of religion, recklessly publishing articles regarding religious questions that go against the policy, thus hurting the feelings of religious believers, resulting in bad effects. Some people in commerce and industry do not understand either the nationalities or the religious policy, and in their ignorance have thoughtlessly designed certain commodities for export that had bad effects.

Some agencies responsible for cultural relics, public gardens, and parks, and some travel agencies have not returned the temples occupied for many years, or have returned some, but not completely, keeping a "tail." The main cause for such situations, aside from the fact that quite a few people are still fettered by "Leftist" influences, is that a number of cadres lack an overall view of policy and usually tackle such questions from the viewpoint of the interest of their own units. In recent years, such questions carried over from the past have been gradually resolved.

To carry out the religious policy correctly and in an all-around way, the main task at present is to oppose incorrect "Leftist" tendencies while paying attention to overcoming incorrect tendencies toward laissez-faire attitudes. We must keep a sober mind, watching out for hostile influences at home and abroad who attempt to make use of religion to carry out sabotage in our country or to interfere with our religious affairs. A few bad elements in our country will collude with hostile foreign powers to engage in sabotage activities or make use of religion to carry out other criminal activities. We must be on the alert, attacking and promptly stopping them.

Another important element in the party's religious work is to strengthen the patriotic united front among religious circles.

During the course of the Chinese New Democratic Revolution, religious patriotic circles, beginning with the May Fourth Movement, joined with the anti-imperialist and anti-feudalist united front. Religious patriots at that time put forth the slogan of opposing the use of religion for aggression by imperialism. During the nationwide movement of resisting Japan and national salvation, even more religious patriots joined the national united front against Japan. During the War of Liberation they made important contributions to the establishment of new China. At the first plenary session of the preparatory meeting for the new Chinese People's Political Consultative Conference in September 1949, Zhou Enlai said this in a speech: "There are many democratic persons who fought on their own against reactionaries in the Guomindang areas; . . . Although they did not organize any political party or organization, they did link up a good many democratic persons for the struggle. . . . Wu Yaozong, a religious person in Shanghai who continuously carried on the fighting, was such a person'' (*Selected Works of Zhou Enlai on the United Front*, p. 125). This is high praise for religious patriots, represented by Wu Yaozong.

Since the founding of new China, the party has continued to follow the policy of uniting and educating in order to get more religious people to join the patriotic united front and work for revival of the national economy, to complete socialist reform, and to construct socialism. The party also unfolded the patriotic, anti-imperialism movement inside religion, to reform the system of feudal oppression and exploitation in the name of religion, and to bring about fundamental changes in the religious situation. Religious representatives always attend the national and local meetings of the CPPCC, which is one form of the united front. They have contributed good ideas on political, economic, cultural, and educational matters. They have represented the legal interests of the various religions, provided supervision for the practice and implementation of religious policy, and put forth proposals at the third meeting of the Third Plenary Session of the CPPCC in April 1962. At that time Zhou Enlai said, in a speech: ''There are now religious units in the CPPCC. There was a time in the past when we committed some errors in this aspect of our work. Some friends in religious circles made criticisms, giving many good ideas that deserve our serious attention.'' Zhou Enlai also spoke about the common basis that brought religious people to join the united front. He said, ''Ideological problems are problems among the people. Religious faith is a long-term issue. We only hope that patriotic religious persons will love their motherland, willingly serve socialism, and study hard. Thus, they still keep their religious faith, but this does not affect the expansion of our people's democratic united front, nor does it hinder the socialist construction of our country'' (ibid., p. 445).

During the ''Cultural Revolution'' the party's united front with religious circles was seriously damaged. After the Third Plenum of the Eleventh Party Congress, the ''Leftist'' mistaken ideas guiding the united front were corrected. Following the shift in the work of the party and the country, the key task of the united front in the new period ''is to bring all active elements into full play, strive to change passive elements into active elements, unite with all forces that can be united with, and, with one heart and one mind, pool the wisdom and strength of everyone to maintain and develop a peaceful, stable, and united political situation, and struggle to build a modernized, strong, socialist country'' (Deng Xiaoping, ''The Task of the United Front and the CPPCC in the New Period,'' in *Selected Works of Deng Xiaoping*, p. 173). The scope of the united front of the party and religious circles has been broadened, the basis for their unity has been expanded, and their tasks have become heavier than before.

In the new historical stage, following developments at home and abroad, in order to solve the problems of Hong Kong, Macao, and Taiwan soon, and to accomplish the great task of unifying our motherland, the party's Central Committee has put forth the idea of ''one country, two systems.'' Therefore, the new stage of the united front includes all socialist workers, all patriots who support socialism, as well as all patriots who agree with unity within our motherland, including religious patriots from Taiwan, Hong Kong, Macao, and overseas who support the unity of the motherland.

In consideration of the fact that two different social systems exist in mainland China and Taiwan, Hong Kong, Macao, and elsewhere, and that under different historical conditions differences exist among the various religions, the religious communities and organizations on the mainland and in Hong Kong should observe the principles of "nonsubordination, noninterference, and mutual respect." This is an important item in our country's policy regarding the Basic Agreement, signed by China and Great Britain, to return Hong Kong to China in 1997. Patriotic religious circles in Hong Kong support the unity of the motherland and have played an important role in bringing about the signing of the agreement. They have also taken part in drafting the Hong Kong Basic Law, playing an important role in the future stability and prosperity of Hong Kong.

The General Program of the Party Constitution, adopted at the Twelfth Party Congress, stipulates that "The Chinese Communist Party is in unity with the workers, peasants, and intellectuals of all nationalities throughout the country, and with all democratic parties, nonparty persons, and all patriotic forces among the nationalities, to develop and strengthen the widest possible patriotic united front composed of all socialist workers and all patriots who support socialism and the unity of the motherland. We will accomplish the great task of unifying the motherland with all the Chinese people, including compatriots in Taiwan, Hong Kong, Macao, and elsewhere overseas" (*Collected Documents of the Twelfth Party Congress*, pp. 80–81).

Resolutely to carry out the policy of freedom of religious belief, to strive for progress in developing the patriotic united front with religious circles, and to unite more closely with all religious believers both at home and abroad—all these have one purpose: to promote the current reforms, opening to the outside, and domestic revitalization, and to achieve the great task of building the four modernizations and the unity of the motherland.

7 | Conclusion

THIS BOOK is an attempt to study the religious questions in the socialist period in China. In the course of our exploration we keenly realized that the study and application of the past and present reality of Chinese society, combined with basic principles, has great significance for opening up reflection on religious questions. In recent years, Chinese academic circles have expressed different views on certain writings regarding religious questions by veteran revolutionaries, such as Marx and others, and the prospect of contention has arisen. This is a lively embodiment of the spirit of the Third Plenum of the Eleventh Party Congress.

The spring breeze of "Let one hundred flowers bloom, let one hundred schools of thought contend" has wafted into the realm of religious research, which for years had been looked upon as a "forbidden zone." This new and happy phenomenon will certainly lead to the flourishing of theoretical research on religion. We will now briefly present our views on how we understand the problem posed by [the allegation that] "religion is the opiate of the people" [*Selected Works of Marx and Engels*, 1:2].

"Opiate" Is a Metaphor Describing the Negative Influence of Religion under Certain Conditions in a Class Society

In the decades before Marx said that "Religion is the opiate of the people," there were in Germany alone quite a few scholars who used various metaphors to describe the numbing effect of religion. Some of them directly used the word "opium," as did Feuerbach, Heine, and others. Thus it is clear that Marx took his wording from those who came before him.

Marx put forth a series of elaborate, original, and profound hypotheses from the point of view of the proletarian revolution. However, can Marx's theory of religion be summed up in one sentence, that is, "Religion is the opiate of the people"? No, Marx himself never summed up his views in this way. He said that, in a class society, "nation and society generate religion, an upside down world view, because they themselves are an upside down world"; we have to change "criticism of the kingdom of Heaven" to "criticism of the world"; and change "criticism of theology" to "criticism of politics" (from "Critique of Hegel's *Philosophy of Right*," which refers to religion as the "opiate of the people," *Selected Works of Marx and Engels*, 1:2). "Only when you have wiped out the shackles of this world can you overcome the narrowness of religion" ("On the Problem of the Jews," *Complete Works of Marx and Engels*, 1:425). These and other well-known references cannot be summed up in the word "opiate."

Even if we say that "religion is the opiate of the people," the complete paragraph is this: "Religious suffering is at the same time an expression of real suffering and a protest against real suffering. Religion is the sigh of the oppressed creature, the sentiment of a heartless world, and the soul of soulless conditions. It is the opium of the people." It is evident that this statement is aimed at the situation of religion in class societies. Later, in his "On the Attitudes of Workers' Political Parties toward Religion," Lenin also said this: "This dictum of Marx's is the cornerstone of the entire Marxist world view on the problem of religion. Marxism always holds that all present-day religions, churches, and religious organizations are institutions of the bourgeois reactionary class for safeguarding the system of exploitation and for benumbing the working class" (*Selected Works of Lenin*, 2:375).

Nowadays, when people cite these words of Lenin, they always quote the former sentence and leave out the latter. They think that since it is the "cornerstone," it can never be shaken. In fact, is not the latter part of this quotation the best explication of the former? "Present-day" refers to that time, the time when religion was used by the reactionary bourgeoisie. We hold that the assertion by Marx and Lenin that religion is an "opiate" was first of all aimed at the situation of religion in Europe at that time (in Germany and Russia where religion was closely linked with the reactionary rule); it was aimed at the negative function of religion in the proletarian revolution.

In addition, what they called "opiate" has two related meanings. First, religion is the "expression of the actual sufferings" and is "the sigh of the oppressed" in class societies. When laboring people cannot free themselves from the sufferings caused by class oppression and exploitation, they seek the illusion of spiritual comfort in religion. Just as people drink to drown their sorrows, so does religion have the anaesthetic function of easing pain.

Second, the ruling class throughout history has made use of religion to benumb [drug] people, making them give up, endure oppression and exploitation, and place their hope in grace hereafter in a heavenly kingdom. This is the way a thief works, first getting his victim drunk, then stealing all of his possessions.

It seems that either of these two meanings of "opiate" would help maintain the reactionary rule of the exploiting classes and harm the revolution. Therefore, the proletariat, when rising in revolt to overthrow the old society, must expose the "opiate" function of religion, arousing and encouraging the working people to struggle for genuine happiness and for the realization of socialism and Communism.

The Historical Functions of Religion Differ and Cannot Be Summed Up in One Word, "Opiate"

As stated above, in certain historical periods, the oppressed classes have used religion as a spiritual weapon and connecting link to unite the people for rebellious movements. In the long-lasting class societies, religion played a passive role with regard to revolution. But it should be noted that, under certain conditions, it is a historical fact that oppressed classes have used religion as an ideological weapon in making revolution.

Engels said, "The middle ages [in Europe] combined other forms of ideology—philosophy, politics, law—into theology and made them disciplines subsumed under theology; therefore, all social and political movements at that time had to take the form of theology. As for the feelings of the people, who were completely under the influence of religion, if they wanted to set off a great storm, they would have to let the vital interests of the people appear under the cloak of religion" (*Selected Works of Marx and Engels*, 4:251).

What Engels means here is that in all social and political systems in medieval Europe, the feudal class had to make use of religion to maintain its rule, and the oppressed classes got their support from religion. This is historically inevitable. The functions of religion under these two circumstances are entirely different and must not be confused.

Apart from that, it should be pointed out that the social functions of religion cannot be viewed from a purely political angle. Religion permeates nationality and becomes part of its history and culture. The literature, fine arts, architecture, and so on of all peoples are affected in varying degrees by religion. The social functions of a culture in the form of religion cannot be summarized as "opium." When people cannot tear themselves away from the treasure house of Buddhist arts at the Dunhuang caves, when they are immersed in the music of a Chinese Daoist liturgical ceremony, when they enjoy looking at the "Last Supper" by Da Vinci, or when they listen to Schubert's "Ave Maria," their feelings are complex and diverse. We must analyze and carry on the heritage of culture in its religious forms and must not look upon everything as "opium" and therefore reject it.

The Functions of Religion in the Period of Socialism Are Even Less Aptly Described as "Opium"

In chapter 5 we made a preliminary exploration of how religion can be in harmony with a socialist society. Since they can indeed be in harmony, it is not right to say that all functions of religion are "opiates," or that religion is, in essence, an "opiate." The crux of the matter is that the exploiting system that existed for thousands of years has been overthrown, there is no longer an exploiting class, and the class roots of religion have disappeared. People no longer turn to religion for comfort because of suffering caused by class oppression and exploitation. Under socialist conditions, neither of the above-mentioned functions of religion exists.

Is there no longer suffering in socialist society, and has religion lost even the least of its passive functions? The answer is, of course there is still suffering. As analyzed above, in socialist society the contradictions of class confrontation have been solved, but there are still plenty of contradictions among the people. There are still many social problems, such as poverty, illness, limited opportunities for higher education, unemployment, divorce, disappointment in love, family disputes, bureaucracy, and unhealthy tendencies. All these will bring short-term troubles to some people, and some will turn to religion for help. Others will become dispirited and world-weary.

This is the passive function of traditional religion in a socialist society. It is even more like this in places where the economy and culture lag behind, and masses of religiously influenced people live in crowded communities.

But it should be stressed that the short-term difficulties of these people [under socialism] are essentially different from the suffering caused by the exploiting systems. Their short-term difficulties can be gradually overcome by the people's own efforts. With the work of certain units and patriotic religious circles, the passive mindset of these believers can be gradually changed, and the passive function of religion can be kept to the minimum.

We hold that under socialist conditions, the social functions and limitations of religion are those described below:

1. Because of the profound changes in the social system and in religion itself, it is now possible for religion, influenced by patriotism and socialist ideology, to be in harmony with socialist society and to make its contributions to that society.

2. Certain traditional religious teachings, regulations, and activities, combined with the conditions on which religion relies for its existence, still exercise a negative influence on believers. Of course there also exists the possibility for religion to be used by evildoers to upset social stability and harm the welfare of the people.

3. While religion as an ideological belief of some of the people can be categorized as an idealist world outlook, it is harmless to society in the personal life of the believer. Social existence determines social ideology. The social functions of religion cannot remain fixed and unchanged. If we can implement a correct policy on religious questions in the wake of the development of socialist material civilization and socialist spiritual civilization, choosing the good and avoiding the bad, the harmonization of religion with socialist society will continue to develop.

While discussing the disposition of "religion as an opiate of the people" and investigating religious problems in the socialist period, we came to feel even more the necessity to stick to the principle of taking Marxism as our guide while proceeding from actual conditions in carrying out multidisciplinary comprehensive studies of religious questions in the socialist period in order to deepen our research work.

Religion should be studied from a philosophical viewpoint, and, since the founding of new China, the research work on religion carried out in our academic circles has been done mainly from the perspectives of philosophy and history of ideology. After several years of practical [field work] study and investigation, we strongly feel that religion in the socialist period studied from their point of view alone will not give the complete picture of religion. If religion is studied from a philosophical point of view alone, attention will be paid only to the differences between theism and atheism and between materialism and idealism, overlooking other factors such as psychology, culture, morality, organization, and economics.

Taking the present socialist construction as a whole, we cannot but attach great importance to these other factors. The introduction to this book presents the thesis that religion is also a substance. We hold that religion, as a social substance, is not only an ideology but also a form of culture, a social grouping, a social community of definite economic substance. We must, of course, engage in a comprehensive multidisciplinary study of this multistructured religious phenomenon in order to make our understanding conform with the realities of religion.

In our recent investigations and studies, in addition to religious philosophy, we have touched upon sociology, psychology, ethics, ethnology, folklore, and so forth. For example, while investigating the causes of people's belief in religion, we discovered that religion is not just a holdover from the old ideology that has lost its grounds for existence in socialist society; this clearly runs against the facts. We have explored the grounds for the long-term existence of religion in a socialist society from historical, sociological, and psychological viewpoints. Also, basing our conclusions on abundant data from our social investigations, we have proved that religion can coordinate with a socialist society. By coordination we do not mean that two different ideological systems, such as theism and atheism or materialism and idealism, can be coordinated or can replace each other; we mean coordination in political and social life, coordination on the basis of patriotism and socialism.

Of course, for religious believers, this coordination cannot be torn apart from their ideology, belief, morality, and behavior that derive from their religious beliefs. Perhaps we can say that the coordination mentioned is drawn not from a philosophical world outlook, but from a sociological viewpoint.

Can one say, then, that we see no difference or contradiction between theism and atheism? No, but we have noticed that in the course of Chinese history, politics and religion have always been separated. In the past, religion did not pose a serious obstacle to China's democratic revolution, and it has generally been like this in some ethnic minority areas as well, where politics and religion were combined. In the present stage of socialist construction, believers and nonbelievers are, in fact, marching forward hand-in-hand along the road of the four modernizations. Differences in religious belief are only secondary and should not be given first place. In his "Economic and Philosophic Manuscripts of 1844," Marx wrote, "If only religious philosophy etc. is the real existence of religion for me, then I can only be a true believer as a religious philosopher, but in doing this I would negate actual religious belief and those who really believe in religion."

We think this is very well said. By "real existence of religion," Marx undoubtedly means, "actual religious belief and actual religious believers."

In China today, how many believers can be called religious philosophers? How many of them really understand religious philosophy? If we seek to understand and study religious questions from the point of view of philosophy of religion only, are we not divorcing ourselves from the religious realities in China today?

A foreign scholar has proposed that religion is a phenomenon consisting of five elements: church, ceremony, belief and concept, special emotional experience, and moral norms. This definition demonstrates that religion is more than an ideology. But this formulation has its serious defect, because it overlooks a most lively element of religion, that is, the believers—whom Marx called "real people believing in religion." We have come to realize through practice [phenomenological field research] that if we want to study, under socialist conditions, the thought, beliefs, morality, and behavior of the "real people who believe in religion," we are sure to touch upon many disciplines. Only by a synthesis of multidisciplinary studies can we scientifically and thoroughly bring to light the features of religion in the socialist period, explore its laws of growth and evolution, and provide our nation with a theoretical foundation for a correct policy.

Second, judging by the theoretical construction of religion, we must follow the course of history and carry out comprehensive multidisciplinary studies. In academic circles in the world today, natural sciences, new disciplines and borderline disciplines of social science, and synthetic disciplines where natural science and social science merge are springing up like mushrooms, enough to make one dizzy, too many for the eye to see.

It is the same with research on religion. Numerous schools are springing up offering a variety of perspectives: religious sociology, religious psychology, religious ethics, religious ethnology, religious anthropology, and so forth, and so the work of religious research is deepened and broadened. Not only in the nations of America and Europe, but in the Soviet Union and Eastern European nations, scholars of religion have summed up their experience and lessons and are paying attention to borderline disciplines. We should admit that we have started too late. It is our belief that we should do more synthetic, multidisciplinary research on religion in order to explore more deeply into the relationship among religious phenomena, Marxism, and the practical situation of China with its Chinese features.

APPENDICES

APPENDIX ONE

To Pi County and Back

Field Studies on Social Sources of Religion
in Northern Jiangsu Province (June 1983)

PI COUNTY is located on the Xuhuai plain, bordering Shandong Province on the north, with cultural traditions and history tracing back to the Han dynasty. Famous men came from here, and legends about them still circulate. For example, it is said that the Huangshe Production Brigade of the Chahe Commune is the birthplace of Huangshigong, who was revered as a celestial being after his death. It is said that Chang Liang, a wise subject of the Liubang Emperor, put his shoes on for him at the bridge. Actually, there is now no bridge either at the East Bridgehead or West Bridgehead of the commune. They say that Liu Xiu (the Guangwu Emperor of the Eastern Han dynasty), while stealing melons from a field here before becoming emperor, had looked this way and that way ("look" and "bridge" are homonyms in Chinese, both pronounced "qiao") to see if anyone was coming his way. Yixu, a place in Daizhuang, got its name because, they say, Liu Xiu slept here, leaning against a tree ("yi" means to lean, "xu" means to sleep).

This place also has glorious revolutionary traditions in modern times. The great Taierzhuang victory in the early stage of the Anti-Japanese War took place in Shandong, close to this county. A portion of the Huaihai Battle, which shocked the world, was fought here. The Huang Botao Army of the Guomindang was annihilated in the Zhanzhuang district of this county. The people of Pi County have made great contributions and heavy sacrifices for the independence of our motherland and the cause of liberation.

This area is extremely poor, with very bad natural conditions, poor soil, and frequent natural calamities. The soil cannot retain water, so drought sets in if the rainfall is low. In times of heavy rains, mountain torrents rush down and, because of its low-lying topography, the county becomes a floodway, destroying the grain crop. In addition, because of the oppression and exploitation of reactionary officials and feudal landlords, crop yields were poor, and the people lived an utterly bitter life for a very long time.

Changes in Standard of Living and Economic Output since the Third Plenum of the Eleventh Party Congress

Like people all over China, the people of Pi County stood up after Liberation. Changes in their life and productivity occurred. But, because of the "Leftist" deviation that prevailed for years and policy errors (such as forced planting of rice on unirrigated land), production gains were slow, food and income levels of the peasants were low, and peasants often used up their provisions before the Spring Festival, forcing some to flee to avoid famine. This situation did not begin to change until after the Third Plenum of the Eleventh Party Congress, and particularly after 1980, when the responsibility system began, raising the initiative of the peasants, and, when good weather prevailed, bringing increased grain harvests year after year. It was time for the summer harvest when we arrived in Pi County, and rich fields of wheat could be seen in every direction.

We visited the Chahe and the Guanhu communes, where the leaders briefed us on the great changes since the Third Plenum. The total crop yield (wheat, corn, and potatoes) of the Chahe Commune was 6.5 million kilograms in 1977, and 13 million kilograms in 1982. In former years, the wheat per person ranged from a low of 5 kilograms to 40 kilograms a year. When coarse food grains were added, the average grain ration per person each year ranged from a minimum of 100 to a maximum of 150 kilograms per year.

By 1980–81, the average food ration per person had risen to about 250 kilograms, and in 1982, over 300 kilograms. When private plots are included, the actual figures are higher. The varieties of food in the diet have also changed. Sweet potatoes, which used to be the main food, have become a commercial crop, sold to wineries, while wheat has become the staple food.

The highest annual per capita income in the past was about 90 yuan; the lowest, about 20 yuan. The average income at that time for the entire commune was about 50 yuan per person. Last year the average income was 160 yuan, and as high as 300 yuan per person when income from private plots and sideline jobs was included.

In the past, it was usually cadres who could own bicycles and wrist watches. Now there are 4,000 bicycles among 7,000 households, and it is common to see people biking to work in the fields. Almost every household has a radio, and most of the young people wear watches on their wrists. More and more families have sewing machines. When new buildings are erected, they are no longer thatched huts, but built of brick and tile.

Since its Third Plenum, the party's line and policy have brought great changes to the countryside. At first, some cadres could not understand the new responsibility system, saying, "We are going back overnight to the pre-Liberation situation after thirty years of hard work." However, the cadres and masses came to understand the correctness of the party's policy after learning the actual facts.

There is a bumper harvest of wheat and barley this year. Yields have increased in every commune and production brigade. The total grain crop of the county reached 250.3 million kilograms, which, was 50.1 million kilograms more than the bumper harvest of 1982, setting a new record. The grain harvest of only one season equals that of the entire year in 1977. All households willingly delivered the government grain quota and sold the surplus for themselves. One peasant, who harvested 1,500 kilograms, said, "I'll fight tooth and nail with anyone who speaks against Deng Xiaoping." It can be seen that the party's line and policy have entered deeply into the hearts of the rural people.

In recent years great changes have also taken place in the spiritual life of the masses. During the ten years of chaos, people were overwhelmed with contradictions, factionalism ran amok, fights broke out, with people using fists and even swords and guns. There were also contradictions between clans, leading to frequent gang fights. Now, since the inauguration of the responsibility system, people have been busy with their own productive labor, and contradictions have greatly diminished. Thievery has clearly gone down. There were many criminal cases dealing with stolen livestock, provisions, carts, and even wheat cut from the fields. Now nobody steals; no one even picks up wheat fallen on the ground. Before the responsibility system was set up, peasants showed little interest in scientific farming. Today, because one's own vital interests are at stake, they are very much concerned about how to use chemical fertilizers and improved varieties of seed grains. The people's initiative for using scientific methods is greatly enhanced.

Relations between the cadres and the people have greatly improved since the Third Plenum of the Eleventh Party Congress adopted the new agricultural policies. Before that, cadres took more than their share and embezzled public funds and properties, while the people choked in silent fury. Some vented their rage on the cadres by destroying crops in the cadres' private plots. A cadre of Huangshi Production Brigade of the Chahe Commune said, "The twenty years of contradictions between the cadres and the masses have basically been solved since we began to practice the responsibility system." The reason is that the fruits of the peasants' labor are no longer under the control of the cadres. On the contrary, cadres will even deliver fertilizers and seeds to the homes of commune members in order to help them increase crop yields.

In recent years both economic production and standard of living have made great progress in Pi County. The changes are enormous when compared with the days when people fled from famine and received relief grain. But when compared with more-developed areas they are still below standard. Peasants are very happy to have steamed bread and salted vegetables cooked with vegetable oil, even after a bumper harvest. They still have to eat some coarse food grains and store part of their flour and rice as a reserve against a possible food shortage or famine. Young villagers generally wear polyester-blend clothing, but in the summer naked children can still be seen everywhere. There are more and more new homes of brick and tile, but the majority are still living in mud-walled huts with thatched roofs. There is electricity in the town where the commune center is located, but many production brigades still have to use oil lamps. Sanitation conditions are poor.

Some new contradictions have arisen in the period of development since the inauguration of the responsibility system. Some richer families have an inside track, getting loans from the bank and buying seeds and fertilizer, while some poor households are short of labor and live a hard life. The party secretary of a brigade in Guanhu Commune said, "A rich family can earn three or five hundred, even a thousand yuan per capita annually, while a poor family may earn less than a hundred, and not be able to deliver the government grain quota or buy seeds and fertilizer. As a result, they have less and less food grain." He went on to say, "The old people who suffered in the past are very worried as they see these poor families get into difficulties." The government is now paying close attention to the needs of the poor.

Culture, Education, Medical Care, and Sanitation

Since Liberation great changes have taken place in culture, education, medical care, and sanitation. In the early years it was not easy for the township government to find a copy clerk. There was only one primary school in Chahe Commune. Today there is a primary school in each production brigade, two junior high schools, and one high school run by the commune. Ninety percent of school-age children are in school. But there are still not enough schools, so many children are unable to go on to junior and senior high. In Guanhu Commune, 99.5 percent of the school-age children are in primary school, 64 percent of primary graduates go on to junior high, and 23 percent of junior high graduates go on to senior high. The percentage of primary graduates in the whole county who enter junior high is 38 percent. Because of the feudal idea that men are superior to women, only 15 to 20 percent of the senior high school students are girls, with 40 percent in junior high, and an equal number of girls and boys in primary school.

In the rural areas of China, some of the people are illiterate.

According to the national census, 37 percent of the Chinese people are illiterate, including some children. Education is rather advanced in Guanhu Commune, but even so, out of a total of 42,000 persons, there are 240 illiterates between the ages of twelve and sixteen, and 1,800 from seventeen to twenty-five.

Money is needed to develop education and culture. At present it is not easy to raise money from the peasants, so the primary school buildings at brigade level are the most dilapidated ones in the township. According to the leading comrade of the county propaganda department, there are five thousand school rooms that are in a dangerous state needing repair. There have been accidents when buildings collapsed and teachers and pupils were injured. Some primary schools of Xinglou Commune are called the "three muds": mud desks, mud stools, and muddy children (splashed with mud). We have visited three of the primary schools in the Xinhua Brigade of the Guanhu Commune, all of them with mud walls and muddy windows. In one, a whole row of classrooms was in a state of dangerous disrepair, with roofs collapsing. With no furniture in the dark class-rooms, children had to bring their own stools.

Primary school teachers are poorly qualified. Teachers in the government-run schools are little better. Many teachers in schools run by the local people are primary school graduates only. Teachers are paid by the local people in schools run by production brigades. They earn very little money and, because they have to work in the fields as well as teach, cannot concentrate on teaching. During our visit to three primary schools in the Xinhua Brigade of Guanhu Commune, the busy farm season was over, but the schools were still closed. According to the brigade cadres, there was a lumber market in front of the primary school on market days, and the teachers forsook teaching for business, earning far more money than their salary. How can these teachers concentrate on their educational tasks?

Since the founding of new China, medical and health work in Pi County has made some progress. The Guanhu Hospital of Xuzhou City is quite well equipped. The hospital at Chahe, set up in 1958, is one of the key hospitals in the county, treating patients from nearby communes. It is making steady progress, with several dozen beds, and departments of internal medicine, surgery, X-ray, and electrocardiography. During the Cultural Revolution, medical cooperatives were organized in the villages, but because everyone could "eat from the same pot," too many people came to see the doctor, and funds were exhausted before half the year had passed. After the Third Plenum of the Eleventh Party Congress, clinics were set up in production brigades, with barefoot doctors under the super-vision of the commune hospitals. Small fees are charged for treatments and injections. Medicines are sold at the normal retail price in order to make some profit. In this way the medical network at different levels is maintained. Some doctors, approved by the authorities, are allowed to carry on private practice.

Since medical costs have to be paid by the patients, peasants needing medical treatment are limited by their rather low incomes. Their living conditions are unsanitary and provide poor protection against illness. According to the head of the Guanhu Hospital, commonly recurring diseases, all related to sanitation con-ditions, are typhoid, dysentery, gastroenteritis, and hepatitis; epidemic encephali-tis "B" and malaria are diseases carried by mosquitoes; and bronchitis and pneumonia are quite widespread in winter and spring. Apart from these, be-cause northern people eat a great deal of coarse grain and engage in heavy physical labor, they often incur intestinal blockages. Cancer is linked to aflatox-ins. If it rains and corn cannot be harvested in time, then aflatoxins are likely to breed. This can also occur in bean oil, salted vegetables, turnips, and beans.

Cases of traffic and farm machinery accidents and poisoning from farm chemicals have been on the increase. Peasants can afford to pay for routine illnesses, and they are willing to borrow money to pay for serious illness if there is hope for a cure. However, if the case is complicated and difficult to cure, requiring loan after loan, they will stop medical treatment and resign themselves to their fate.

In short, if the villages of northern Jiangsu want to change the conditions of sanitation and culture, improve the level of education, and provide effective safeguards against diseases, they have to make unremitting efforts to raise their income by increasing agricultural productivity.

Backward Superstitions and Customs

A great many peasants in northern Jiangsu made their contributions, some even giving their lives, in the war against the Japanese invaders, and later in the War of Liberation. They have made profound changes in their spiritual life since Liberation in building a new life. But in the struggle to change social traditions and do away with superstitions, we often resorted to simple coercion and commandism instead of solving the ideological problems. In addition, the rural economy, culture, and education have lagged behind, providing fertile soil for superstitions and backwardness even today. These backward ideologies reappear whenever they find an opportunity. Certain old traditions are quite stubborn.

At the time of Liberation there were many temples in the villages of northern Jiangsu, such as the Grandma Temple, Fire God Temple, Guangdi Temple, and Temple of the God of Wealth. At the time of land reform these were abolished and all superstitious sects and secret societies were banned. But ideas of ghosts and gods are deeply rooted among the people, and all kinds of superstitions are rampant. Almost every household kept a memorial tablet of some kind of female celestial being, a piece of red paper on which was written "Throne of Lady Huang the Second" (yellow weasel), "Throne of Lady Hu" (fox), "Throne of Lady Yu the Second" (snake), and "Throne of Lady White" (snake). Matching couplets framed the tablets, with sayings such as, "Quiet in the house, peace through the year." When traditions were changing and superstitions were being eliminated, these female deities could not stay. Before removing the tablets some people burned incense and prayed, saying, "Now the new society will not allow me to pay my respects to you. Allow me to send you to study arts in the high mountains." Some people, in fact, only covered the tablets with white paper.

Another stubborn custom not easy to change was holding ceremonies in memory of ancestors. On New Year's Day, during the Qingming (Pure Brightness) Festival, and on July 15 of the lunar year, families would visit the graves of their ancestors and burn paper money and incense. During the the Qingming Festival, mud was placed on top of the graves; this was called "adding trees to the forest." If mud was not placed there, it meant that the generational succession would be broken. Sometimes rows of weeds were placed in front of the graves to represent generation after generation.

Sorcerers, shamans, witches, geomancers, and blind fortunetellers were all banned, but they have again gained some ground in recent years, although they do not flaunt their activities publicly.

Although the temples and tablets have been removed, superstitious activities will come back again on a big scale if given a chance. An outstanding example is the incident of "Yellow Stone bestows celestial medicine" that took place in the Yellow Stone Production Brigade of the Chahe Commune. The Yellow Stone Brigade once had a temple of the "Old Man Yellow Stone" that had been there for ages. It was destroyed during the War of Liberation, and only a few stone tablets remained. But the place where the temple had been is still considered to be sacred by the local peasants. They strongly believe that Old Man Yellow Stone still blesses and protects the area. Every year on February 25 of the lunar year, beginning at midnight on the day of the temple fair (which has been moved to the town of Chahe and now is a normal trading fair), there are always hundreds of people going to the site of the temple, burning incense and repeating their vows to the deity. A myth suddenly surfaced in February and March 1979, saying that Old Man Yellow Stone had returned and would offer treatment to the sick. It is said that about thirty thousand people came from the local county, nearby counties, Shandong and Henan provinces, and even riding on motorcycles from Shanghai. While burning incense they knelt on the temple site, presenting eggs and cakes, and praying for themselves and for their family members, saying, "Cure our illnesses and we will never forget you after regaining our health." They prayed for celestial medicine by rolling up white paper in the shape of a tube and waiting for the wind to blow some dust, considered to be celestial medicine, into it. This event lasted for more than ten days. The area surrounding the site of the destroyed temple was full of people, and the crops in many adjoining fields were ruined. People came from almost every household in nearby villages. Only after the cadres had taken many days to teach them were they convinced to stop coming to this event.

Other superstitious rumors are easily circulated. In 1981 a rumor went around that people should make a flour cow and present it to the Goddess Wangmu. In fact what was done was to ask the daughter-in-law to make a big dumpling in the shape of a cow and take it to her mother's home to ward off disaster. It was also said that the mother should make a white sleeveless blouse for herself to avoid calamity.

Recently another traditional myth suddenly surfaced, to the effect that the paternal grandmother should make yellow trousers and the maternal grandmother should make a yellow sleeveless shirt for the boy to wear to ward off disaster. As a result, all the yellow cotton cloth in the nearby commune was quickly sold out.

In April this year a rumor suddenly arose while pupils were going to receive injections against encephalitis "B" that a savage with a red nose and big eyes would come to give injections to children—in the navel of girls and the temple of boys, causing the boys to die slowly and rendering the girls infertile. Of course the young students ran away when they heard that injections were about to be given, and the whole project was stopped for a time. Only after carrying out some ideological education were these superstitious rumors wiped out.

Because of their beliefs in gods and ghosts, peasants are opposed to cremation. To avoid cremation, peasants no longer put on public funeral ceremonies, but clandestinely place the remains into a coffin and bury it deep in the ground.

A serious obstacle to birth control is the traditional view that men are superior to women, and that the family line is passed from one generation to the next through the male children. Peasants also have practical reasons for wanting male children. Male workers have become the main breadwinners of the family since the advent of the responsibility system; more male workers mean more income. A couple with no male children is likely to get into trouble, with no old-age security and nobody to fetch water. Birth control is a national policy, and special cadres are in charge of implementing the policy in each commune. Still the peasants are not convinced. Some go elsewhere to give birth to babies. Time and again female infants are thrown away or drowned.

On the other hand, peasants put on a big show for weddings. Mercenary marriages have gained ground, and marrying a wife has become a heavy economic burden. When a young man becomes engaged, he has first to "pass the red," that is, give some small presents, before he sends the betrothal gifts. These small gifts include two to four dresses, shoes, and stockings. After that he has to send big gifts, worth about 500 yuan, including a watch, a bicycle, a sewing machine, and about twenty lengths of cloth.

When the girl goes to her fiancé's home after the engagement, the boy's family has to give banquets for three or four days, each one with four small dishes and eight big ones. When the girl leaves, again she gets a suit of clothes and a pair of shoes. She also gets a cash present of at least 50 yuan, sometimes 100 yuan or more, on their first meeting. At the time of the Autumn and Spring festivals, the boy again gives cash gifts of 50 yuan to 100 yuan.

In the past, the gifts could be carried by hand, but now the boy must use a carrying pole or a barrow to take the meat (ten kilograms or more), fish (only carp will do), chickens, wine (more than ten bottles, in even numbers only), cakes (at least eight and as many as twenty packages), and cigarettes. For the wedding gifts the boy has to provide a three-room house built of brick, while the girl's family provides a dowry that includes a big wardrobe, a chest of drawers, suitcases, a desk, square and round tables, a bicycle, a sewing machine, sofa, radio, and so forth. One room would be too small to hold everything. Both families have to give wedding feasts, generally ten or twenty tables, sometimes as many as forty or fifty by the boy's family, and ten or twenty tables by the girl's. When the bride goes to the bridegroom's home, she rides on a barrow or a tractor decorated and covered with a quilt. Sometimes a car or truck is used. This shows the improvement in village life, while it also illustrates the difficulties that arise when customs change.

The Style of the Party and People

During the ten years of chaos, factionalism ran amok in the northern Jiangsu villages, and ideas about the old patriarchal clans came back. Disputes among people increased, and the general mood of society was very bad. Since the Third Plenum of the Eleventh Party Congress, stability and solidarity have returned, the general mood of the society has turned for the better, and disputes have decreased. Except for the problems of birth control and cremation, relations between cadres and the masses have been increasingly relaxed.

However, new contradictions have come up since the responsibility system was instituted, such as disputes and fights over land boundaries. It is not easy to convene a meeting, because everyone is busy with his own work: announcements are made through the public address system, but the results are not very good. Cadres are also busy with farming their own contracted land and do not know how to adapt their leadership role to the new situation. Although the income of peasants has seen some increase, it is still very limited. Aside from the money they pay into the common fund, they are unwilling to support funding for the needs of collective welfare, culture, and education.

Because of the unequal status between men and women, and for other reasons, such as money problems, there are many family disputes. Since it is so expensive to wed a girl, she is looked upon as a treasure. If she bears a male child, she becomes all the more precious, as if she were the mother of an emperor, and the young mother can vent her spite upon the mother-in-law. Apart from problems in the relations between women in-laws, there are also numerous quarrels between husband and wife and father and son. Since the responsibility system began and farm chemicals were distributed to each household, cases of suicide by swallowing chemicals have happened from time to time.

We talked with a number of cadres who are party members. Most of them are easy to get along with. They are on very good terms with the people, working diligently and showing concern for the masses. But, because of the damage inflicted by the ''Gang of Four'' on the party's working style, we heard many negative criticisms. If you want them to do something for you, it is said, it will depend on the gifts you give them, or your relationships. Some cadres have become rich. A party cadre from a local commune said jokingly to us, ''Your social sciences research institute should take up a new academic discipline called 'relationships.' '' Cadres often eat and drink to excess, are prone to boasting and exaggeration, resort to cheating, and deceive their superiors and delude their subordinates. Some higher officials prefer to hear good things rather than bad, so their subordinates send in exaggerated reports. The commune party committee puts its efforts mainly on improving production and neglects ideological education, paying little attention to propaganda work.

A party secretary of a commune committee said with emotion, "In the early days after Liberation, cadres made special efforts in ideological education; everywhere we could hear singing loud and clear, but now we hear it no more. Cadres are all too busy with their own production work." Some grass-roots party branches can scarcely get a meeting together. A few party branches are controlled by evildoers. Obviously, the general mood of the party has turned for the better, but there is still need for fundamental changes.

Social Origins of Religion

Marxism believes that social existence determines one's consciousness, and that consciousness is the reflection of one's social existence. Marxism always studies religious ideology in the larger context of the entire social life. It should be done this way, not only in a society of class exploitation, but also in one where exploitation has been abolished.

Although great changes have taken place in recent years in economic production and daily life in the villages of Pi County, production is still at a low level. People are not yet able to free themselves from the threats of natural disasters or of various diseases. The levels of education, culture, health care, and sanitation are held down by the state of the economy. Therefore, people are unable to control their own fate. The fact that many people believe in religion because of sickness reflects this reality. In the villages, male workers play the leading role, and most women cannot completely free themselves from the sense of oppression and contempt embodied in the idea that "men are superior to women." This is why most religious believers are women. For various social reasons, conflicts of interest between individuals cause discord within families and between neighbors. After finishing school, young people have little chance to make full use of what they have learned, and they lack opportunities for culture and recreation. These are some reasons why peasants and young people turn to religion for comfort.

Before Liberation all five religions could be found in Pi County: Buddhism, Daoism, Islam, Catholicism, and Protestant Christianity. With over 120 temples, Buddhism and Daoism were particularly prosperous. Various superstitions were popular as well. After Liberation, the influence of religions and superstitions was greatly weakened. However, a simplistic policy of arbitrarily banning religion was adopted, with the result that all those temples mentioned were taken over for other uses during land reform, and all religions came under assault during subsequent historical movements. Religion was totally suppressed during the ten years of chaos.

Meanwhile, production was making slow progress due to both natural and man-made disasters, so that the soil for religious ideology to some extent still exists. Ideas of ghosts and gods that have been in people's minds for thousands of years will not die out easily. Therefore, once the policy on religious freedom was restored, Protestant Christianity, with its special flexibility and adaptability, has replaced other religions in many areas and continues to grow quite rapidly.

In addition, the ten years of chaos harmed both the party's status and the general mood of society. Religious commandments and moral doctrines as practiced now by numerous Christians have a definite influence. Many cadres and others say that Christians do not fight or swear, they neither smoke nor drink, and there are few disputes between them and their neighbors or within their families. Because Christians are quite honest and do not steal, production team leaders usually ask them to watch the fields prior to harvest and put them in charge of the grain barns. Christians often perform good deeds, such as returning money that they find on the street, and they find pleasure in helping others. They get up very early or stay up late at night to attend their religious services, and good order prevails in their churches and meeting places. All this imperceptibly helps to spread religious influence.

In short, observing and analyzing religious phenomena cannot be separated from social life, and religion may be taken as a mirror of society. In a complicated way, it reflects problems of building material and spiritual civilization in the villages today. If we overlook this fact and think we can handle religious questions by simply placing arbitrary limits on religion, that clearly is not realistic and is against Marxism: "Under socialist conditions, the correct and fundamental way to solve the problem of religion, under the prerequisite of protecting religious freedom, can only be gradually to eliminate the social and ideological sources on which religion depends by an enormous development of socialist economy, culture, and science, and by a great leap forward of socialist material and spiritual civilization. Such a great cause cannot be accomplished in a short time, not in one, two, or even three generations. That is to say, it will take place in the struggle of several generations over a long historical period, including believers and nonbelievers" ("Basic Viewpoint and Policy on the Problem of Religion of Our Country in the Socialist Period," in Selected Essays on the United Front in the New Period, pp. 214–15).

We feel strongly that this essay, the result of our investigations, is a scientific work that conforms to historical materialism. Only by taking this direction can religious work [of the party and government] do away with both idealist and "Leftist" influences and go on to greater achievements.

A Survey of Productive-Labor Projects in Buddhist Monasteries of Fujian

IN APRIL and May 1984 we conducted field research on Buddhist activities in Fujian Province. This essay is a systematic report of those investigations.

Before the "Cultural Revolution" there was already a tradition in Fujian Province of monks and nuns working for income-producing projects belonging to the temples and monasteries. For example, the Buddhist Association of Fuzhou had already developed textile weaving, bamboo crafts, sewing, metalwork, bookbinding, paper-box making, rope making, and so forth—eight handicraft factories with over five hundred Buddhist workers, including monks and nuns and men and women believers. Their productivity was excellent.

The temples and monasteries in the suburban districts near the city had organized farming work for the monks and nuns; they raised rice and vegetables, established fruit orchards and tea plantations, and raised medicinal herbs, with the goal of economic self-sufficiency. Other temples and monasteries in the mountain areas also carried on agricultural production with good results.

During the ten years of turmoil all was ruined, the factories were moved away, and agricultural production ceased. After the Third Plenum of the party's Eleventh Central Committee, the current religious policy was gradually put into effect. When the provincial religious work units and the Buddhist Association restored religious activities, they also set up a variety of productive-labor projects for monks and nuns in monasteries and temples, each one adapted to the particular local situation. This was done in the tradition and spirit of "one day without working means one day without food."

Now, aside from a minority of temples and monasteries that have established rice mills, sewing units, incense factories, and so forth, and some newly opened handicraft work, the most important projects are in agriculture and services. The temples and monasteries in the mountain districts all have projects for expanding agricultural production, such as rice, peanuts, yellow beans, vegetables, orchards, tea plantations, medicinal herbs, tea-oil plants, and timber.

The temples and monasteries in urban or tourist areas operate various kinds of service projects staffed by monks and nuns, such as hostels, small shops, restaurants, tea stalls, and photo shops. Now, with their well-managed productive-labor projects, most of the temples and monasteries in the province are able to "use the monastery to support the monastery." Some raise more food than they need for themselves. Some have surplus income beyond their living costs. Some allocate extra funds from their production projects to repair temple and monastery buildings. Many of the monks and nuns have a new self-image and a new spirit. They are proud that they are "self-supporting workers" and that they make a contribution to the "four modernizations" of our country. The situation and the experiences of the monks and nuns who take part in productive labor in this province are described below.

An Overview

Monks and nuns in temples and monasteries in the mountain districts of Fujian have the best record in production. These temples and monasteries are located in the mountain districts quite far from the cities, so not many Buddhists go there to worship, and contributions from overseas Buddhists are small. To put it another way, they do not rely chiefly on selling incense and charging fees to support their livelihood; rather, they solve the problem of self-support through productive labor. Most of these temples and monasteries are self-sustaining, not only in food, but also in their other expenses. The living allowance of the monks and nuns is going up, and the agricultural output of some temples and monasteries exceeds that of the average farmer or production brigade of that region.

Some of the tea plantations, forests, and orchards operated by neighboring units, brigades, and communes over a period of years were not well managed and were not doing well. When they were given over to the Buddhist monks and nuns to manage, production increased greatly, so people's communes in several other districts contracted their fields and orchards to the temples and monasteries, often with excellent results. Some of these are described below.

The Buddhist Anyang Yuan (Retirement Home)
of the Chongfu Temple in Fuzhou City

The sixty-five elderly nuns living in the Anyang Yuan can be divided into three categories. One group consists of those who are no longer able-bodied but are cared for by the temple. There are forty-five of these. There are ten in the second group, those who work as service personnel, taking care of the general work in the temple and caring for the daily needs of the old people. Ten other persons make up the third group, those who take part in productive labor, operating the crematoria, placing the ashes in repose, and raising rice and vegetables.

Altogether the temple has 10 mu of land. In 1983 they planted 8.5 mu in rice and harvested 13,000 jin of rice, averaging 1,500 jin per mu. Two mu of vegetables provided all the food they needed. In addition they have three crematoria and one ossarium. Their entire income for 1981 was 24,190 yuan: 4,390 from agricultural production, 16,800 from the crematoria and ossarium, and 3,000 from admission fees. They had a surplus after total expenditures of 22,590 yuan, which included the living allowances for the elderly nuns, wages for the service personnel, medical expenses, and other costs.

The temple and monastery take full responsibility for the elderly nuns living in the retirement home, including food, lodging (each person has a small room), medical care, and a living allowance beyond their own resources (each person receives eight yuan a month from the people's government for the "five guarantees" [pledged by the government for all elderly persons: food, lodging, clothing, medical care, and burial]). The temple itself provides 18 yuan for personal allowance, plus 21 yuan for food and 5 yuan for miscellaneous expenses. The service personnel receive from 35 to 40 yuan a month. Those who work in production projects are paid according to their labor, each person averaging over 50 yuan a month. This temple has earned a surplus beyond its own needs since 1981.

Zhiti Temple, Ningde County

Zhiti Temple, located on a high mountain, now has forty-four monks. Formerly, monks had a hard life there, often resorting to sweet potatoes [rather than rice] for their main food. In recent years they have opened up new farmland and tried various enterprises that have brought big improvements in their livelihood.

They now have 40 mu of agricultural land on which they raise rice, manage forests, and cultivate tea plantations, herb gardens, and other crops. They have built a power plant to generate electricity for their enterprises and lighting for their personal needs. They harvested over 30,000 jin of rice in 1983, including more than 2,000 jin given over to the government as their grain quota. Added to that was over 15,000 yuan in income from tea, medicinal herbs, and other products.

In addition to their room and board, each monk received an average of 21 yuan per month. Because their production and management was done so well, they received special commendation from the provincial Buddhist Association and other units.

Jinbei Temple, Ningde County

Jinbei Temple, with four monks and two nuns, has plans to expand to ten persons. Because they have only a little over 8 mu of land, they planted 1.2 million tea plants in 1980 with the goal of self-support. In 1981 their income from the sale of tea was 14,000 yuan. Added to this was income from jasmine flowers, vegetables, and over 5,000 jin of rice. In 1983 the total income was over 16,000 yuan. They are now expanding production by planting 2 million tea plants, with plans for 5 million more next year. They also have plans to replant 5 mu of higher-altitude tea land in bamboo, jasmine, oil vegetables, and fir trees, aiming for a target income of 10,000 yuan per year. Because their production work has been done so well, they have received high praise from local religious work units and the Buddhist Association.

While their work in agriculture has been profitable, they also have a very fine spirit. Refusing to use the money for themselves, the monks and nuns hold to a simple lifestyle. Aside from their food and clothing, which is provided by the temple, each person receives only twelve yuan a month for personal use. They are admired for contributing most of their surplus income for repairing temples and monasteries and preserving famous ancient buildings. Moreover, in addition to earning income from tea production for their own needs, they are contributing to our nation's total output of tea for export, so the local tea administration gave them 3,750 yuan for help in expanding their tea production this year.

White Cloud Temple, Tailao Mountain, Fuding County

White Cloud Temple has more than twenty monks who work 14 mu of land planted with rice, sweet potatoes, yellow beans, tea, and medicinal herbs. In 1983 they harvested over 32,000 jin of rice from 4 mu of paddy land, 7,000 jin of sweet potatoes, 1,600 jin of yellow beans, and 2,000 jin of tea leaves. In 1984 they planted 50,000 more tea plants, and they have plans to plant fir trees, pine trees, and bamboo. Now the monks have surplus income beyond their own needs for food and other living costs. They have a newly built two-story building and have improved their present living quarters.

Lingfeng Temple, Fuding County

Lingfeng Temple now has thirty monks and eighteen nuns, many of them elderly. There are three persons between the ages of fifty and seventy, and thirteen over seventy. In all, only thirteen are able to work fulltime and four halftime. They have 33 mu of cultivated land and 5 mu of other land, plus 150 mu of forest land. They raise rice, sweet potatoes, tea, sugar cane, vegetables, and jasmine plants.

In 1983 they harvested 38,000 jin of rice from 22 mu of paddy land and gave 1,300 jin for the government grain quota after selling 3,250 jin. The total income from agricultural enterprises for the year was 14,210 yuan. Added to that was 8,773 yuan net income from the vegetarian restaurant and other tourist income, for a total annual income of 22,983 yuan. Of that total, 61.7 percent came from production projects. Because they manage their projects well, they now have surplus income beyond their own needs.

In addition to the food and living expenses of the monks and nuns, those who are elderly receive 30 yuan apiece for their personal use each year. Each able-bodied or halftime worker receives an annual share of about 300 yuan. The remaining surplus is used for construction, such as repairs, building of barns, sheds, bridges, repairing the altar, and carving new Buddhist images. They have also installed their own electric generator for illumination and for equipment used in production.

Pingxingcan Monastery, Fuding County

Pingxingcan is a newly built monastery that had been the Pingjiang Buddhist Tea Plantation. They now have sixteen monks and five nuns, most of them elderly. Among them only five are between the ages of eighteen and thirty, with fourteen between fifty and seventy and two over seventy. Only five are fully able-bodied, seven are semi-able-bodied, and the rest are unable to do any manual labor. They have 14 mu of agricultural land, including 3.3 mu planted in paddy rice and 15 mu in sweet potatoes. In addition there are tea plantations, forests, and fields planted with yellow beans, turnips, rape, ginseng, tea, vegetables, and so forth. They now are self-sufficient in grain and vegetables. In 1983 their total income was 5,811 yuan, 90.5 percent of that, or 5,511 yuan, coming from farm production.

In addition to their food, the monks and nuns receive 72 to 120 yuan per year for their labor. Their standard of living is not high, but they have enough for building and repairs, because the monks and nuns insisted that they would not accept their share of the temple's total income for the last three years. This kind of spirit of enduring hardship in order to start new enterprises has been praised by Buddhist circles.

Xinghai Temple, Zhonghua Mountain, Liancheng County

Xinghai Temple has more than twenty monks. Their productive land was given to them by the Xinchuan People's Commune. In 1978 the tea-oil plantation of the commune, located on mountain land, was planted with 3,500 tea plants. In 1981 the party and government, the United Front Work Department of the county, and other related work units decided to give this mountain land to the monks of the Zhonghua Mountain Xinghai Temple to manage. In addition, they gave all of the equipment needed for cultivation and production, including a rice mill, tractor, electric generator, milling machine, and 1,203 square meters of buildings. This action was taken to help carry out the policy of freedom of religious belief.

The two parties agreed that from 1985 on, the income would be divided into ten parts, 30 percent going to the commune and 70 percent to the monastery. Now, in addition to the 3,500 tea-oil trees, they have more than 16 mu of farmland, which includes 200 peach trees, 500 pear trees, 160 orange trees, and

2.5 mu of vegetables. They also have opened a brick and tile factory. Productivity has steadily risen with the help of nearby Buddhist laypersons, sometimes as many as one hundred in one day, who often volunteer their labor, bringing their own food and farm tools.

Some monasteries and temples that lack cropland have become tourist areas and have organized the clergy to provide services for visitors. The Yongquan Temple at Gushan, Fuzhou, and Nanputuoshan Temple in Xiamen have been particularly successful in such ventures.

Yongquan Temple, Gu Shan, Fuzhou

There are about sixty monks at the Yongquan Temple. Since cropland is limited, they cannot expand crop production beyond what is now planted. Land now cultivated includes 3 mu of paddy rice, 6 mu of vegetables, 8 mu of fruit trees, and a few other smaller crops. The priority now is to meet the needs of visitors, with such service enterprises as restaurants, cold-drink shops, and service shops. Income from these enterprises for 1982 and 1983 was 383,939 yuan, sufficient to provide for the basic needs of the temple without outside financial help. Each monk received from 30 to 40 yuan a month for living expenses.

Nanputuoshan Temple, Xiamen

There are about fifty clergy at the Nanputuo Temple at present, ten of them veterans (including some with responsibilities in general affairs in the temple enterprises), and thirty-seven novices enrolled in seminary studies. In addition, there are over seventy laypersons who come from outside as day workers.

The general-services section is organized into two departments: one includes the larger collective enterprises, the vegetarian restaurant, small bookshop, photography shop, and so forth. The services section receives income from selling entrance tickets, guest hostel fees, offerings for incense, and contributions. Monks who work in service projects receive an average pay of 50 to 70 yuan a month, with additional bonuses and other benefits such as retirement pay. Monthly income from the enterprises averages about 4,000 yuan for entrance tickets and over 4,000 yuan for incense offerings.

The living expenses for seminarians come from these sources. In addition to receiving their clothing and bedding, seminarians receive a monthly personal allowance of 30 yuan, but when contributions from overseas Chinese Buddhists are added, the average rises to about 50 yuan a month.

At present, aside from the wages and personal allowances of monks and workers, the main expense is for repairs to the temples and monasteries, and for regilding the Buddhist statues. After these expenses, there is still a surplus, making this one of the wealthier temples in Fujian.

Some Lessons Learned

We summarize here some of the experiences of [government] religious work units that have organized productive enterprises staffed by Buddhist monks and nuns in various parts of Fujian Province.

Continually Carry on Education

The religious work units never stopped educating the monks and nuns who took part in productive-labor projects. They used every kind of meeting, such as Buddhist representative assemblies, nuns' discussion meetings, and study meetings. For example, a provincewide call was made to all monks and nuns at the Third Plenum of the Fujian Provincial Buddhist Representatives Assembly to take the road of self-support, to "eat their own food" (*zishi*), to carry on the fine tradition of rural Buddhism (*nongchan*), and enthusiastically to foster habits of productive labor, thereby "adding bricks and tiles" to the building of socialism.

It was clearly stipulated in the constitution adopted by the Fujian Provincial Buddhist Representatives Assembly that "all Buddhists in the province will be mobilized for active participation in the socialist modernization of our country under the leadership of the Communist Party and the people's government, in order to build a high-level democratic, civilized, socialist nation that is great, strong and modernized."

The religious district of Fuzhou City disseminated the results of the Third Plenum of the Eleventh Party Congress at many meetings, stressing the shift in emphasis, namely, that the main priority for the work of the party would be to build the spirit of socialist modernization. Henceforth, all monks and nuns would be asked to serve the "four modernizations" of the motherland by taking part in productive labor to the full extent of their capability.

The Buddhist Representatives Meeting of Fuqing County asked each Buddhist monk and nun to join the love-country, love-religion self-support projects, to protect and preserve ancient cultural treasures, and to make their contribution to the "four modernizations." The constitution of the Fuqing County Buddhist Association set for itself the task of "organizing all Buddhists in Fuqing County to take part in productive labor, using local materials and conditions to develop productive projects." The "patriotic covenant" of the monks and nuns pledged that they would "resolutely build a foundation for economic self-sufficiency for each temple and monastery by expanding the production of grain, edible oil, tea, timber, medicinal herbs, and other products, with the goal of achieving a surplus beyond their own needs as a contribution to the nation's 'four modernizations.' "

Ningde County decided to use the study method to carry out education of the monks and nuns to be patriotic and law-abiding, and to raise their understanding of the glory of manual labor, with the goal of making their temples and monasteries self-supporting. Through constant thought education, and emphasizing such Buddhist teachings as "One day without working means one day without food" and "[To serve] our country in all seriousness is at the same time a joy," the monks and nuns were receptive. As a result, the zeal for economic production of the great majority of monks and nuns rose dramatically, and they gradually came around to thinking right about "self-support through economic production" and "the glory of manual labor."

Create the Right Conditions for Monks and Nuns Who Take Part in Productive Labor in Temples and Monasteries

To do productive labor well requires a productive base. Some [government] religious work units got together with all related parties and studied the local situation. In some cases they recovered the land that had been occupied by other units; in other cases they gave a piece of uncultivated mountainland so that the monks and nuns could plant crops.

The Pingxingcan Temple of Fuqing and the Jinbei Temple of Ningde both requested mountain land for cultivation from the religious affairs offices of the respective counties.

The Tianwang Temple of Ningde, with the full assistance of the religious affairs units of the county government, has recently recovered for its own use land that had been occupied [by other units].

The Yongquan Temple of Gushan had its land completely taken over by a local rural production brigade during the "Cultural Revolution." Part of that has been returned, and they are negotiating for the rest.

Xinghai Temple on Zhonghua Mountain in Liancheng County recovered a piece of land that had been used by the commune for raising oil vegetables. This was facilitated by the county government without any cost to the temple. Many cadres working in religious affairs units give high priority to carrying out the policy on religion by recovering property belonging to temples and monasteries.

Utilize the Unique Features of Temples and Monasteries That Are Particularly Suited for Income-Producing Projects

One significant experience of productive-labor projects in temples and monasteries has been the utilization of unique features and advantages of each place. When the size of the land area is small but the location is close to a city, there will be more visitors, so the monks and nuns have organized appropriate service enterprises. For example, the Chongfu Temple in Fuzhou has set up a crematorium and ossarium. Yongquan Temple on Gushan, near Fuzhou, and Nanputuo Temple in Xiamen have opened service enterprises, such as vegetarian restaurants. Those temples located far from cities on high mountains have less visitors but more land, so they give priority to opening new land for cultivation and setting up production enterprises.

For example, several temples and monasteries in Ningde County have planted grain, fruit orchards, bamboo groves, medicinal herbs, and so forth. Since the age and physical strength of the monks and nuns differ from person to person, the various projects are designed to meet those differences. Temples and monasteries with a majority of physically weak, elderly monks and nuns cultivate vegetable fields, whereas those with religious personnel who are stronger raise paddy rice and operate other enterprises. Monks with special skills are given work suited to those skills.

There are many elderly monks and nuns. For example, among forty-eight religious personnel in Lingfeng Temple, only thirteen are fully able-bodied, four are semi–able-bodied, and the rest cannot work. But because suitable work was arranged for all who were able, productivity of the temple is very good, and the living standard for the monks and nuns has improved steadily year by year.

Another example is that of a master monk in the Jinbei Temple, Ningde, who was an expert in growing fruit trees, so a contract was signed with the county fruit department to plant fruit trees.

Carry Out Technical Instruction and Promote Scientific Agriculture

Religious work cadres from cities and counties often visit temples and monasteries to instruct them in scientific information, sending them technical books on agriculture and urging them to subscribe to periodicals. They also show films— entertainment films first, followed by scientific films. The purpose is to raise the agricultural skill levels of the monks and nuns.

Insecticides Conflict with Buddhist Teaching. In Ningde County there were some temples and monasteries that raised paddy rice using methods that were better than the neighboring production brigade's, but their harvest was no better, because the monks and nuns were unwilling to use insecticides. They believed they would be killing living beings, and thereby contravening the Buddhist commandments. After the religious affairs cadres of the county had convened a number of meetings, distributed scientific books and materials, started classes in scientific agriculture, and showed films on the use of insecticides and pesticides, they took the monks and nuns to see the good harvests of farmers who used pesticides. After seeing with their own eyes the actual results of using pesticides, they realized this was the way to increase their crop yields. They discussed the question, "Is it really taking life to use pesticides against insects? Is it really against the teachings of Buddhism?"

After these discussions, they all agreed that harmful insects are like evil persons, and it is not contrary to Buddhist commandments to destroy them; so they gave up the idea that killing insects is taking life. This year the monks and nuns in Ningde County agreed unanimously to use insecticides and to follow scientific methods of cultivation, with the result that their harvest is larger than that of their neighbors.

Hold Regular Meetings to Commend Vanguard Workers
and Exchange Experiences

Each year all local Buddhist associations convene meetings of representatives from temples and monasteries to exchange experiences in production projects, to commend vanguard workers, and to improve production. The Fujian Buddhist Association convened a large meeting at the Fahai Temple in Fuzhou January 4–9, 1984. Monks and nuns representing all the temples and monasteries in the province reported on various projects and exchanged experiences. Awards were given to seventeen temples and monasteries for their leadership in productivity, and to seventeen persons for their outstanding productivity and hard work.

In the latter part of April, the Buddhist Association of Ningde County convened a "Meeting of Temples and Monasteries to Exchange Experiences in Production Projects" at the Zhiti Temple. Delegates gave reports on accomplishments, everyone exchanged experiences, and certain temples, monasteries, and individuals were chosen for special awards. This kind of meeting is certainly effective in keeping the momentum going.

Tianwang Temple in Ningde is an example. Seeing the good return on tea planting of the Jinbei Temple, they studied their methods and then planted 600,000 tea plants, inviting a monk from the Jinbei Temple to give them guidance.

At the provincial meeting of temples and monasteries for exchange of experiences and ideas, the delegates carefully worked out a plan for every kind of production project for the year 1984. These included projects already in place that could be enlarged to make greater contributions to the nation. Some delegates said that we should not be content with simply doing our own projects well; we should also actively help monks and nuns of other temples and monasteries to carry on the good traditions of Buddhism, raising the productivity of each temple and monastery to the point where they can truly achieve "self-sufficiency through their own efforts" and "use the monastery to support the monastery."

Benefits Resulting from Economic-Production Projects of Temples and Monasteries

Productive labor by monks and nuns fits in with the demands of the times. It is in the fine tradition of Buddhism, it helps carry out the spirit of "the monastery supports the monastery," it allows monks and nuns to be self-sufficient in food, it helps protect our country's historical sites, and it contributes to the "four modernizations." This is the direction to go and the road to take for Buddhism during the period of socialism in China.

Carry on the Fine Buddhist Traditions

It is traditional in China for monks and nuns to engage in productive labor. Early in the Jin dynasty, monks were engaged in farming. After the Tang dynasty, the

Baizhang Sect of Chan Buddhism established the "Hundred Rules," which made it clear that "one day without work means one day without food." Since then, monks and nuns, following this fine Buddhist tradition, have engaged in productive labor. Because the vast majority of Buddhist monks and nuns throughout history have believed and accepted this, they have happily taken part in productive labor.

The reaction of monks and nuns in Ningde County is an example. They say, formerly we did not do much actual productive labor; instead, we relied on donations from Buddhist laypersons and on fees for Buddhist religious rites, with the result that we were never free from [economic] anxiety, and people looked down on us. Even worse, we were not observing Buddhist tradition, because we had forgotten it. Now, by engaging in productive labor, we have revived this fine Buddhist tradition, changing the opinion of the general public toward us, and achieving what we had really hoped for.

Set the Direction for the Development of Buddhism under Socialist Conditions

Despite the Buddhist tradition of monks and nuns taking part in economic production from the Ming and Qing dynasties onward, Buddhism went into a decline, and monks and nuns "made their living from the dead," offering prayers for a tranquil afterlife, telling fortunes and gradually separating themselves from productive labor.

Prior to Liberation, most monks and nuns did very little productive labor. After Liberation, during the nationwide land reform movement, monks and nuns were also allocated cropland. Many of them began to work the land and became self-supporting workers who raised their own food. From this experience onward, monks and nuns have taken part in economic production, thus setting the direction for the future development of Buddhism, while at the same time responding to the demands of society under socialism. "Nonworkers do not eat" is a policy of socialism. Monks and nuns are citizens like everyone else, and therefore they must adhere to this policy, which is also in full accord with the Buddhist tradition that "one day without work means one day without food." This, then, should be the direction for the development of Buddhism, for it suits both the demands of our times and the teachings of Buddhism.

Earn One's Own Living, Use the Monastery to Support the Monastery, and Lighten the Burden of Our Country

Another step in carrying out the policy of freedom of religious belief is to open some Buddhist temples and monasteries so that Buddhists can have places to resume their regular religious activities. Units related to this matter have already said that reopened temples and monasteries should be self-supporting. To do this right, the monks and nuns should take part in productive labor. In this spirit, Fujian Province has called on all monks and nuns, to the extent of their physical health and strength, to engage in productive labor, with significant results. At present the basic condition for each temple and monastery in the province is "use the monastery to support the monastery."

Ningde County, where most of the monks and nuns are earning more than enough for their own personal needs, is a good example. Not only are the working monks and nuns earning enough for a good living standard for themselves, they are also supporting their elderly colleagues who cannot work, thus relieving society of this burden.

The Chongfu Temple in Fuzhou also has well-managed projects that support forty-five elderly monks and nuns in the retirement home whose final years can now be lived in tranquility.

Preserve Historical Antiquities and Contribute to the Four Modernizations

Aside from providing for their own livelihood by productive labor, monks and nuns in Fujian use their surplus income to preserve antiquities by repairing and restoring temples and monasteries, many with long histories. For example, construction began on the Zhiti Temple in Ningde County in A.D. 862, near the end of the Tang dynasty, and was completed more than a thousand years ago in the year 971, during the Song dynasty.

Temples and monasteries in Fuqing County, such as the Chaoming Temple and pagoda, are nearly one thousand years old, tracing back to the Southern and Northern Liang dynasties. These ancient buildings had been in disrepair for many years and suffered additional damage during the Great Proletarian Cultural Revolution, when most of the Buddhist statues disappeared. If repairs had not been made soon, there was danger that the remaining precious antiquities would disappear forever. But now those temples and monasteries with well-run economic enterprises are taking some of their earnings to repair the buildings and to replace the missing Buddhist statues. This has already brought significant results in the overall preservation of the cultural antiquities of our country.

In addition, temples and monasteries with well-run economic projects contribute to the Four Modernizations. Many of them have planted orchards for the production of fruit juice, which adds to our country's exports. The monks of Jinbei Temple have planted many fruit trees to increase their production of fruit juice. The grain, fruit juice, and medicinal herbs sold by the monks of Zhiti Temple each year are worth 5,000–6,000 yuan, which is a significant contribution ["adding bricks and tiles"] to the Four Modernizations.

Remaining Problems

There are still some problems with regard to the economic-production projects of temples and monasteries in Fujian.

1. The expansion of economic productivity of some temples and monasteries is limited by the fact that only a portion of their occupied land has been returned to them, and they do not have sufficient cropland.

2. Some of the new monks and nuns fear hardship and manual labor. They would rather roam around than stay in one place and work. Some of them openly say that they are unwilling to work, and that they prefer to travel and stay at big temples and monasteries.

3. The problem of recruits [new religious personnel] must be solved. Most temples and monasteries do not have enough monks and nuns. In some of them, most of the religious personnel are elderly and unable to work. As a result, the morale of the able-bodied monks and nuns suffers, because they feel that they are not able to support their elderly colleagues by themselves.

4. How can temples and monasteries that are tourist attractions or are located near big cities and have utilized the advantages of their location to open up money-earning projects change the current situation in which they are dependent on income from selling incense and contributions by visitors?

Why Some Young People Become Buddhists

IN RECENT years, with the implementing of the party's policy on religion, religious activities in monasteries in various parts of the country have been restored. A number of young people have enthusiastically embraced Buddhism, some even applying to live in monasteries and become monks or nuns.

For example, in Fujian, a province with a long history of Buddhism, the number of monks and nuns exceeded 3,800 in 1982, shortly after the implementation of the policy on religion. Some were new converts in the latter years of the Cultural Revolution. Besides these, there are many young people now who want to study to become monks or nuns. One Buddhist seminary aroused widespread interest when news of its opening was made public. Many persons wrote letters asking about the nature of the study program and requirements for admission. In a few months over two hundred letters were received applying for admission to study or to become monks or nuns. Some of the applicants were young women, some even high school students. In their letters they said that they "admired very much the professional monks and cherished the hope to become devout Buddhists." Others wrote saying that they were "facing the decision on what road to take in life," and, "believing in Buddhism and admiring eminent monks," they were determined to take the examination and strive for the goal of a lifelong religious vocation.

Backgrounds varied among the applicants, from high school students to unemployed high school graduates, cadres, and workers, but the vast majority were young villagers. These young people were "born and grew up in the sunshine of the new society." What, then, made them so eager to become Buddhists? Why is Buddhism so fascinating to them that they would want to say goodbye to their dear ones, leave home, and come to live a lonely and boring life?

In our search for answers, some comrades from the Institute for Research on Religion of the Shanghai Academy of Social Sciences, helped by persons in Buddhist circles and supported by the religious affairs sections of various regions, have interviewed, since 1982, some young monks and novices, both men and women, in a number of places. We present here a preliminary analysis of their reasons for believing in Buddhism.

The Influence of Buddhist Families

A very important reason that some of these young people came to believe in Buddhism is the influence of family members who are Buddhists. Buddhism has a long history and widespread influence in China. Although our society has experienced world-shaking changes since Liberation, religious thinking as an ideology continues, and will continue for a long time in our society, to affect the minds of some people. The elderly, particularly those who came from the old society and had a strong belief in Buddhism, are deep-rooted Buddhists; even disasters such as the ten years of chaos cannot make them give up their belief. The religious faith of these people will always affect those around them, in particular their family members.

A seventeen-year-old boy from Hubei said that he had often listened to his grandfather tell stories. Since the grandfather was a Buddhist, he liked to tell Buddhist stories. As a result, the child wanted to become a monk. As time passed he grew up and his belief in Buddhism deepened, until at last he decided to become a monk and applied to study in a Buddhist seminary.

In another case, a young man from Hunan said, "My parents were faithful Buddhists throughout their lives. Under their influence I made up my mind while still a child to learn about Buddhism and to become a monk. I read the scriptures and prayed to Buddha." It was the influence of his parents' Buddhist ideology that led to his deep-rooted Buddhist faith and his decision to give up his job and enter the Buddhist seminary.

A young junior high school graduate in Jiangxi came from a Buddhist family that had practiced vegetarianism since his grandfather's time. His parents had studied Buddhism each morning and evening. His interest in Buddhism grew from his childhood years, when he lay in bed watching his parents at their studies and listened to their chanting. At the age of ten he began to study Buddhist scriptures under the instruction of his parents. His father's religious teacher, a Buddhist monk, often explained Buddhism to him, and eventually he became a young monk.

Other young people were led to a religious vocation by parents or other family members who became monks or nuns. One young man from Ningxia often visited his mother in the monastery after she became a nun in 1961, and his brother who became a monk in 1975. Through their influence he finally made the decision to become a monk himself.

These examples show that one of the most important reasons for young people's religious belief is the influence of older family members. Of over one hundred monks and nuns in a certain Buddhist seminary class, more than half were influenced by Buddhist family members or relatives. In some cases, every member of the family became a monk or a nun. In others, several brothers became monks. Some who grew up in temples, nurtured by Buddhism, became monks when adults.

Generally speaking, these young believers are more pious and their religious knowledge is more thorough [than that of their predecessors]. They are the core group of a whole cohort of young believers. The very important question is how to unite with these young people, how to help them to build a firm, patriotic ideology and bring their initiative into full play so as to contribute to the Four Modernizations.

The Influence of Buddhist Culture and Works of Literature and Art

Religious culture is part of a national culture. Buddhism has a long history in China. Some of our country's best culture is crystallized and preserved in Buddhist culture. The development of Buddhist philosophy has enriched the ideological history of our country, and Buddhist arts, including architecture, painting, and music, continue to scintillate today. Buddhist culture is attractive to some young people, arousing their interest in studying Buddhism and eventually leading them to religious belief.

For example, there was a young worker at a certain factory who had won the title of Excellent Youth League Member and Advanced Worker. Because of his love of literature and the arts he became interested in Buddhist culture. Later he mailed his application to study in a Buddhist seminary. In his letter he said that he wanted to study in a seminary in order to pursue research on the Buddhist dharma; he wished to probe into the essence of Buddhist dharma to learn more of its value in terms of culture and scholarly studies.

Another young man, a farmer, said: "Buddhism, along with ancient medicine, architecture, martial arts, and calligraphy, is part of the brilliant cultural heritage of the motherland. There should be successors [to those who created this heritage]. I am still young and should learn something [of that heritage]." So he applied for admission to the Buddhist seminary.

Another example is that of a twenty-year-old man from Wuxi who said, "I like reading the ancient literature of our country. I love philosophy, logic, literature, calligraphy, painting, music, martial arts. I know very well that much of the cream of our cultural heritage can be found in Buddhist scriptures. Because we lack trained personnel, this precious cultural heritage is not properly cared for." He would like to study in a Buddhist seminary to acquire relevant knowledge, he said, so that he could pursue a career in this field.

Most young people who think this way have some education and knowledge already and love studying. They hope to absorb the splendid cultural heritage of our nation, and they cherish certain ideals and ambitions. But their basic reason for applying to enter Buddhist seminaries is their hope to further their studies.

They are not as pious as those who choose to become monks through family influences, and they lack the ideological preparation for a lifetime vocation as a monk. Still other young people come in contact with Buddhism and find their interest aroused by reading books, magazines, and works of literature. A seventeen-year-old senior high school student said, "Except for reading about monasteries and monks in books and newspapers, and seeing them in films, I have never seen a real monastery or monk. I have learned from my reading that some monks stood up and fought fearlessly and relentlessly against reactionary rulers, some even giving their lives for the motherland and people. The film, *Shaolin Temple*, is an example of this."

Another man who is studying Buddhism in a certain temple first came into contact with the religion by reading novels. His interest in Buddhism was raised even higher by reading books on predestination, and he finally made up his mind to become a monk. When he was eighteen his parents wanted him to marry, but he was unwilling. He held firmly to his Buddhist beliefs, kept to a vegetarian diet, and finally became a monk.

A monk at a certain monastery in Sichuan loved reading fairy tales when he was a child—stories about fate, predestination, retribution, and reincarnation. Through his reading and the influence of his family he came to the point where he believed that Buddhist teachings give a thorough and sensible explanation of human life and of the universe itself. As a result he became a Buddhist and entered a monastery.

From these examples we can see that not all young people who wish to study in Buddhist seminaries or preparatory classes, or to enter monasteries, are necessarily religious believers. Quite a few of them are merely curious, and, feeling that there are gaps in their knowledge, are searching for answers. Thus, some people come in touch with religion simply out of their strong desire to learn something. Therefore, our comrades who carry on ideological work, particularly among young people, must be concerned when they see young people enter monasteries or come into direct contact with a religion. They should analyze the motives, lead young people to know what religion is, and deal with it in a correct way. Only in this way can they help to implement the party's religious policy and the cause of socialism.

There are other matters that deserve our attention, such as the question of how to reinforce research on religion, including the history of religions, ideologies, culture, and the present state of affairs [in religion]. We also need to broaden young people's understanding of religion so that they can deal with religion in a correct way. Religion is a complex social phenomenon, and for a variety of reasons it is shrouded with layers of man-made veils and thus appears quite mysterious. Most of our young people today, including college students, have no idea of what religion is all about.

A certain university surveyed some of its students and found that most students do not have the least knowledge about religion or "know very little" or are "very vague" about it. Young people have a very strong desire to learn, and some young people want to learn about religion. This is only normal. We regret that their desire cannot be met, with the result that they come to know and judge religion by hearsay, or by reading certain literary works. Some of them turn to religious organizations or actually go into the temples and monasteries. Therefore, it is proper to make available some knowledge of religion, to introduce some facts about religious history and religious culture to young people. This will help them come to a proper understanding of religion and will also help to implement the party's religious policy.

Another university offered a special study unit on religion in the course on historical materialism. After they had heard the lectures, many students said this special study unit had filled in some blanks in their fund of knowledge. Some of them said that the lectures "made us more fully aware of the beginnings, the nature, the essence, and the normal forms of religion, enabling us to get a clear comprehension of religion so as to understand the party's policy on religion."

Turning to Buddhism in the Search for Release from Despair and World-Weariness

Socialism has eliminated exploitation and oppression and the social sources for religion. But the many contradictions that remain in actual life often bring problems and disasters to people. One often meets individuals who encounter these problems in the course of their daily lives. Different people approach these contradictions in different ways. Some press onward in the face of difficulties and become stronger. Others, not daring to face real life, lose faith in life or lose courage because of setbacks and turn to religion in the hope of gaining spiritual comfort. Based on our surveys, the social and personal reasons why young people turn to religion can be summed up as follows.

Problems of Love and Marriage

Love and marriage are major events for young people. True love and a happy marriage make life richer and happier, but disappointment in love or an unsuccessful marriage bring endless troubles and pain. How does one deal with the wounds of a broken love affair? A person of strong will can bury such troubles in his heart and transfer his feelings to other spheres. But certain young people take love to be the total content of life. When they suffer disappointments they can find no way out, and life becomes meaningless.

For example, a young man in a certain place lost his mother when he was very young. He became acquainted with a fellow student in junior high school. They kept each other company for a long time and were dear to each other, just like sister and brother, and they finally fell in love. Later the girl married someone else and the young man was devastated. After that, he felt that "being young has little meaning for me" and decided to become a monk.

In another instance, a young man in Jiangsu Province about twenty years of age suffered heartbreak because of disappointment in love. He had never thought there would be such sadness and sorrow from a broken love affair, so, lacking the courage to fight against fate, he began to think about becoming a monk. He asserted that he would never fall in love again and would give up the thought of marriage to avoid a repetition of his spiritual trauma. He would become a monk and seek a new life. He did avoid the pain of another disappointment in love, but he did so by choosing to flee from love a second time.

The Problems of Going on for Higher Education and of Finding a Job

The hope and ideal of many young people is to go to college. Of course it would be nice to have the chance for further study, to acquire more knowledge, and to make a bigger contribution to one's country and people. But one need not go to college to do that; even if one fails to enroll in college he can make contributions in an ordinary job just the same. However, some young people collapse after one setback, such as failing to pass college entrance examinations, or they find life meaningless simply because they do not like their job. For example, a certain young high school graduate failed twice in the college entrance examinations and was waiting at home for employment. He felt depressed and finally turned to religion for help. He said, "The superior socialist system can never salvage my fate. I will find only disillusionment in this world, so I must find my place and live a quiet life."

A young monk now in a certain temple in Sichuan received a similar blow when he failed to pass the college entrance examinations. Although he got a job, he thought it was meaningless, saying that young people hope to do something earthshaking. But when they see others entering college and see themselves as inferiors, the only way they can find spiritual surcease is to take the road of Buddhism, and thus he became a monk.

Another young man, originally a student in a big city, settled down for many years in the countryside. Later he was transferred to a mine where the work was hard and conditions poor. When he saw that some of the classmates who went to the countryside with him were sent back to the city while others entered college, he sighed over the way fate treated different people in different ways. In addition his mother died. Lacking a warm home, feeling miserable, depressed, and disillusioned with the world, he came to a monastery asking to become a monk.

Problems of Psychology and Environment

Life environment can have great influence on the emergence and formation of religious psychology, particularly for some young introverts. When they feel unable to adapt to their environment, they become sick of the world.

A certain young villager came to take his father's place in a job in the city. He was all alone, without family or relatives nearby, and "for the first time he tasted the bitterness of the world and the difficulty of living in society." There are high buildings and broad streets in the city, but for this young man from the country-side, with "not even a small room of his own to live in and no place to walk freely, he suffered as if shut up in a cage." Besides this, the young man "could not bear the sight of people intriguing against each other and selfishly pursuing personal gain. He did not want to live with ordinary people and soil his pristine character." And so he "cut off all worldly goals and decided to devote his life to Buddhism, to burn himself like the incense in the temple."

A young factory worker thought he was "weak," "a sacrifice to political movements," and "the undeserved target of his leaders' anger" as well, so he lost confidence in himself. After several years of reflection he despaired of life in the real world and turned to Buddhism as the only way to "wash away worldly sorrows." Some people come to believe in religion for purely psychological reasons. Most are young women who are generally lonely introverts and prefer to live quietly by themselves.

There was a young woman living in a big city who believed that her own disposition required that she live in a quiet environment conducive to a refined state of mind. This was incompatible with her life in a noisy city. She yearned for a place of retreat and chose Buddhism as her shelter from real life. She said her fondest wish would be to leave her worldly life and convert to Buddhism.

Another woman, who was fond of calligraphy, painting, and music, said, "These would remedy the emptiness in my mind and heart." She felt that everything worldly was disgusting and prosaic. She wanted a quiet and solitary life, and her only hope was to become a nun.

These true stories show that a rich material life is not necessarily equivalent to an abundant spiritual life. While building a socialist material civilization, we must pay adequate attention to the building of a spiritual civilization that is rich and varied. Those young people who cannot adapt themselves to the world and feel empty-hearted deserve our concern and love; we need to find activities that fit their special needs, raise the level of their culture and ideology, and enrich their spiritual life.

We have listed above the main reasons why some young people become dispirited and world-weary. We need to learn how to cultivate and educate young patriotic believers in religious circles. At present, most patriotic religious believers are aware of the changes from the old society to a new one. They have long received patriotic education and built a strong foundation on patriotism. Whatever the circumstances, they will be firm in their love of the motherland and of their religion.

When we look at the actual situation of young believers, we find that many of them have turned to religion because of setbacks encountered in daily life. Many have come to find the world and its ways repugnant and hide themselves from reality. It is a difficult task to give these young people an education that combines "loving the nation" and "loving one's religion." If we can find a good solution to this problem, it will strongly influence how people in religious circles hold to the patriotic road while at the same time loving their religion.

The Influence of Fatalism and Superstition

Fatalism is an idea that has long been current among the Han people. Even women and children know the so-called truisms, "What will be will be, don't try to resist it," and "Life and death are predestined, wealth and poverty depend on the will of heaven." Such sayings still affect the younger generation of new China. Some young people say, "It won't do not to believe it, neither will it do to believe all of it." There is a family in a certain county of Fujian who believed the fortuneteller when he said they were predestined to become monks. So the husband and wife, together with their child, have abandoned family life for religious vocations in Buddhism.

A twenty-year-old young man also believed that he was destined to become a monk. He sold his properties and became a monk. His wife remarried, and a good family was destroyed. Still other young people believe in Buddhism because of preposterous sayings and fantastic ideas. For example, while recruiting new students, a certain Buddhist seminary found that some of the young applicants claimed that they wanted to become monks and nuns because they were reincarnations of monks and nuns, or they were born of Guanyin [the Goddess of Mercy]. Some claimed that they had a "vision" while praying behind closed doors, and came to ask for [divine] "instructions." Some were originally "protecting the incense and the lamps" at a "celestial palace" on a certain mountain, and after being forbidden to do this by the public security officers, wanted to go to Emei Mountain to "cultivate their moral character" or to "cultivate themselves according to the teachings."

There were two young men in a certain place in Jiangxi Province studying Buddhism from their "adoptive mother." This "adoptive mother" was very mysterious. It was said that she lived on fruit and water only. She earned money by telling fortunes, physiognomy, and curing illnesses. In fact she was something like a witch. Another young man said he would find a way to put "God" in people's hearts to enhance the beauty of their hearts. The ideas of these young, earnest Buddhists sharply diverged from traditional Buddhist teachings.

Most of these young people came from culturally backward countryside and mountainous areas. Since their own cultural standards were low, they could easily be influenced by superstitions. Furthermore, they knew very little about Buddhism and did not know the difference between religion and superstition. The facts of these cases should tell us that education for this kind of young person should start from the very beginning: that is, they should be given more scientific and cultural knowledge and be helped to do away with superstitions, to understand dialectical materialism, and to build a correct outlook on life.

We should do more to help people distinguish superstition from religion, and to cultivate their ability to tell the difference between normal religious activities and illegal, superstitious religious activities in order to implement the party's policy on religious freedom. We should ban illegal, superstitious practices that are harmful to people's physical and mental health.

Other Influences

There are still other reasons why some young people come to believe in Buddhism. For example, some want to enter Buddhist seminaries or training classes because they think it would be nice to be a high-ranking monk who can go abroad. Some want to use religion as a springboard to enable them to move from the countryside to the city and find a position there. Some even publicly acknowledge that they come to study Buddhism for economic reasons.

Some young villagers cannot stand working on the farm at home and yearn for city life. Under the pretext of becoming a monk they want to go to the monastery in a big city in order to enrich their experience. Some Fujian young people have done this. They first became monks in a small temple in their native town or village; next they went to a temple in Fuzhou or to Nanputuoshan Temple in Xiamen; after that they paid visits to other famous temples, monasteries, and mountains. They would stay longer at the good places, while soon leaving the places they did not like as well. All this had nothing to do with genuine religious belief; they simply lived on Buddhism. A small number of people could not stay on in their home place because they had committed some crime. They hid themselves in the temples to get away from legal punishment. There are few such people, yet there have been some.

Young people who believe in Buddhism for these reasons are not genuine religious believers. Although they temporarily stay in temples and monasteries for personal reasons, once they get what they want or find out it is impossible to get it, they vacillate. Of course, it is possible that some will change and become sincere Buddhists after all.

It can be seen from our analysis that there are many reasons why young people become Buddhists. The depth and breadth of their belief vary according to their experience, life circumstances, and cultural level. In socialist society religion is a long-lasting social phenomenon. As an ideology it exercises influence not only on those who came over from the old society, but on some of the young people who grew up in the new society as well. These are the ones who will become the core believers of the various religions; therefore, their living situation, their ideological changes, the reasons for their belief, and their activities both in society and in their religious groups will be closely connected with the development and changes of religion in the future. To overlook this will be detrimental to our future work.

The Current Situation of Daoism in Qingchengshan, Sichuan Province

QINGCHENGSHAN is located fifteen kilometers southwest of Guang County in Sichuan Province. Daoists call it "The Fifth Wonderland," or "The Wonderland of Nine Rooms for Celestials." According to legend, Zhang Lin of the Han dynasty climbed the mountain, preached there, and erected buildings. This is said to be the way in which Qingchengshan became a Daoist center.

Qingcheng means green city. The two peaks, Qingcheng and Pengzu, form an axis with two lines of green ridges running southward, embracing what seems like outer city walls from both sides like a chair or dustpan. Outside the walls are crimson cliffs that even strong and vigorous monkeys cannot surmount. Inside the walls there are green trees year-round. The place looks exactly like a city, and so it is called Qingcheng.

Through dynasty after dynasty about seventy temples and monasteries have been built here. Six principal temples still exist: Jiafu Temple, Guchang Temple at the Tianshi Cave, Zushi Hall, Shanqing Temple, Yuanmin Temple, and Yuqing Temple. During the ten years of chaos [the Cultural Revolution], the temples and monasteries were closed and the Daoist priests were dismissed and driven out. When the party's policy on religion was eventually reinstated after the Third Plenum of the Eleventh Party Congress, temples and economic production facilities were gradually returned to the Daoist priests, and religious activities have resumed. Guchang Temple at Tianshi Cave, where the local Daoist Association is located, has been repaired with the help of the government. The mountain path from Qingchengshan to Shangqing Palace has also been repaired and widened. The "Nine Turns," which made access very difficult, are now wide enough for two people to climb abreast safely.

There are about fifty Daoist priests and nuns now at Qingchengshan living in the temples. Ten of them are elderly, while the rest are young men and women. In addition, there are about one hundred lay Daoists and workers of different ages helping them maintain the temples.

Not long ago, Qingchengshan enrolled a number of young believers who had offered themselves for lifetime religious vocations. Candidates must meet these criteria: They must be willing volunteers, have family approval, be unmarried, and be under age thirty, with senior high school education. In lieu of an examination, they must write an article explaining what they know about Daoism. After moving into the temple for three months of study, labor, and community life, paying for their own board, they are examined by the head priests.

The young novices who have been admitted are wearing Daoist clerical robes. Master Zhang Zhilin teaches their class Chinese, while Master Zhang Zhiyi teaches *wugong*. They chant the scriptures morning and evening, accompanied by drums and gongs. During the day they work at various jobs. Ten students have been sent to Beijing to study under sponsorship of the Chinese Daoist Association. The first graduates have returned and are in charge of daily routines at Guchang Temple.

One young nun had been orphaned during the "Cultural Revolution" when her mother, a teacher, died from unbearable insults. With no means of livelihood, she despaired of life in the outside world and decided to become a nun. Another nun, originally a junior high school teacher of Chinese language and literature, came to the mountain for rest and therapy after falling ill. After recovering her health, she became a nun.

When asked why they had become Daoist believers, the young novices said they did so to provide successors to the older generation. Of course, there were other reasons. Some liked the freedom and quiet of the mountain, some wanted to become skilled in *taiji wugong*, while others came to find a livelihood.

Current income-producing projects at Qingchengshan are of two kinds, production and services. They produce wine, soda water, and tea, and offer services to visitors and tourists. The milky wine is made from *zonghua yangtao* (*actinidia chinesis*) and pure water from a mountain spring, using a secret recipe. The wine has a sweet fragrance and taste, is pure in color, highly nutritious, and harmless to human health. With a loan of 30,000 yuan, they built a factory and started making their Dongtian Brand wine in 1982, a beverage that has become essential for high-class banquets. Dongtian Wine won the prize for significant scientific and technological achievement in Sichuan Province. Every cent of the loan was paid back the first year of production. At present Qingcheng produces 60,000 kilograms of yangtao which is converted into 100,000 kilograms of yangtao juice, which in turn becomes 200,000 kilograms of wine.

Gong tea leaves are picked from the Daoist tea plantations of Qingcheng. Since Qingcheng is situated at the right altitude above sea level, with the right temperatures and a cloudy, foggy climate, this species of tea thrives. Tea manufacturing here began in the Tang dynasty. It was designated "Gong Tea" (meaning tea used for tribute) in the reign of the Kangxi Emperor of the Qing dynasty. The tea-processing factory is now furnished with modern equipment and has an annual output of 2,000 kilograms, which barely meets the demands of the market. Services for visitors provide another source of income. These include admission tickets, a restaurant, overnight accommodations, etc. With a million visitors a year, the admission tickets alone, at 20 fen [cents] each, provide 200,000 yuan. Overnight lodging also brings in significant revenues.

These solutions for the problem of self-support offer great potential for development. Fu Tianyuan, chairman of the Qingchengshan Daoist Association, said, "After Liberation, Daoism could no longer rely upon donations and fees for casting lots based on scriptures as before. Daoism must be self-supporting and create ways to sustain itself."

Zhou Enlai, Zhu De, Chen Yi, Deng Xiaoping, and other leaders have visited the mountain since Liberation. Foreign friends, such as the king and queen of Sweden and friends from Canada, Australia, France, and West Germany, have visited this scenic spot. Premier Zhao Ziyang came to the Qingchengshan Tianshi Cave on June 21, 1985, and showed great interest in its scenery, historical relics, and recent development.

With the help of the people's government, the lingering problems of Qingchengshan were solved at the end of 1985 when responsibilities were allocated as follows: the government will take care of the mountain, the priests will manage the temples, and the tourist trade will be conducted outside the temples. By solving the problems in this way, the doubts of religious believers were effectively eliminated, their unity [with all the people] was strengthened, their patriotism was reinforced, and their support for the four modernizations was brought fully into play.

A Survey of Christian Retired Workers in a Shanghai District

The place where we conducted our survey is a workers' residential district in Shanghai. We had heard that the number of retired staff persons and workers (many of them former women workers in the textile mills) in this district had increased in recent years, with frequent house meetings in the small streets and lanes. With the help and support of related departments and units, we conducted surveys, visited a number of Christians, and compiled statistics, using one of the local neighborhood committees as a key point.

Within the area supervised by this neighborhood committee, there is an independent party branch with 98 members, and 1,269 households with 5,179 persons, of whom about 800 have retired. Forty are Christians, of whom 34, or 85 percent, are elderly; of the 34, 82 percent are women. There are 29 retired Christian workers, 3.6 percent of all retired persons, probably a typical ratio for this area of the city. Of the 40 Christians, an equal number are new Christians who converted during the Cultural Revolution and old Christians whose faith predates the Cultural Revolution (see table 1).

Why Elderly Workers Become Christians

After retiring, elderly workers hope to keep fit. Many go to the parks and grassy places for daily exercises to keep in good health and avoid illness. Crowds of them go there, limbering up and moving about, chatting and talking about their aches and pains. Some older Christian sisters [women Christians] are always urging others to go to the house meetings to "listen" (at that time there were no churches in that district, so Christians gathered in homes for religious services; later, churches were repaired and reopened). These older workers knew very

Table 1

Number of Christians and Time of Conversion in a Shanghai Residential Neighborhood

| | Number of Christians | | | Time of conversion | | |
	Total	Men	Women	Total	Before Cultural Revolution	During or since Cultural Revolution
Elderly						
Retired workers	29	6	23	29	14	15
Women at home	5	–	5	5	2	3
Middle-aged and youth						
Workers	6	4	2	6	4	2
Total	40	10	30	40	20	20
Percent	100	25	75	100	50	50

little about Christian teaching, but after hearing the fantastic "witnessing" of the Christians, their interest in Christianity gradually increased. "Save me, Jesus," and "I beg of you, Jesus," are the "doctrines" they most easily accept.

We relate here some of the reasons why these people have become Christians:

1. Some who are critically ill, having tried all possible medical solutions, turn to Jesus for help. Many of these retired people have been factory workers since childhood who suffered bitterly in the old society. They stood up after Liberation, but their many years of hard labor took a heavy toll, and they now suffer from poor health. They hope that they may soon be healed, and they beg Jesus for his blessing, fantasizing that he will give them some kind of special medicine. After their religious conversion, they found spiritual sustenance that renewed their hope for a medical cure. Spiritual factors have a lot to do with the therapy of chronic diseases, and some of the Christians have indeed recovered their health after converting to Christianity. But, concerned that they may not be sufficiently pious to ward off the return of illness, they become even more earnest in their faith in the hope that God will bless them and everything will go well for them and their families.

For example, a certain retired worker had serious gastro-enteritis and often had to skip meals because of the terrible pain. She suffered greatly and was filled with dread, fearing that she might have cancer. Her hope and confidence were restored after her religious conversion, and she felt physically better. She believed this was a divine miracle and thereafter never wavered in her faith. Eleven out of sixteen of the new Christians in this district accepted the faith because of their own illness or that of family members. They make up 68 percent of the new

Christians, so we can see that this is an important reason why elderly persons become Christians.

2. Conversion to Christianity because of family troubles. Some retired workers were spiritually depressed because their family had turned cold due to bad relations between husband and wife, mother and son, or mother and daughter-in-law. When they saw the harmony and good fellowship among Christians, they accepted the faith in their search for emotional sustenance. For example, a certain elderly woman, a retired textile worker, who lives in this district had no children from her second marriage. When her first husband's son was transferred back to Shanghai from Xinjiang, her present husband often beat her and threatened to get a divorce because of contradictions about children, housing problems, and relations between mother and daughter-in-law. She suffered greatly and finally became a Christian. After her conversion she became a different person, dealing with the contradictions of their household with cheerfulness, patience, and forbearance. Not only did she become a faithful Christian herself, she urged others to believe, and most Christians living on that lane were converted as a result of her persuasion.

3. Conversion because of spiritual trauma from political movements. A woman who lives here, now over sixty, was a staff person in a law court. Her husband was sentenced to reform through labor, and, although she had completed the necessary procedures for divorce, she was treated as a member of a counterrevolutionary's family and sent to Gansu Province, together with her son and mother-in-law. She returned to Shanghai in 1960 without any means of support. After several bad years she got a job in a neighborhood service center. Again, during the "Cultural Revolution" she was criticized and denounced, her house was searched, she fell ill with hemiplegia, and her son and daughter-in-law would not live with her. In 1979, when her husband was rehabilitated, she should have had a peaceful life once again, but her heart was broken when he went to live with another woman. Through the counsel of a friend, she finally became a Christian. When we visited her, she said, "I think of nothing now, and seek nothing but peace and comfort in my Lord. I have done far too little, and I still have distracting thoughts, but my soul finds peace in my Lord."

4. Seeking peace for one's last years on earth and a "final home" after death. Some elderly people have lived a good life, with things going well even in their latter years. But they converted to Christianity anyway. For example, an elderly lady named Hu, now over 70, became a Christian in 1979. She said she had led a happy life and had become a Christian, hoping for a happy "afterlife." She not only attends house meetings herself several times a week, but she also invites other elderly women to go with her, so that eventually they all can go to "paradise" together.

5. Some retired workers convert to Christianity, not because they have met with sufferings, but because of the testimonies of devout Christians. For instance, when they join the group exercises in the park, they often meet with

zealous Christians. Christians visit sick people in the neighborhood and give their testimonies. For example, there is a well-known Christian in this neighborhood district nicknamed "Old Jesus." Since retiring she spends her time going around the neighborhood telling about the "wonders" of Jesus, and some people have been converted through her testimonies. Six of the thirty-three retired workers who live near her (18 percent of the total) have become Christians.

6. Conversion because of physical loneliness. Elderly people are likely to have a psychology of loneliness that is closely related to physical changes in their lives and the fear of death. When workers retire, they leave their busy, ordered working lives behind and live an empty and lonely life. Many do not know how to fill up their time; they cannot adjust to a life with nothing to do, and they suffer from ideological emptiness. Due to the generation gap, too much leisure time, and few household chores, they feel lonely and isolated. Even in a family where two generations live together peacefully, the common language between the two is quite limited, while in other families there are quarrels over housing and money problems. All this contributes to the feelings of depression and loneliness of the older people.

As for those who have no children, life is even more lonely and unhappy. Spiritual emptiness leads to worry, and worry, in turn, brings on spiritual emptiness. As a result, these people show great interest in the Christian house meetings. Our studies showed that these people usually retire between fifty and sixty, while some women retire before fifty in order to give their job to one of their children. At this age, people are still vigorous and need something to do. Some play cards, while others attend church services or house meetings to escape from their sense of emptiness and anxiety and to seek spiritual sustenance.

The Response of the Masses to Christian Behavior

Most of the retired workers who became Christian lived a hard life in the old society, and only after Liberation did they stand up and find personal security. Now most of them own their own homes. Despite their Christian faith, they have strong feelings for the party and love socialism. Some of them say, "The Communist Party saved my physical life, and Jesus saved my soul," or "I rely on the party while alive, and on God after death." This shows their trust in the party for this life, and their illusory faith in God.

There is a Christian woman who thought of nothing but Jesus and went about urging people to go to the house meetings to hear Christian preaching. She had no interest in the public welfare of the neighborhood. But since she heard members of the district Christian Patriotic Three-Self Committee say that Christians should both "give glory to God and help their fellow men," she has become active in neighborhood cleanup, doing good deeds for neighbors, and helping people overcome difficulties, receiving high praise from the neighborhood committee.

Although these Christians attended house meetings when the churches were closed, most of them have said they would support the Protestant Patriotic Three-Self Movement. They willingly and enthusiastically volunteered their labor and gave money for the repairing and restoration of the churches following the implementation of the party's policy on religion and the reopening of the churches.

Many Christians handle their relations within the family and with their neighbors in the spirit of "love" and "forbearance" embodied in Christian morality. One retired worker said, "In the past, I attached too much importance to money, causing problems in the family, and tensions with my children. After becoming a Christian I relaxed and my relations with my family and neighbors greatly improved, because our Lord said that we should love others."

Another Christian bought some beer recently. When he got home, he discovered that the clerk had given him an extra bottle. Because of an uneasy conscience he could not sleep well, and early the next morning he returned the bottle to the shop.

Types of Christian Lifestyle

There are three types of Christian lifestyle in this district: (1) Most Christians, except those who have difficulty in moving around, attend church services every Sunday. Some go to big churches at a distance, but most attend the nearby church now that it has been repaired and reopened. (2) Another type of Christian meets regularly for prayer in groups of five or six, which go from house to house, with no fixed meeting place, fixed time, or regular membership. The people of the district are impressed with one of these persons, a woman who visits neighborhood homes after she has done her household chores, praying and caring for the sick. (3) Another type of Christian practice is to meet regularly in specific homes. One example can be seen in the homes of two elderly Christians, where there are often from two to six people praying and reading the Bible.

Before the nearby church was reopened, there were two regular house meetings, one in the home of a pious Christian couple. Long after their marriage, and following the healing of a debilitating illness, they became Christians and a child was born to them, reinforcing their faith. They have plenty of space in their home, and meetings are held there several evenings each week, with ten or more persons each time, all of them elderly or unable to walk any distance. When we visited them, they were holding a worship service. They were friendly and enthusiastic as they welcomed comrades from the Patriotic Three-Self Committee. Neighborhood cadres say their meetings are sober and quiet.

The other meeting place is the home of a retired woman worker. She has a two-story house where mother and daughter live together. Since the downfall of the "Gang of Four," well-attended meetings have been held there two or three times a week; the largest group, over one hundred, was in 1981. There is usually a preacher, a song leader, and a person responsible for financial offerings. The worshippers are mainly older persons, most of them from the local neighborhood, but often others from outside the district. Some of the preachers are "independent preachers" who go from place to place.

Some Comments

The ratio of genuine religious believers to those who believe in ghosts and gods among the Han people is not very large, and this analysis confirms those facts. According to the statistics of this neighborhood committee, the ratio of Christians to total residents is 0.8 percent, and the ratio of retired Christian workers to total workers is 3.6 percent. In our survey of the retired non-Christians, we have found three types: The first are those who have stood up, both politically and economically, and have received some years of education, so they do not believe in religion. These are mainly party members and neighborhood cadres. The second type are those, mainly women workers, who, after retiring, are busy with housework and caring for their children and grandchildren; others, mainly men, spend their time playing cards and chess. They do not need religion for spiritual sustenance. The third type are "fatalists," a common expression for those who accept the idea of "destiny."

Some who believe in "fate" object to religion. In this neighborhood there is an eighty-year-old grandmother, with four children and many grandchildren, who has long been the head of the neighborhood committee. All members of the family are on very good terms with each other and live a happy life. When she told others why she was not a religious believer, she said, "It's no use to worship gods. I have never believed in them. A person's destiny was prearranged long ago, and praying to the gods cannot change it." Although this is a simple statement, it does express the reason why some Chinese people have no religious faith. Although "fatalism" is also a kind of religious idea, it really is contrary to religion. However, when "fatalists" meet with insuperable problems, they often turn to religion and an omnipotent God as a source of hope.

We chose this particular neighborhood district for our investigation mainly because we had heard there were many Christians among the retired workers. In the course of our survey, we learned that there had been five or six Christian churches here before Liberation and on into the 1950s, which explains why there are many Christians among the workers in the area. Many of the older Christians converted and joined the church in the early 1950s. After the many Shanghai churches consolidated their services into a few churches, the number of churchgoers decreased year by year. One reason is that the "Leftists" contravened the religious policy after 1957. The other reason is that the number of employed people increased after 1958, and more people were occupied elsewhere, with little spare time to attend church. In the ten years of chaos, all churches were closed, and the textile mills in this district were heavily damaged. Some Christian workers were attacked. For example, two of the textile workers in the district were treated as counterrevolutionaries, but not for religious reasons. They were subjected to public criticism and denunciation both in the mill and in the neighborhood and were placed under the supervision of the masses. Since they were Christians, other Christians were also affected.

After the implementation of the religious policy by the Third Plenum of the Eleventh Party Congress, the policy of religious freedom was restored, Christians could attend public religious services, and house meetings were revived (due to the fact that nearby churches were not reopened until Christmas of 1982). Meanwhile, large numbers of workers have retired in the years since 1978, giving them plenty of time for religious activities. The older Christians not only attend house meetings themselves but urge non-Christian women to attend as well. In a short period of four years, the number of new Christians is now equal to those long-time believers. Both old and new Christians told us that this new scene is now the normal atmosphere since the removal of "Leftist" influences and implementation of the policy on religion. Retired workers have ample time to attend house meetings, some of them going to several meetings and several church services a week. They believe that they will draw closer to God and save their soul sooner by frequent church attendance and listening to preaching. Judging by what we have seen and heard, Christian activities are both frequent and lively.

Some comrades have been worried about the conversion to Christianity of retired workers who suffered greatly in the old society and then stood up in the new one. Some even think that, by becoming Christians, they have "forgotten their class origins." After our own visits and investigations we believe that the class sources for religion have disappeared in socialist society, but the ideological and social sources will long remain, and some people are bound to turn to religion. The conversion to Christianity of these retired workers is linked to family, social, and economic problems, as well as to their political, cultural, and ideological levels. Most of the retired Christian workers had little concern for politics, and after retirement ideological emptiness is likely to set in. They are likely to turn to religion when confronted with seemingly insoluble personal problems. Most of them are illiterate or semiliterate, lacking understanding of culture, science, and hygiene, so they easily turn to religion when they fall ill. When they accept religious faith after retirement, they are looking for physical and mental health, for "happiness after death" and "paradise in the life hereafter." Some retired workers become Christians simply to find something "substantial" to fill their lives, because they have nothing else to do. These retired workers have experienced life in both the old and new society, they love the party and socialism, and even when they convert to Christianity they still trust the party and support socialism.

On the basis of our surveys, we believe that it is both absolutely necessary and fully possible to carry out correctly the policy of freedom of religious belief through the guideline, which is propagated by patriotic religious organizations, "give glory to God and benefit all mankind." This will lead these retired Christian workers to love both Christianity and the motherland, and make their contribution to the building of the two civilizations [material and spiritual]. We must be careful in our work not to place religious faith in opposition to faith in the party and support for socialism. Only in this way can we help bring about unity among the masses and open up new aspects for building socialism.

APPENDIX SIX

The Church at the Foot of Changbai Mountain

A Survey of Christianity among the Korean
People in the Northeastern Provinces

OUR COUNTRY has about 1,780,000 compatriots of the Korean national minority living mainly in the three northeastern provinces: about 200,000 in Liaoning, 400,000 in Heilongjiang, and 1,100,000 in Jilin (including 700,000 in the Yanbian Korean Autonomous Region). In some cities there are regions where the Korean minority people live in compact communities, such as Manrongdun in Shenyang, where only 1 out of 608 families is of the Han nationality, and all the rest are Koreans. In this region the agricultural economy is quite well developed, and culture and education are widespread.

About one hundred years ago the Korean people began to emigrate into the Northeast. There were three large movements of people: (1) In early times, poverty-stricken peasants waded across the border river to open up wasteland; (2) early in this century Koreans, including many heroic resistance fighters, took refuge in our country after the Japanese imperialists occupied Korea; (3) in the 1930s, Japanese militarists organized an immigration after they had occupied the northeastern provinces [Manchuria].

In 1945, following World War II, more than half of the Korean settlers, particularly those in better economic and cultural situations, left China for Korea, Japan, and North America. Therefore, almost every Korean family in the Northeast now has relatives abroad.

Korean compatriots have made special contributions to the founding of new China and to the improvement of friendship between Korea and China. There are places in the Yanbian region where one can see gravestones of revolutionaries in almost every village. They heroically gave their lives in the Anti-Japanese War, the War of Liberation, and the War to Aid Korea against America. Korean compatriots have made great sacrifices for the independence, liberation, and prosperity of our motherland.

In June 1984, we made surveys of the present state of Christianity among the Koreans, mainly in Shenyang, Manrongdun and its suburb, Sujaidun, and Yanji City in the Yanbian Autonomous Region.

I

Forty or fifty years ago, the Koreans living in the Northeast had many religions, but today they are mainly Catholic or Protestant Christians; very few of them believe in another religion. According to information from several comrades, and our own impression as well, there are more Protestants, their religious activities are more lively, and they are spread over a wider area than the Catholics.

Korean Protestantism was introduced from Korea in the latter years of the nineteenth century. In the early days there were five or six denominations, the strongest being the Presbyterians. The churches in Korea today still follow the Presbyterian system. Each church is governed by an elected committee, called the session, with religious affairs under a full-time pastor, an elder, who does the preaching and presides over church services and rites. The Protestant churches prospered in the 1930s. Later the Japanese invaders organized the ''Manchurian Korean Protestant Church'' to strengthen their control over the church; on the other hand, they forced the people to worship Shintoism, and Christians were cruelly oppressed. The Protestant churches revived after the Japanese surrender, but, because of anti-Communist rumors, most pastors [elders] soon fled abroad, taking with them the wealth of the church, and church activities were paralyzed.

After Liberation, Korean Protestantism was also affected by erroneous ''Leftist'' influences. Soon after the defeat of the Japanese (Yanbian was never then under Guomindang rule), ''Holy Bibles'' were burned and churches torn down. Take, for example, the influential Xita Church in Shenyang: in spring 1951, just as a worship service was ending, people from the local cultural center suddenly burst in, driving out the believers, locking the gate, and occupying the buildings and property. The Christians were forced to hold services thereafter in other places. During the ''Cultural Revolution,'' all religious activities were declared illegal. Nevertheless, there were always Christians and their families who continued to meet clandestinely for religious services on dark nights or in basements with all doors and windows tightly closed.

After the Third Plenum of the Eleventh Party Congress, the policy of freedom of religious belief was restored, and the Xita Church, on Christmas Day 1979, was the first to revive worship services. Local governments and departments of religious affairs made great efforts to carry out the religious policy. Some cadres said, ''We will treat Christians as our own brothers and sisters. All are friends, whether believers or nonbelievers.'' Other cadres, seeing that the Korean churches had suffered much destruction, gave them special attention in carrying out the religious policy. In the past four years, twelve Korean churches and meeting places have been restored and reopened. There are now two Korean pastors and eight elders, but they all live in Shenyang, Yanji, Tielin, and Longjing. Churches are concentrated in towns or cities near Shenyang and Yanji and are unable to meet the needs of the many Christians in the region. In 1982 and 1984, respectively, the "Holy Bible" and a hymnbook were published in the Korean language. The Korean churches are the most vigorous and are growing faster than those of any other national minority.

Great changes have taken place in Korean Christianity since the founding of new China. During the period of reactionary rule, there were a few Korean Christians who colluded with the Japanese puppets and the Guomindang government, seizing control of some church institutions. Take, for example, the ex-elder of the Manrongdun church, a certain Han Chinese. He had joined the reactionary Independent Party, and during the Guomindang period he was head of the village and school. He was in a position to control education, politics, and the church in the entire village and was executed after Liberation. At that time, some local people did not have a good impression of Christianity because some Christians held reactionary political views. But today the leaders of Korean churches in every place are retired workers or staff personnel, with some still at their posts. For example, Elder Jin of the Yanji Church is head of the shoe and hat section of a state-owned department store. Deacon Jin of the Tumen Church is director of a clothing factory. The two elders of Longjing Church are retired workers. They have all been praised for their good work. The situation in the villages is the same. There are many Christians in Shijing Village, where the leader of their meeting place [worship center without a resident pastor] is Deacon Jin, the new leader of their production team.

A good many Korean Christian families, including those of several pastors, have won the honor of being named a "Five-Good Family." This shows that Christians conform to the prevailing moral norms of social life and neighborhood relationships. The party branch secretary of Manrongdun told us this story. On the evening of May 18, 1984, a big fire broke out in the village, spreading to six homes, of which two were gutted. After the fire, a number of Christians, without urging from anyone, immediately collected money, clothing, and food for the victims. Most of the Christians were women, who refused to give their names. These women, many of them elderly, have no independent financial means; their contributions came from their personal savings. The party secretary has great respect for the public example set by the Christians.

We found that the good behavior of the Christians not only draws the praise of people, but also attracts them to their faith. It also leads new believers to follow suit, doing good deeds themselves and improving their own conduct. The changes that take place in these people are themselves a further means of spreading religious influence. For example, a member of the Longjing Church volunteer training class told us that he became a Christian in 1980. His teenage daughter had objected to his attending the class, so his heart was not in it, and his mind wandered, thinking about his busy farm work. One day he unexpectedly received a letter from his daughter telling him that several Christians had helped her with her farm work, and she wanted her father to focus his attention on studying the "Holy Bible." As a result, he now places great value on his Christian faith, and his eldest daughter has said that she wants to become a Christian.

Another member of the volunteer class, a woman, said that her husband often got drunk and beat her until her nose turned black and blue and her eyes swelled shut. Later, he "heard that the Bible gives advice on how to be good, and he saw that Christians are honest." Both husband and wife converted to Christianity, the husband gave up drinking, and now they have a peaceful family. In recent years, through hard work they have prospered, and their house is now a center for religious meetings. The changes in the material and spiritual life of this couple have attracted many others to turn to and to accept the Christian faith.

Two Korean young men, barely twenty, and unemployed after finishing high school, had fallen into bad habits such as drunkenness and fighting. One of them had taken part in stealing weapons from an army unit, had stolen funds, and had twice been imprisoned. Friends and relatives had tried in vain to help him. But now he has changed since becoming a Christian and has cut off all contacts with former bad friends. Both young men have said that they now "want to be persons of value," and to "seek after real values in life."

The experience of these misled youths shows that the ten years of chaos have sown seeds of confusion about life values in the minds of some people, and when the years of chaos ended and society did not solve their livelihood problems, some young people had lost the ability to distinguish good from bad. When these young men were converted to Christianity, people thought it was a "miracle." The father of the once-imprisoned young man (himself a cadre in a production team) thought it was a fine thing for his son to join the church and allowed him to attend the training class for church volunteers.

Since the reopening of the churches, the number of Korean Christians has not increased as dramatically as in China proper, but recently it has shown a tendency to increase following implementation of the policy on religion. In fact there are many family worship services in villages where problems such as language, physical conditions, and distance from the city churches make it difficult to go to church. In April 1984 the Religious Affairs Office of Liaoning Province sent cadres out to make a survey of the meeting places of the Korean Christians near Yingkou. The number of Christians is certainly larger than was thought, for they discovered at least thirteen places as they made careful visits deep into the villages.

II

Korean Christianity in Northeast China has its own characteristics, quite distinct from that of the Han Chinese, due to differences in language and historical background.

1. It has distinct national [ethnic] features. Most churches in the Korean districts were set up and run by the Koreans themselves, notwithstanding the fact that early in the century American missionaries opened churches, schools, and hospitals. For a long time the northeastern provinces were occupied by the Japanese invaders, so these churches were influenced only in a small way by Western missions. Many of the Korean Christians now feel that they became "three-self churches" long ago, because immediately after the surrender of the Japanese imperialists, these churches became fully self-governing and self-supporting. On the other hand, they do not have much to do with the Han Chinese churches. Take Shenyang, for example: up to this day, even Koreans who speak Chinese would rather go a long distance to a Korean-language church for worship and baptism than to attend a nearby Han Chinese church.

In those churches used by both nationality groups, the religious affairs, finances, and personnel are handled independently of one another. The Koreans use Korean Bibles, and they sit on the floor with men separated from the women, as is their custom. Both Christians and non-Christians observe Korean national ceremonies, customs, and habits. The church organizes picnics and visits to nearby parks for every traditional national festival. Korean Christians have a special feeling for their national [ethnic] churches. After the Cultural Revolution, as soon as they heard that the churches were to be returned to them, they organized volunteer repair teams, and even the old women came to carry baskets of earth and rubbish on their heads during the initial clean-up. The Xita Church in Shenyang used to be called the Jerusalem of Korean Christianity in the northeastern region—the Holy Land. Today it is the center for information about all the Korean churches in the region and is the place where the Korean-language "Holy Bible," which they all use, is published. When Korean Christians from outside China come to this region, they always visit this church. It truly is the central church for the Korean Christians of northeastern China.

The Korean Christians have now joined the Protestant Patriotic Three-Self Movement. A "Three-Self" committee or group has been formed in each church and meeting point. But there are differences among them regarding the way they understand and respond to the policy of patriotism, anti-imperialism, and church autonomy. Therefore, it is important to help the Korean churches to develop in a healthy way. At present, the Xita Church selects patriotic materials from Christian books and magazines published in China and reprints them in the Korean language, a service that is warmly welcomed.

2. There is a strong foundation on which the faith is passed from one generation to the next. Although the number of Korean Christians is less than it once was, today's church families can trace back through many Christian generations. The religious influence permeates their lives. Although religious activities were cut off for over twenty years, and even longer in some places, their firm religious faith survived times of suffering without wavering, growing even firmer after the implementation of the religious policy following the Third Plenum of the Eleventh Party Congress.

A Korean woman named Li, a model worker in Liaoning Province, was separated from her father, a church deacon who left for South Korea thirty-seven years ago. She was only eight years old at the time, but she still remembers the hymns and Bible stories her father taught her. He was a widower, an honest man and a devout Christian who lived a spartan life and spent all his money and energy preaching and helping the poor. Through his example his daughter was led to believe in Jesus. Six years ago, communications between the father and daughter were restored. Although she did not accept his invitation to meet him outside China, she did accept his counsel to become a Christian and help with church work. She was baptized and urged her three sons to accept Christianity, even urging her eldest son to study for the ministry. She goes to the Xita Church every day to help with mimeographing and has become a good church worker.

Some elderly Christians go to the church for prayer at four o'clock in the morning, and some high school girls have very strong faith. A young girl student lives with her grandmother, whose house is a Christian meeting point in Shijing Village, Longjing County. She studies hard, won third place in the joint provincial junior middle school graduation examinations, and publicly testifies to her faith among fellow students.

Korean churches are giving high priority to recruiting and training young clergy. Elderly Christians, many of them retired, now fill positions of church leadership as deacons and elders. Many young Christians have applied to join a theological training class. Yanbian churches have organized such a training class for two successive years, taught by deacons, elders, and other volunteers; most of the students are children or grandchildren of former elders and deacons. Most religions seem to be handed down through the families of believers, and this seems to be even more true for the Korean Christians.

Korean compatriots have a rather high cultural and educational level. It is said that they will send their children to school no matter what the cost. All the Christians have had schooling, and the content of their religious faith is rather healthy; one seldom hears anyone talking about ghosts and demons, or any other banned talk, either inside or outside the church. They don't speak about exorcising demons and faith healing now as they used to, as a means to attract people to the church.

3. They have many channels for communicating with people abroad. Most Christian families have relatives who live outside China, and these are seen everywhere in the cities and villages. Besides these, forty to fifty foreigners have visited the Xita and Shenyang churches this past year or two, and twenty more have gone to the Yanbian churches. The churches use these opportunities to share church news with the visitors, and to enhance international relations for the benefit of the four modernizations of China and world peace. In this opening to the outside world, there are, of course, people who become Christians through friends and relatives, and some who receive books sent by overseas friends. This is only natural. In the homes of some Christians, we have seen gifts, such as

"Holy Bibles," hymnbooks, and photographs of relatives who are pastors or preachers overseas. But we have also heard of anti-Chinese, anti-Communist foreign influences making use of religious channels for attempting political subversion in China. Because of the key geographical location and the particular historical background of the Korean nationality, their contacts with the outside world present certain complications. For example, certain overseas missionary agencies use modern communications, such as radio, to send in propaganda, broadcasting from morning to night, and making use of national [ethnic] feelings to stir up dissension. Some visitors, aiming to sabotage the policy of self-government and self-support and restore foreign influences over Chinese Christianity, sow discord among some Christians by tempting them with offers of gifts, and interfere in local religious matters. They invite large groups of friends and relatives to feasts, pass out gifts, make promises of money, and try in every way to ingratiate themselves with the local churches. Some even go so far as to lead religious services, conduct ordinations, and even set up new religious sects. Others, trying in vain to get the Korean churches to deviate from the patriotic line, vilify patriotic pastors, saying they are false pastors and theirs are false churches.

One or two reactionaries or special agents have made use of religion and national [ethnic] feelings to infiltrate politically and collect information. Since such activities seem to be more evident among the Koreans than among churches elsewhere in China, this matter deserves special vigilance.

In the wake of the implementation of religious policy in the spirit of the Third Plenum of the Eleventh Party Congress, the positive factors of the Korean Christians at the foot of Changbai Mountain have been brought into play. They are doing their part in fostering international relations and building the four modernizations. As relevant documents have pointed out, if we are to build a socialist material and spiritual civilization, it is of utmost importance for national stability, for the solidarity of all national minorities, and for the development of international relations while resisting the infiltration of foreign influences, that religious questions be handled correctly.

Religious Faith of Fishing People in Qingpu County

The Importance of Implementing the Policy
on Religion for Bringing Unity with the
Masses of Believers

ON MAY 2, 1983, the most impressive groups among the Catholic pilgrims going to the church on Sheshan near Shanghai for religious services were the fishing people from Qingpu County. At about five o'clock in the morning, over two thousand believers came in groups from various fishing brigades of Qingpu County. After assembling at the foot of the hill, they formed a line and slowly walked to the top of the hill while chanting the prayers, entered the church, which was still under repair, and took part in the Mass. When the Mass was ended, they descended halfway, to the Pavilion of the Three Saints and the Pavilion of the Holy Mother. There they knelt in groups, again chanting prayers in unison. Some of them walked prayerfully along the newly repaired Way of the Cross [the fourteen stations of the cross]. For the entire morning they immersed themselves in a strong religious atmosphere.

Ours is a socialist country. New China was founded over thirty years ago, and the fishing people still devoutly hold to their religious faith. Why is this? Is it beneficial or not for the cause of socialism that they maintain such a pious faith and carry on religious activities such as "pilgrimages"? This essay is an inquiry into these two questions.

Believers for Many Generations

Qingpu Catholics, of whom most are fishermen, numbered between nine thousand and ten thousand shortly after Liberation. About one-third of those have died in the past thirty years. Those who were thirty years old then are now over sixty, and onetime teenagers are now in their forties. These believers, in their forties, fifties, and sixties, now form the main body of Catholics.

Before Liberation, Chinese Catholic churches were controlled by foreign forces. The church considered all who had joined the church as "church members" [jiaomin—people of the church] and required all parents of newborn children to take them to the church to be baptized by the priest within three to eight days after their birth.

The Catholic fishing people of Qingpu are also called "net-boat Catholics." Their boats are their homes. They make their living from aquatic products such as fish, shrimp, and crabs, wandering about on the rivers of Qingpu County. Because their nomadic way of life sometimes prevented parents from taking their newborn children to the church for baptism within the time prescribed, the church required that they take the child in such cases to a lay Catholic who had been examined and authorized by the priest to administer baptism. Later, the parents would take the child to the priest for formal baptism. Catholics today who are middle-aged or older joined the church in this way, by baptism soon after their birth.

There is no precise historical record of the first generation of Catholics in Qingpu. According to *The History of Missionary Work in Jiangnan*, a book about the Catholic fishing people written by missionaries in the Jiangnan [south of the Yangze River] region, one can see from odd bits of information that there were Catholic fishing people in this region of rivers and lakes in the reign of the Kangxi Emperor.

The number of Catholics dropped sharply during the hundred years following the ban on Catholic religious activities issued by the Yongzheng Emperor, but the faith survived, and some missionaries remained, hiding on boats by day and coming out by night.

A Catholic named Wu of Baihe Village, now eighty-three years old, can still recall stories his grandmother told him about the night-time activities of those missionaries. The fishing people of Qingpu have a religious history of two or three hundred years. Their religious faith has been passed down by their ancestors from generation to generation. Now, when they are asked about the history of their religious faith, they are unable to give a clear picture of the first generation of believers, but they will answer forthrightly, "We come from a long line of believers; we have been believers (lao jiaoyou) for a long, long time."

From Youthful to Adult Believers

In the old society, two and even three generations of "net-boat Catholics" lived together on a small boat in a cabin not big enough for a four-foot bed. In ordinary times these "multigeneration believers" (shidai jiaotu) had their own family worship on their boats, such as "morning lessons" and "evening lessons." On Sundays, called "the Lord's Day" by Catholics, they "read the special Sunday prayers" on their boats when they could not go to church. These religious activities carried out on their boats were only a part of their religious life.

At that time most of the fishing people were members of the churches in Tailaiqiao, Yangyuyu, and Zhujiajiao. The same "parish priest" was in charge of the churches in Yangyuyu and Tailaiqiao, and the Zhujiajiao church had its own "parish priest" beginning in 1945. Any church that had its own "parish priest" was called a "parish church" (huikou). The principal activities of a parish church were to "fulfill the four precepts": Mass on Sunday, and on important festivals such as Christmas; fasting on Friday; "confession" and "holy communion" at least once a year; and contributing money for the support of the church.

Dates for special church services were fixed by the "parish priest," and on those occasions the fishing families traveled by boat to the point nearest the "parish church" to which they belonged to take part in the special activities, which took from a few days to more than a week.

In addition to "fulfilling the four precepts," these churches also had their "major" and "minor" festivals. The major festivals were Christmas, Easter, the Assumption of Mary, and the Local Church's Special Festival. The "minor festivals" were Lent, the Month of our Lady [May], Pentecost, Birthday of Our Lady, All Saints' Day, and All Souls' Day. On those occasions all fishing families were expected to row their boats to the churches and attend the religious activities.

May was the Month of Our Lady [literally, "Holy Mother"], the month for Catholics of the Shanghai region to go on pilgrimage to Sheshan. The parish priest required that the Catholic fishing families of Qingpu attend the "Day of Pilgrimage to Worship Our Lady," and hundreds of boats docked at the foot of Sheshan Hill. Family after family climbed the hill to take part in worship.

The middle-aged and older Catholics have learned from their parents through the years the prayers, Bible readings, kneelings, and forms of worship, so they know the rites and ceremonies from habit.

In the old society most children of net-boat Catholics never went to school, but went instead to "Bible class." Even before they joined a Bible class, they had already heard the Six Daily Prayers and the Questions and Answers on Doctrine [Catechism], so in two or three months, or, at most six months, they could recite everything from memory after attending the Bible class.

When they had completed the class, they were interviewed and tested by the parish priest. They could recite the Six Daily Prayers, but they could not understand them very well because they were written in classical Chinese. The Catechism was written in modern Chinese, so at least they could recite and understand the questions and answers about doctrine after completing the Bible class, and the chief Catholic doctrines were rooted in their minds.

After the Six Daily Prayers and the Catechism came the First Confession (confessing their sins to the parish priest) and First Holy Communion (the first time they could receive the "sacred host" from the parish priest during the

Mass). Before these two "first" occasions, they could not take part in the holy ceremonies with their parents. After First Confession and First Communion these children became complete young Catholics.

These children returned to their boats after First Confession and First Communion and lived a life just as they did before the Bible class. Only those whose families were better off could study at the Catholic Wangdao Primary School, which was run by the Tailaiqiao Catholic church, the seat of the parish priest in charge of all the Qingpu Catholics. Students at the Wangdao Primary School all lived in the school and had to attend frequent religious functions at the local church. In addition, the class on religion was one of the main courses offered at the school. The children were even more influenced by what they saw and heard in the Catholic classes, rites, and services there.

Both the children who returned to their boats after they finished the Bible class and those who studied at the Wangdao Primary School had to be confirmed when the bishop came to inspect the church. At that time, the bishop came to Tailaiqiao every four years. When he came, all the Catholics who belonged to those churches came by boat to the place where the bishop would lead the church functions. Children who had not been confirmed following First Confession and First Communion had to be confirmed by the bishop. According to the Catechism, "confirmation has the purpose of assuring that those who are confirmed have a 'firm belief,' will be 'brave soldiers of Jesus,' and will 'prove their faith by their words and deeds, and even by the sacrifice of their lives.' " Thus it can be seen that confirmation is really a "vow" by these children to show their firm belief in the religious doctrines. Today's Qingpu Catholics who are middle-aged and older all were confirmed while teenagers as proof of their "firm belief."

The influences of family, society, and education in one's childhood are very important for one's growth in later years. Qingpu's Catholic fishermen who are now over forty have lived on boats since childhood, having little contact with the outside world. They only went to the churches, and the main influences in their lives were religious. Religious ideas were deeply embedded in their minds and became the norm for their words and deeds.

When the children of net-boat Catholics wanted to marry, they had to go to the church and ask the priest to perform the marriage ceremony. Before the wedding they had to be interviewed and examined by the parish priest, just as they did after the Bible class. Today's Qingpu Catholics who are over fifty have all passed this "examination" and have moved through the stages from "young Catholics" to "adult Catholics."

Examples of Religious Ideology

The religious experience described above makes devout believers of the Qingpu Catholics, with the result that their way of looking at everything comes under this religious influence.

In the past hundred years, imperialism used the Catholic church in its invasion of China. Qingpu's Catholic fishermen knew nothing of this fact of history. They only knew that Catholicism was the "true religion," not that it was being used by the imperialists. In facing the problems of wealth and poverty, happiness and suffering, the Catholic "teaching" wanted Catholics to believe that everything was arranged by God, and so this is what they believed.

For example, following this Catholic "teaching," they looked on the real world as a place of misery because God made it that way. People suffered because of their sins, and their misery was God's punishment. The only way out was to submit to what God had arranged and endure suffering in this world so as to acquire everlasting happiness in the next world.

Before Liberation there was nothing to safeguard the life of a fisherman, wandering about the rivers and lakes in a small boat under constant threat of accidents. They believed the Catholic doctrines because, on the one hand, it helped them to endure the temporary sufferings of this world, while, on the other hand, they believed that "praying for blessings and protection from God, Jesus, and the Blessed Mother" was efficacious.

A certain Catholic fisherman named Zhang, from the Chengjian Brigade of Jiefang Commune, still believes that his family avoided a terrible incident at the time of the Japanese puppet regime due to God's protection. At that time Shanghai was under the heel of the Japanese invader, and civilians had to show their so-called good conduct certificate when they passed sentries. The father of this fisherman was carrying to Sijing shrimps he had caught for sale. He forgot to bring his certificate with him and was caught by a Japanese sentry and dragged to one side. The soldier made him kneel and drew his sword. It is said that Zhang's father kept saying, "Jesus save me." Although the Japanese did not understand what he was saying, when he saw the cross suspended from his neck, he said, "All right," and released him.

During the Anti-Japanese War, the representative of the Vatican to China and the bishop of the Shanghai Catholic archdiocese ordered Chinese Catholics to obey Japanese rules and not revolt. When the Japanese saw the cross on the chest of this man, obviously he thought the man would not rebel and let him go. But this man, Zhang's father, believed that it was because he kept saying, "Jesus save me," and that "Jesus had protected him." Thus the family became even more pious, and when, on occasion, something especially good happened to them, such as making a good catch of fish, shrimp, and crabs, they would associate their good fortune with "God's beneficence" and become even more devout.

In the old society Qingpu Catholics, under strong religious influence, endured their sufferings because they believed that "God had arranged things" that way. On the other hand, they prayed for "protection from God, Jesus, and the Blessed Mother" to save them from sufferings. Day after day and year after year it was like this. For many of them, their faith grew even deeper and more pious as time went by.

From Liberation to the Eve of the Cultural Revolution

After Liberation, the Catholic fishing people of Qingpu moved from the old to the new society, taking their devout religious faith with them. Many Catholics did not dare to show their patriotism or draw close to the government and party, because there were people inside the church who spread false rumors that the Communist Party wanted to wipe out religion; moreover, leaders of the church in Shanghai, acting on instructions from the Vatican, gave orders to Catholics not to endorse the party.

In 1953 and again in 1955, struggle campaigns in the Catholic churches cleaned out the imperialist and counterrevolutionary elements, removing the heavy weight of stone that had pressed down on the Catholics. But a number of the Qingpu Catholics still did not know that the purpose of the struggle against the imperialists and counterrevolutionaries was to protect proper religious belief. They mistakenly thought that the imperialists and counterrevolutionaries using the guise of religion were their "church elders" (*shenzhang*), and they dared not draw a line of demarcation between themselves and these enemies.

They gradually came to know that the acts of these imperialists and counterrevolutionaries using the guise of religion were illegal and harmful to the people of China and were unacceptable because they were contrary to the doctrines and regulations of the church as well. Only then, following the Christian teaching of love for others, and the fourth of the "Ten Commandments," which says that one should love one's country, did they denounce the evildoings of the imperialists and counterrevolutionaries using the guise of religion. Having drawn a sharp line between themselves and their enemies, their consciences were clear.

However, just when the Qingpu Catholics began to follow the patriotic road, "Leftist" influences began to appear, and proper religious activities were confused with superstitious activities in the process of implementing the religious policy. On the pretext that religious activities would "hamper production," measures were taken to reduce the number of churches and religious activities. The fishing people dared not go to church for fear of being despised. They carried on their religious practice and Bible reading on their boats. After 1958 one could "catch sparrows on the doorstep" of the Catholic church in Tailaiqiao.

On Christmas 1964, the church at Zhujiajiao, with less than one hundred believers attending Mass, was desolate. This did not mean that the Catholic fishermen had given up their faith; it showed that they were again doubtful about the religious policy, and that there was a barrier between them and the party and government. During the period of the campaigns to wipe out the imperialists and counterrevolutionaries using the guise of religion, it had not been easy to bring the Catholic fishing people around to loving both religion and country, even using patient education. Now "Leftist" influences were pushing them back away from the road of loving their country and their religion, causing heavy losses in the unification work with Catholic believers.

Catholic Faith Holds Firm during the Cultural Revolution

At the beginning of the Cultural Revolution in 1966, Catholic churches in Qingpu County were closed or destroyed. Catholics consider their churches to be "holy sanctuaries" (*sheng tang*), that is, sacred places. After 1958, due to "Leftist" influences, the Catholics had already come to suspect the religious policy. When the Cultural Revolution broke out and they saw their "holy sanctuaries" destroyed, what would they think? At the time of Liberation they had feared that the party and government would "exterminate religion," and now, with all the churches closed, was it not true that religion was being exterminated? That would be a bitter disaster for Catholics, and now it finally was happening.

At the same time that churches were being destroyed, religious believers were deprived of their civil rights: they were not allowed to read the Bible, to wear "holy medals," to place "holy pictures" in their boats, or to have rosary beads or religious publications. All holy pictures, holy medals, and rosary beads had to be "handed over." Moreover, some devout Catholics were publicly criticized and denounced, even imprisoned.

For example, the small fishing boat of a Catholic who belonged to the parish of the present deputy leader of the Baihe Fishing Brigade was searched four times, and his religious books, which he had used since he was a fifth grader at the Wangdao Primary School, and his three treasured silver chains with "holy medals" were all confiscated. He was framed by a special agent and imprisoned for two months.

Another Catholic, now fifty years old, was called a "monster and demon" and had all his religious books confiscated just because he had studied in a church primary school and had been acquainted with the missionary priest there.

The Catholic named Zhang, mentioned above, who believed that "Jesus had protected him" and saved him from a calamity during the Japanese puppet regime, was called a "bourgeoisie" and criticized and denounced for eight months.

The "ultra-Leftists" believed that China had become a "country without religion." They did not know that it is precisely times like this, when churches are destroyed and Christians assaulted, that the faith of devout believers is strengthened. Their firm faith gave the Catholic fishing people of Qingpu courage when they were wrongly attacked. Now they are all saying that they followed the example of "Jesus, who was nailed to the cross and died," and that their sufferings were their "gift to God," believing that God would compensate them. When they were not allowed to read the Bible, many of them resorted to silent reading in their hearts. Others, together with their whole families, and even groups of boat families, read aloud while sailing out of earshot of the shore. They used every means to hide the few rosary beads and holy medals that had escaped detection. Thus it turned out that while the "ultra-Leftists" attempted to stifle religion by administrative methods, the final results were exactly opposite to what they had intended. This proves that banning religion by administrative decree will not work.

Violating the Policy on Religion Gave Opposition Forces an Opportunity

The post-Liberation patriotic anti-imperialist movement among the Catholics was carried out unevenly. Some of the Qingpu fishing people had their awareness raised in varying degrees, while others received no education in patriotism and anti-imperialism. There were Catholics among those who were assaulted during the Cultural Revolution who, indeed, had taken the road of loving the motherland and loving religion after the patriotic anti-imperialist movement. To assault these Catholics was to assault core members of the patriotic forces. The Catholic situation was complicated; religion was often used as a front for evildoings. Qingpu fishing people who had not received patriotic anti-imperialist education usually had only a vague understanding of the difference between proper religious functions and illegal activities using the guise of religion. They were easily cheated, and after the religious policy was trampled [by the ultra-Leftists] the core group of patriotic Qingpu Catholics collapsed, making it even easier for someone to deceive them.

In March 1980, before any of the Shanghai district churches had reopened, Qingpu Catholics heard the rumor that the "Blessed Mother" would show her power and presence by appearing on Sheshan Hill surrounded by a halo. For over ten years they had not gone to Sheshan to worship the Blessed Mother, so, when they heard the rumor passed around by some people, they quit working and went to Sheshan to see the "apparition and radiance of the Blessed Mother." When they arrived at Sheshan, the people who had spread the rumor, hiding themselves among the crowd, shouted reactionary slogans, breaking, smashing, and abusing the government.

This happened just when the policy on religion had been restored at the Third Plenum of the Eleventh Party Congress, but chaos and instability prevailed among the Catholic fishermen. Illegal activities under the guise of religion carried on in the dark, together with the circulating of rumors, split the Shanghai churches just when they were striving for independence and self-government.

Unite Devout Catholics by Carrying Out a Workable Religious Policy

The "ultra-Left" line violated the religious policy and caused religious believers to lose trust in it completely. The only way to gain their confidence was to truly carry out the policy and make believers see the actual implementation. By doing this, the questions caused by their ignorance, such as the illegal activities carried on under the cover of religion, could be more easily resolved.

As a result of the sincere implementing of the religious policy by the Qingpu

government and party committee, the Qingpu Catholics saw the following actions take place: sixty-five cases of unjust and false verdicts were corrected after
reexamination; cadres visited them time after time, making friends with them
and talking earnestly heart-to-heart in order to untie the knots in their thinking;
Catholics who had once taken the road of loving the motherland and religion, but
who were scattered during the "Cultural Revolution," were located and welcomed home; a number of priests, nuns, and lay Catholics were elected as
people's representatives to the Qingpu and Zhujiajiao CPPCC; some Catholics
were taken on trips by relevant [government and work] units; and, before the
Zhujiajiao church reopened, local Catholics were allowed to go to Shanghai to
attend Mass in reopened churches, provided that it did not interfere with productive labor. This was done not only without condescension by the leaders of
relevant units, but with their support.

In addition they [the Catholics] saw that relevant [party and government]
units made a clear distinction between the two contradictions [antagonistic and
nonantagonistic] with regard to those Catholics who had been deceived by rumors of "the apparition and halo of the Blessed Mother" and had gone to
Sheshan. Ideological work was patiently, sincerely, and painstakingly carried
out, helping Catholics draw lessons from their wrong actions and encouraging
them when they made a little change or progress. Believers were deeply moved,
uniting and educating many of them. Some Catholics who had been fooled told
of their bitter experiences after gaining a better understanding, while others even
exposed some who had engaged in illegal activities, struggling with them face to
face. The chaotic situation among Qingpu fishing people rapidly changed, and
negative factors became positive ones.

The decisive factor in regaining the confidence of the Qingpu fishing people
in the religious policy was the return to them of the Zhujiajiao Catholic church,
its repair and reopening, and the restoration of normal religious activities. In
December 1980, with strong support from the Religious Affairs Offices of
Shanghai and Qingpu County, and with the help of the Shanghai Catholic Patriotic Association, the first meeting of the Qingpu Catholic Representatives Committee was convened, and Qingpu Catholics announced the founding of the
Qingpu Catholic Patriotic Association, formed by Catholic laypersons, priests,
and nuns. Before the opening of the meeting, the broad masses of Catholic
fishing people (in response to their insistent demands) had already been given
back the Zhujiajiao Catholic church, which had been taken over by a work unit,
and had begun to make repairs.

After its founding, the Qingpu Catholic Patriotic Association worked actively
with the government to carry out the religious policy and speed up repairs. They
chose Christmas Day, December 25, 1980, the biggest festival of the Catholic
year, as the reopening day. On that day more than a thousand Catholics came to
the first church in the Shanghai suburban districts to celebrate Christmas after
reopening. Catholics who had not been able to attend Mass for more than ten,

some even twenty, years and felt "uneasy in their conscience" attended midnight Mass and dawn Mass as well. They were so happy that they thanked the government, party, Religious Affairs cadres and the Patriotic Association from their hearts. Many believers shed hot tears as they expressed their thanks to cadres and members of the Patriotic Association.

In the wake of this, the Qingpu Catholics' understanding of the party's and government's implementing of the religious policy deepened, their patriotic awareness was raised, and their relations with cadres became more and more intimate and friendly.

Some Catholics had been doubtful about the religious policy, and, under the influence of the Vatican's sabotage activities, harboring misgivings about loving the motherland, loving religion, and self-government and independence of the church, had not been willing to attend religious services in the churches. But now, more and more, they began to shed their doubts and misgivings and take part in the activities of the Patriotic Association, attending meetings and study sessions, and going to church for normal religious activities. Since the reopening of the Zhujiajiao church, churchgoers have numbered between two thousand and three thousand on the big Catholic festivals, and over four thousand for the annual Sheshan pilgrimage.

At the beginning of this report we stated that about two thousand Qingpu Catholics went to Sheshan on pilgrimage on May 2, 1983. It should be noted that these were the second group. The first group of nearly a thousand went on May 1. In addition to attending normal religious services, the number of Qingpu Catholics attending the big festivals grew from one thousand in 1980 to four thousand in 1983. This shows that they are uniting around the party and the government and making their contribution to the four modernizations with greater enthusiasm than ever before.

After Gaining a Better Life

In the old society most Qingpu Catholics suffered hardships. They were called "fisher beggars." Every year at Spring Festival time they usually went ashore to "beg for New Year's cakes." They were also called "thief boats" because, when they had nothing to live on, they had no choice but to go ashore and steal vegetables and squash from the fields to ease their hunger. With no provisions in the boats and only rags to wear, they drifted on the waters the year around. Neither girls nor boys on the boats could marry someone who lived ashore. While the peasants suffered, then, the fishing people suffered even more.

After Liberation, the Catholic fishing people stood up. Now the majority of fishing families have moved ashore into new villages prepared for them. Following the development of marine culture projects, the aquatic production brigades, where fishing people are concentrated, can spare some of their labor force and unemployed youths to work in industries operated by the brigades. For example, some fishermen from the Baihe Aquatic Brigade are working in the leather-shoe factory, the box factory, and the sand-washing plant run by the brigade. In recent years, the income of every household has increased. Many have bank deposits of more than a thousand yuan. Bicycles and sewing machines are very popular, and many have television sets and tape players. Take the Zhaoxian Aquatic Brigade, for example: in 1981 they bought twenty television sets at one time. Their living standard is steadily rising, and they like to describe it as "a sesame plant that puts forth blossoms joint by joint, higher and higher."

Qingpu fishing people clearly know that they owe all the benefits gained since Liberation to the leadership of the Communist Party. They remember the kindness of the Communist Party as their production output grows and their living standard rises. But, at the same time, they remember that they are "multi-generation Catholics," and that man has a "soul" as well as a physical body. They believe that their "soul" will rise to "paradise" after the death of their physical bodies. Devout believers have no doubts about the "soul" and "paradise"; all is contained in one word, "faith." In the old society they lived a hard life and yearned for "everlasting blessings in the next world," while on the other hand they asked for the "protection of God, Jesus, and the Blessed Mother." Today, as they live a better life, they still yearn for "everlasting blessings in the next world." Thirty years after Liberation, with their lives much better, Catholics still judge good and bad on the basis of whether it will help or hinder their "soul" to go to "paradise." They think it is really good if it is good for their soul; if it is contrary, they worry that their soul will go to a frightful "hell."

Qingpu fishing people had been worried about the "extermination of religion" after Liberation because they feared that it would prevent their "soul" from rising into "paradise." During the Cultural Revolution they suffered a "religious calamity." They did not attend public religious services, but in fact they held onto their religious faith because they did not want their "soul" to be turned away from "paradise" because of apostasy. Going to "paradise" is their ultimate goal. After the Third Plenum of the Eleventh Party Congress, they saw the real implementation of the policy on religion, and once again they can go to church to make confession and to take holy communion so their "soul" can go to "paradise." Now their conscience is clear and they feel that their situation is fine.

Catholics think that a good life refers only to the physical body, while that which is good for the "soul" refers only to that which helps the "soul" go up to "paradise." "Good for the body" does not hinder "good for the soul," and the same thing applies the other way around. This may be a new requirement of Catholics under socialist conditions, and a new Catholic trait as well. What they mean when they say that "good for the body" does not hinder "good for the soul" is this: even though their living is easy now, they must not stay away from church services; while "good for the soul" does not hinder "good for the body" means that they must do well in their productive work, not neglecting production by attending normal religious activities. Can they attend normal religious activities and not affect production? The practice of Qingpu fishing people in recent years proves that it can be done. People have seen that whenever the Qingpu Catholic Patriotic Association holds a meeting, they always call on Catholics to do well in their productive labor. Whenever Catholics take part in large-scale religious activities, they first discuss how to avoid affecting economic productivity.

Today, the main activities of the Zhujiajiao church are the celebration of Christmas and Easter and the "pilgrimage" to Sheshan in May. These activities are well-organized; they don't just drift along without leadership. Those who are at work generally do not attend religious services until they have worked overtime to fulfill their duties. In the past three years they have always fulfilled or exceeded the production quota. One devout Catholic, an expert at catching fish and prawns, said he was "more diligent in his work than before" after his demands [to authorities] to go to church were met. He is taking the lead in his work, studying new fish technology, and getting higher and higher yields.

As Qingpu Catholics have come to understand from their personal experience that a better life does not keep their soul from going to paradise, they are making big strides forward on the road of loving both the motherland and the church, and of running the church independently. Today they are no longer *jiaomin* (church people) like the Catholics of before, under the control and direction of foreign forces. In the past they thought that religious faith meant obeying the pope and the Vatican. Now, after political study, many Catholics hold that the pope is also a human being, and pure religion for them is to believe in God, not the Vatican. They are vigilant against infiltration by hostile foreign religious influences and the few persons who use religion to carry out illegal activities. In the past they did not dare to come close to the party and the government, while today they know that religious believers are one component of the Chinese people, and all people must support the party's leadership, obey the government, love the country, and abide by the law.

Take a Catholic from the Zhaotun Production Brigade, for example. He said, "The party and the government opened the church, and my soul has found peace. Since Liberation I have earned a happy life; I have a television set and a sofa at home. Hereafter, God will take care of my soul and the people's government will take care of my body. I will contribute to the four modernizations and be a Catholic who loves both my motherland and my religion."

There are both religious believers and nonbelievers among the people. Religious belief or nonbelief is a difference in ideology. Differences in ideology may not, indeed should not, be a barrier to solidarity. Today's Qingpu fishing people joined the church in childhood and have firmly held to their devout religious faith. They also love their socialist motherland, work diligently in physical labor, fulfilling and even overfulfilling their production quotas, and contribute to socialist construction and the four modernizations. For all these reasons, people should reevaluate them and look at them in a new light.

222 RELIGION UNDER SOCIALISM IN CHINA

New Believers in the Past Three Years

In this report we have mainly described Qingpu Catholics over age forty. The religious situation of their children and grandchildren between the ages of eighteen and forty is quite different from theirs. Children born into fishing families before 1955, the year when Catholic counterrevolutionaries were rooted out, were baptized and joined the church soon after their birth just like their parents. But they have not attended Bible classes. Of the children born after that year, some were not baptized immediately, while others were only given conditional baptism. Children born in the 1950s and early 1960s are now twenty to thirty years old. They generally fall into two types: those whose parents taught them to read the Bible privately, and those who never studied the Bible at all. After the reopening of the Zhujiajiao church, those who had been conditionally baptized went to the church to be formally baptized by the parish priest and thus become full church members. Those who had not been conditionally baptized but had learned something about the Catholic faith went to the church, were baptized, and became church members.

In the past three years, there have been fifteen hundred new Catholics baptized or rebaptized by the parish priest. These new Catholics did not know very much about the hows and whys of Catholicism, and some knew nothing at all. Some of them said that they were willing to be baptized and join the church through the influence of their families, particularly their mothers. They think that the "Ten Commandments" are helpful, teaching people to do good and guard against evil, so they joined the church because they wanted to observe the "Ten Commandments." The demands of these new Catholics for a religious life are much less strong than those of their parents. Every evening when they read the "evening lesson" at home, the middle-aged and older Catholics want to finish the reading, but the young ones hope they don't have to read that long a time, and they soon disappear from the family gathering. They have no heart for Bible reading when there is a particularly good television program. During the year, they mainly attend services on Christmas and Easter, and they go on pilgrimage to Sheshan. They are very interested in these activities and do all kinds of service work then, particularly singing in the choir, which is composed mainly of young people.

In our survey of new Catholics in the past three years, we discovered that the depth of piety of Qingpu Catholic fishing people is changing. In the past, the whole family read the Bible together and went to church together. Today it is not rare to see that in a given family, some take part in religious activities, while others do something else. This tendency will continue.

In China today there are now about three million Catholics scattered in different places and circumstances. Judging by Catholic history before Liberation, there must be many "multigeneration Catholics" like those in Qingpu County. These "multigeneration Catholics," just like the Qingpu fishing people, devoutly hold to their religious faith while at the same time playing an active and useful part in socialist construction. The important thing for us to do is earnestly to carry out the policy of religious freedom, to be completely forthright with them, to do a good job in educating and uniting with them, and to make them feel that they can be both ''good for the body'' and ''good for the soul'' in their daily life and thus take love for the country and love for their religion as the driving force for contributing to socialist construction.

Adapting Islam to Chinese
Socialist Practice in Xinjiang

RELIGION is a complex social phenomenon. In old China it was under the control of the ruling classes, who used it for their own purposes, with serious negative effects on social progress. Since Liberation, after the profound transformation of the economy and society, and major reforms in the religious systems, religion in China has experienced fundamental changes. Contradictions related to religion are mainly contradictions among the people [nonantagonistic contradictions]. Religion, as a social ideology and as a belief held by a portion of our people, will continue to exist for a long time. Religious believers are only a minority of the people of China. But in Xinjiang more than half the people are Muslims. Therefore, in both theory and practice, it is important to study the relationship between religion and socialist practice, and, in Xinjiang Province, to study the relationship between Islam and the developing construction of Xinjiang.

I

There are ten Muslim national minorities in China, and all ten can be found in Xinjiang. Three of them—the Dongxiang, Sala, and Bao'an—moved to Xinjiang from the eastern provinces after Liberation. Based on the size of their populations, beginning with the largest, these ten groups are the Uyghur, Kazakh, Hui, Kirgiz, Dongxiang, Tajik, Uzbek, Tartar, Sala, and Bao'an. These ten peoples are all Muslims, but, owing to differences in their way of life, environment, social influences, ways of economic production, and religious history and customs, there are differences in the depth of their religious belief and religious practices. Even members of the same national minority are influenced in the way they practice their faith by where they live, whether in cities or the countryside, near cities and towns with convenient communications, or in remote mountainous areas, as well as by their occupations, whether farmers, workers, intellectuals, or cadres.

From May to July 1983, we carried out a sample survey of 207 Uyghur households in two compact rural communities in the Kashi area. In villages A and B, 92.1 percent of the adults surveyed took part in religious services (see table 1). Of these, there were more women than men, more elderly than middle-aged, and even fewer among the young. Fewer Uyghur workers living in Kashi City went to services than in the Uyghur villages. The results of our survey can be compared with those of an earlier one made by our Nationalities Research Institute (see table 2). It is easy to see from these statistics that fewer urban workers take part in religious activities than people in the countryside.

From May to July 1984, we conducted field research on Islam among residents of two Kazakh villages in Yili, made up of both farmers and herdsmen (table 3). I visited every person and every household, with the following results: 21.55 percent of the adults regularly participated in religious activities, of whom there were more men than women; they were mainly people over age fifty, with very few middle-aged or younger. Among the 102 Uyghur, Kazakh, and Hui Muslim workers of the Yili woolen textile factory surveyed by the Nationalities Research Institute, 50.99 percent took part in regular worship services. Of those surveyed, 30.39 percent could recite from the Qur'an, and 26.4 percent observed the Islamic rules on fasting, either fully or in part. Most of this group were Uyghur, and very few Kazakh; therefore, it is difficult to compare their situation with data obtained from the two Kazakh villages. The number of workers from the Kashi cotton textile factory is different from those of the Yili woolen textile factory, as well.

Although these Muslim nationality groups surveyed all believe in the same religion, they show differences in many respects, while they do have common factors that derive from their religious faith.

1. Islam is closely connected with the national [ethnic] character of the believers and shows strong national [ethnic] features. Islam was introduced into Xinjiang more than a thousand years ago, and Islamic customs have long been absorbed into the national [ethnic] culture of these believers. In a Muslim family, people take part unconsciously, from birth to death, in the various religious activities that come along, such as the giving of an Islamic name, circumcision, and funerals. Some religious activities must be observed according to the ethnic custom, such as the special reading (*nika*) at weddings, and worship services for festivals, which must be observed by all the males, even children as young as five or six. They have several meals a day, and after each meal they will say "duwa" to thank Khuda [Persian for Allah] for his beneficence. Usually these people, particularly the elderly, connect Khuda with whatever happens to them in their daily life and work, including their successes and failures. Every one of these people, even those who do not read the scriptures and those under age eighteen, never cease to praise the True Lord. This is a powerful social force, and many people accept the Islamic faith under these subtle influences.

Except for the Yi-chan sect, no other sect in Xinjiang has formal requirements for membership. It can be said that when a Muslim child is born, he is

Table 1
Male and Female Residents of Two Villages Who Participate in Religious Activities

| | | | | No. of persons taking part in religious activities | | | | | |
| | No. of persons surveyed | | | Men | | Women | | Subtotal | |
Location	Men	Wo-men	Sub-total	Num-ber	Per-cent	Num-ber	Per-cent	Num-ber	Per-cent
Vill. A	134	143	277	115	85.8	132	92.3	247	89.2
Vill. B	126	133	259	120	95.2	131	98.5	251	96.9
Total	260	276	536	235	90.4	263	25.3	498	92.6

Table 2
Participation in Religious Activities by Workers in the Kashi Textile Mill and Residents of Two Rural Villages

| | | Those who recite scriptures | | Those who practice fasting | |
Occupation	No. surveyed	Number	Percent	Number	Percent
Workers	88	54	61.3	26	29.5
Peasants	536	484	90.3	338	63.1

Table 3
Adults Who Take Part in Religious Activities in Two Kazakh Villages in Yili

| | | | | No. of persons taking part in religious activities | | | | | |
| | No. of persons surveyed | | | Men | | Women | | Subtotal | |
Location	Men	Wo-men	Sub-total	Num-ber	Per-cent	Num-ber	Per-cent	Num-ber	Per-cent
Vill. A	143	143	286	35	24.48	24	16.78	59	20.63
Vill. B	174	148	322	48	27.59	24	16.22	72	22.36
Total	317	291	608	83	26.18	48	16.49	131	21.55

a Muslim. This is why some people consider the term ''Muslim'' to be equivalent to the Islamic national minorities.

2. Islam has a profound social and ideological foundation among its believers. Muslims believe that, besides the real society of this world, there is a supernatural heavenly garden [paradise] and a fiery hell. They believe that the real

world is temporary, and the heavenly garden on the other shore is everlasting. In the village of Kashi, when we made a sample survey of 100 Uyghur high school students, asking whether a person's soul lives on after death, 95 of them answered in the affirmative. In the village of Yili we put the same question to 159 Kazakh junior high school students, and 128 of them, that is, 80.5 percent, answered, yes. The foundation of their religious epistemology is belief in the everlasting soul. The replies of the junior high school students represent their own thinking but also reflect the minds of the adults in those villages.

At present, most people above the age of fifty or sixty, including activists, model workers, and basic-level cadres who worked on land reform and the movement to organize cooperatives in the period after Liberation, take part in religious activities. A number of basic-level cadres who have not yet reached the retirement age say that they will live a religious life after they retire. In their hearts they are constantly concerned with the problem of whether their souls will go up to heaven or down into a fiery hell after their death. While young and full of sap they mistreated people and handled some things wrong under the misguided influence of the "Leftists." Now they are old and demoted to the level of ordinary people, old folks living at home with no work to do. They have relaxed their self-imposed strict ideological demands. Looking back on their past in a repentant mood, they do not review their record in a correct way, but spend their time hoping for a final "good result," that is, to go to heaven. These people are most regular in worship and are highly influential.

3. In the past thirty-five years, all national minorities, in their religious activities, have traveled the same rough road. Our party has always practiced the policy of religious freedom. But in the course of carrying it out, problems have occurred. From the year of Liberation [1949] to 1957 we abolished the religious system of exploitation and carried out religious reforms while upholding the party's policy of freedom of religious belief. Religious activities were carried on in a normal way during those years. In 1958, during the Great Leap Forward, mosques were severely damaged. In the ten years of domestic turmoil, almost all mosques were destroyed, and imams were denounced. Since the Third Plenum of the Eleventh Party Congress, people's hearts have been won over by the party's implementation of all policies, including the policy on religion. According to surveys made in three successive years, Muslims from all national minorities are quite satisfied with the party's policy on freedom of religious belief. Since 1979, the number of people attending Islamic activities has greatly increased, for many reasons.

First, religious believers have revived normal religious activities because the policy on religion is being carried out. Religious feelings that were suppressed for many years were suddenly released. The number of people attending religious services has increased with a rush, just as a spring will stretch beyond its normal length when pressure on it is released.

Second, their attendance at religious services since the inauguration of the responsibility system in agriculture is protected in a material way, because the standard of living for rural people has greatly improved, giving them more flexibility in arranging their time. A person's first need is to fill his or her stomach. With one's stomach rumbling with hunger, who can think about attending worship services? When people all "eat from the same big pot," their time also belongs to the collective, and there is little time left at their own disposal. Nowadays people are much freer than before to decide whether they will work in the fields, attend religious activities, or take a rest. The flourishing of the Mali Muslim sect in southern Xinjiang is directly related to the improved economic situation. In the past, only one member of the family could ride the donkey to the mosque for services. Now every family has a vehicle drawn by a donkey, horse, or ox, and the whole family can ride to worship. Some even go by cars or tractors, with several families riding together.

Third, political and ideological work in the villages has weakened, due to its failure to keep up with the changing situation. Some people turn to religion because their spirit is unsteady.

Fourth, religion in this area is spread widely in hundreds of thousands of homes, and religious activities are thriving. Religious policy restricts the propagation of religion to temples, churches, and mosques, but it cannot be so sharply limited when an entire people group is religious. In certain places in recent years, nonbelievers were put under spiritual pressures. For example, religious believers would not shake hands when they met them, they would not pay neighborly visits to non-Muslims on holidays, nor would they attend their funerals. In certain areas where there are large population movements, imams would appear without having a residence registration and without proper occupations; they moved from place to place, setting up small meeting points for reading scriptures and in general stirring up a religious atmosphere.

II

The Marxist world view is opposed to any kind of theism; but in political action it is fully possible, in fact it is absolutely necessary, for Marxists to form a united front with religious believers in the common struggle for building socialist modernization. Our field surveys show that Islam can coordinate with socialist practice and play its role as long as we can implement the party's policy on religion and do our work well.

1. From the political viewpoint, socialism represents the basic interests of all of China's people, including the Muslim minority nationalities. The intrinsic difference in comparing socialist society with slaveholding, feudalist, and capitalist societies is that the social phenomenon whereby some people oppress and exploit other people is wiped out. In the process of carrying out land reform, cutting rents, and opposing local tyrants after Liberation, we seized the land that had been taken over by people in the feudal upper ranks of religious circles and

redistributed it to the peasants who had little or no land. We abolished religious taxes (*wushouer*), enabling 550,000 households with more than 1,900,000 peasants to acquire 7,200,000 mu of land, 70,265 head of livestock, more than 390,000 farm tools, more than 190,000 houses, and 9,340,000 catties of grain. These people stood up and began to live a new life.

As a result, socialism and the Communist Party were loved and supported by the broad masses of the Muslim national minorities. One liberated peasant, Kurban Tulumu, expressed the class feeling in a vivid way by wishing to go to Beijing on his donkey to see Chairman Mao.

What is this "heavenly garden" [paradise] that Muslims talk about? They say that it is larger than this real world, a seven-story heaven. There are two rivers running through it, with water whiter than milk and the fragrance of musk. The people there use household utensils made of gold and silver, and the food they eat is something we have never tasted. This heavenly garden is not beyond the imagination of real people. Muslim comrades from the Xinjiang national minorities have seen that only the Communist Party could make them masters of the land, and only the socialist system could give them a comfortable living and create a "heavenly garden" on earth where fragrant flowers bloom in all directions. Elderly persons recall how people were filled with political enthusiasm in the early days after Liberation, and attendance at Islamic services decreased.

2. From an economic point of view, the interests of believers and nonbelievers coincide. The eagerness of all the people to get rich, including Xinjiang Moslems, is seen in the way they take part in socialist construction and the struggle to achieve the four modernizations. The favorable turn in the Xinjiang economy, particularly economic progress in northern and southern Xinjiang, is without question due to the cooperation of believers and nonbelievers under the leadership of the party.

In 1983 we gave an examination to 100 Uyghur third- to fifth-graders, and this year we examined 225 Kazakh students from the same grades. Their answers to the question "How can one have a happy life?" are given in table 4. The children's answers correspond closely to those of their parents and other adults. In our surveys we discovered that 90 percent of the Muslims assume that a happy life depends both on one's own labor and on Khuda [Allah]. On this point, where we take the view that one can get rich by one's own labor, most Muslims will agree, at least in part.

3. With regard to the relationship between Muslims and non-Muslims, we assume that they will stand shoulder to shoulder and unite in the cause of progress. Relationships between most national minorities in Xinjiang and the Han people are the same as relationships between Muslims and non-Muslims. One time, while discussing relations between Muslims and non-Muslims, Marx said: "The Qur'an is the basis for Islamic law, which, combining the geography and culture of all dissimilar ethnic groups into a simple formula, divides them into two categories by nation and ethnic group—orthodox and heterodox believers.

Table 4
**Primary Students from Two Villages Reply to the Question
"How Can One Have a Happy Life?"**

		By one's own labor	Rely on Allah	Mainly rely on Allah, but also on one's own labor		Mainly rely on one's own labor, but also on Allah		Mainly rely on Allah, but also on one's own efforts	
	Number of persons surveyed	Number	Percent	Number	Percent	Number	Percent	Number	Percent
Village 1	100	7	7.0	7	7.0	36	36.0	50	50.0
Village 2	225	17	7.6	31	13.8	112	48.8	79	35.1

The heterodox are *ha-er-bi*, that is, enemies. Islam preaches that the heterodox are not protected by the law; moreover, a condition of permanent hostility is set up between the heterodox and the Muslims.''

Since its introduction into China, Islam has been influenced by Chinese culture and historical and ethnic traditions, and from the beginning Muslims in China have come from the national minorities. Therefore the usual hostility of Muslims to nonbelievers has undergone basic changes in China. The unity and cooperation of Muslim and Han workers have always been good throughout the history of Xinjiang. They have gone through thick and thin together, sweating together on the farms and shedding blood together to protect their territory. During the thirty years since Liberation this sharing of weal and woe has further developed through the education and practice of national unity. Now the idea that the Han people and the national minorities cannot be separated is deeply embedded in their hearts.

4. There is nothing contradictory between the socialist code of conduct and certain Muslim moral norms. Although the starting points and the connotations are different, the end result can be the same. For example, in dealing with person-to-person relationships, the Islamic faith requires that its believers speak the truth, do good deeds, respect the elderly, give alms to the poor, aid the victims of natural calamities, care for orphans and widows, help each other, and so forth. As for themselves, Muslims are required to observe strict self-discipline, avoid doing bad things, refrain from smoking, drinking, gambling, stealing, and so forth. Objectively, this certainly is beneficial for social stability and order and for building socialist spiritual civilization.

According to our surveys in Kashi, 78.8 percent of male adults in the two Uyghur villages did not smoke, and 99.6 percent did not drink alcoholic beverages. In the two places studied in Yili, 67.2 percent of the adults did not smoke (although women in the Xingyan pastureland region do smoke), and 87.8 percent did not drink. The people and cadres of the two Kashi villages said there had never been a case of drunkenness in recent years, and there was rarely a case of children failing to respect parents. What does it matter if religious believers do not understand the norms of socialist morality from the Communist viewpoint, when their behavior conforms with the requirements of socialist material and spiritual civilization, even though it is based on Islamic teachings and traditions?

The past thirty years of history have proven that it is fully possible for Islam in Xinjiang to adapt to the practice of socialism in our country and to play the role that it should.

He Yanji
Center for Religious Research
Xinjiang Social Studies Institute

The Rich Soil on Which Christianity Grows in an Anhui County

IN RECENT years, [Protestant] Christianity has been growing and spreading in the region around my native town in a certain county of Anhui Province. This is a phenomenon that deserves study.

A General Survey

Before Liberation there were only two Protestant churches and one Catholic church in the county seat (which became the prefectural center after Liberation), and a few small churches scattered in nearby small towns. The influence of Christianity was neither great nor deep-seated.

After Liberation, members of the clergy took other jobs, churches closed down, and residential church properties were turned over for other uses. Today, most people under forty do not know what Christianity is.

Following the "Cultural Revolution" in the early 1970s, Christianity began to revive, but not in the open. Believers were few, mostly older women. In the years 1976 and 1977 during the "[party] line education" movement, Christian activities were attacked and Christians, guarded by local militia, were assigned to "study classes" or placed in solitary confinement to confess their crimes. Those in "study classes" were deprived of their personal freedom, and, in addition to bringing their own food, were forced to pay an extra one or two yuan each day for the guards' expenses. People greatly feared being sent to these study classes, because while they were there they had no gainful employment and so could not afford to pay for the expenses of the classes. Some even lost their family savings.

In the spring of 1977 a certain work team engaged in [party] line education discovered some Christians praying in secret. Viewing this as a counterrevolutionary activity, the deputy team leader, after launching an armed attack at night, found that the group consisted entirely of elderly women who had scattered in fright.

After the fall of the "Gang of Four" and the implementation of the party's religious policy, formerly clandestine Christian activities came into the open, and more and more people became Christians. In some places whole families and villages converted.

I have visited their religious services. One visit was made on March 1 (January 15 of the lunar calendar). That was the local market day, and many Christians gathered in the market square in the morning for a preaching service. Because of the size of the crowd they had to break into groups, dividing over eight hundred persons among the homes and courtyards of three of the Christian families. Moreover, it was evident that this was not the total number of Christians in that locality, for some of the Christian men did not attend public services, and some families only sent one person as a representative. All these religious activities were voluntary, with no [church] organization whatsoever.

In villages where there are no churches or special places for services, Christians from a small area often gather in one of the Christian homes for services, thus forming a Christian meeting point. There are many such meeting places. A number of Christians who do not attend congregational worship, but only pray at home, are considered to be the same as long as they are faithful to the Lord.

There are still no resident full-time pastors here. The preachers are volunteers or persons with some status locally. Very few of those who preach have been Christians for more than ten years, while the majority are newly converted middle-aged persons who have had only a smattering of education.

Of the above-mentioned eight hundred people who attended the worship service, only one had a Bible, printed long ago, which was considered a treasure. A few had notebooks in which were copied some verses or chapters from the Bible and some hymns (in fact, some had been crudely set to popular tunes and melodies). I have seen a small two-thousand-word pamphlet about three inches by four inches called "Questions and Answers about Christianity" [a catechism], which is circulated among the Christians and copied by many. Only one Christian had a picture of "the crucified Jesus," which had been woven from silk in a Hangzhou factory. As for their form and content, it must be said that these religious activities, despite the fact that Christianity came from abroad and has been a man-made religion from early times, were quite natural and spontaneous.

Who Are These Christians?

Some of the Christians are workers, a very few are cadres and teachers, while the vast majority are peasants. There are more women than men. I have compiled statistics for one meeting place, where 73.8 percent are women and 26.2 percent men, but these figures are not very precise, because many men who are unwilling to be publicly known as Christians do not attend public religious activities.

As for the age range of Christians, there are more elderly than middle-aged or young people. At the above-mentioned meeting place, women over fifty numbered 53 percent, middle-aged women from thirty to fifty were 25.9 percent, and young people 21.1 percent.

I once put two questions to a group of twenty-nine men at a meeting place: (1) When were you converted? and (2) Why do you believe in Christianity? Five of them replied that they came just to have a look (it's possible that some did not reply honestly). Of the other twenty-four, only one had been a Christian for more than ten years, while 95.8 percent had converted within the past four years.

When asked about their motive for becoming Christians, thirteen (54.2 percent) of the men [who said they were Christians] replied that they accepted the Christian faith in order to ask the Lord to bless and care for persons suffering from illness—their wives, parents, themselves, or other family members.

Two answered that they became believers to get the Lord's help in controlling a bad temper. Five replied "peaceful belief," meaning there was no illness or suffering in their families, but they felt that it was good to have religious faith, so they followed others and became Christians. Three became Christians because Christianity teaches people to do good. One answered that he came to believe through reading the Bible. These last eleven men made up 45.8 percent of the group.

As for education, the great majority of the middle-aged and elderly were illiterate or barely knew a few words without true reading ability. Quite a few of the young Christians were primary or junior middle school graduates, while three of those I met had graduated from senior middle school.

How the Christians Worship

Worship services are generally held on Sunday mornings when the weather is good. After breakfast Christians come one after another to the [open-air] meeting place. Some come early to arrange benches and planks as seats. They do this without pay. Some elderly Christians who cannot walk are taken in carts (wheelbarrows or small cargo carts) by their children or grandchildren. Those few who are too sick to get down from the carts lie there listening to the preaching.

Before the worship begins, some Christians, men and women, young, middle-aged, and elderly, take turns singing "holy verses" or "hymns." Some sing solo, others sing in pairs or trios. It is said that some had never opened their mouths in front of people before, but here they sing lustily facing the congregation. Some of the music for these holy verses and hymns is taken from local folk tunes, others are melodies taken from the old-style primary schools, some are original, made-up tunes, while some have no tune at all.

The service begins at 9:30 when most of the people have arrived. At first someone explains a certain chapter or verse from the Bible. If the person has a Bible or a handmade copy of the scripture passage, he or she reads a few sentences and then freely explains its meaning. The Christians keep very good order, and silence reigns over the open-air meeting area.

After a period of speaking, there is reading and singing, and then more speaking. The speaking is combined with singing, just like the local storytelling that is accompanied by a small drum. Next comes the period of prayer. The worshippers do not kneel, but only bow their heads. But some say that they do kneel when there are not so many people.

The last element of the service is confession to God. Some speak out loudly, confessing their sins, the punishment and retribution that they merit, and pledging never to sin again. The service lasts about one and a half to two hours.

There is no payment made by new converts. I don't know what is meant by eating the "holy meal" [*sheng can*, i.e., Holy Communion].

Local cadres generally do not interfere with Christian services. But there are a few cadres who put pressure on them, saying that such meetings hinder production, so they vary their modes of worship to avoid censure from the cadres, meeting in the daytime during the farmers' slack season and, during the busy season, in the evenings in small groups.

The Main Content of Their Preaching

The most frequent sermon topic is filial piety. Originally a moral precept of the Confucian school, filial piety has been given great emphasis in Christian preaching. This is clearly linked with the failure of sons and daughters to care for their parents and to poor relationships between mothers-in-law and daughters-in-law, phenomena that can be blamed on the sabotage and interference of the counterrevolutionary clique of Jiang Qing and Lin Biao. At the outdoor preaching place the preacher sang this [rhymed] "holy hymn," which brought a strong response from the congregation:

> We exhort you to be filial; it is not easy to repay parents for their kindness.
> They cleaned your dirty bottom and held you out to urinate. Who knows how often they lay [with you] in your wet bed?
> When her son was ill, your mother feared for you; she neither slept nor ate, but prayed day and night. Only after she nearly died of worry did her son recover.
> When he was four or five, she was always watching out for him, afraid he would swim in the river or climb a tree in search of birds' nests.
> When he reached the age of fifteen or sixteen, he became impolite, neither respecting the elderly nor loving the young, and forgetting his parents' kindness.
> When her son married and prospered, he indulged himself in eating and drinking.
> When he had a baby son, he embraced him and provided him with beautiful clothes and hats, calling him pet names while taking walks with him.
> You love your own children, why do you forget how much your parents loved you?

Sweet water cannot be taken from a bitter well; brambles will not grow grapes, nor pumpkin vines grow yellow silk.
There is reward for evil and reward for good; the moving cart leaves its tracks, and the unfilial parent will have unfilial progeny.

The content, language and tune of this song all come from local folk tradition. It is a perfect popular art that arouses such strong response from the Christian congregations because it strikes at a social problem that has long concerned the Christians. About half of the holy poems and holy hymns that I have seen are like this.

Another frequent topic for preaching is forbearance, forgiveness, and obedience. Here are the words of a certain song, called "Keep One's Way":

When struck, I do not strike back;
When abused, I do not retort,
Nor do I get upset or sulk.
I smile when rebuked.

Forbearance and obedience are Christian teachings, and forgiveness is [also] advocated by the Confucian school. The Christians offer new explanations when they preach. The Bible [they say] tells people to obey those in power because they represent God's will; thus the preacher offers a new reason for obedience to the cadres.

Other doctrines are preached apart from these. In the words of its followers, Christianity advocates that one should "Show filial piety to parents, respect to the elderly, and love to the young; do not believe in superstitions; do not worship idols or burn paper money as offerings for the dead; do not steal; do not profit at others' expense; do not strike others or abuse them; give up evil and return to good; eliminate the false and keep the true; hold firmly to the truth."

Naturally, "Do not believe in superstitions" means the feudal superstitions that have long prevailed in the countryside, such as belief in geomancy, ghosts and demons, celestial beings, fortunetelling, and divination. "Do not worship idols" means to worship only Christ, not idols such as the God of Wealth, the Earth God, boddhisattvas, the Heavenly Lord, the Dragon King, and other heretical idols. By "Hold firmly to the truth" they mean to hold firmly to the religious position of Christianity.

Their Preaching Methods

During the [outdoor] worship services, the preacher both speaks and sings, first reading a passage of scripture, then expounding on that, then singing a couple of hymns. Music for the services includes trios, duets, solos, and congregational singing, which sometimes has a leader and sometimes not. The entire worship service is relaxed and pleasant, unlike services held in a church, which are solemn and serious. This kind of service, which combines speaking and singing, resembles *dashu*, a popular form of storytelling accompanied by rhythmic beating on a small drum, which draws large audiences in Anhui Province.

Sacred verses and songs are often sung to the tunes of local folk melodies, such as "Sing the Fifth Watch" (also called "Sing a Bit at the Fifth Watch"), "Flowers Bloom in December," and "Ten Words of Advice."

The lyrics for the first two verses of "Ten Words of Advice" are:

> First, parents-in-law are urged to listen carefully, never quarrel with daughter-in-law.
> She is the one to grind the flour, knead the dough, and husk the rice.
> She makes three meals each day and boils water over a smoking fire.
> She is always busy spinning and weaving and mending garments until late at night.
> Do not give her less to eat and wear. The Lord is pleased when you love your daughter-in-law.
> Second, daughters-in-law are urged to listen carefully, and never to quarrel with parents-in-law.
> They are elderly, unable to move around and work. Spare no efforts in caring for them; give them food and drink.
> The true God will bless you with long life; you will have daughters-in-law just like yourself, and a virtuous daughter who enjoys a good name.

The wording is rough and the tune is simple, but it is effective, because it is easy to understand, to learn, and to sing.

Christianity is a religion imported from abroad. To attract the masses and take root and grow in the local soil, it does not use the high-level Christian culture from abroad; rather, it uses artistic forms long prevalent among the people, things they love to see and hear. Aiming at social problems that concern people most, it revises and develops Christian teachings, making Christianity something locally born and bred both in form and content.

The Influence of Christianity on Social Life

The popularity of Christianity has produced certain social effects. These are seen not only in the increasing number of Christians, but also in the influence of Christian teachings on the actions of Christians and the impact of its spiritual force on social life.

1. Since Christianity preaches against "superstition" and "worshiping idols," many Christians have given up belief in traditional gods and spirits of heaven and earth; they no longer kowtow in the Lunar New Year ceremony, shoot off fireworks, pray to the gods for healing, or solicit help from witches and shamans. They no longer give homage to the god of the planet Jupiter when

breaking ground for a new house, nor believe in geomancy at the time of death, or in sackcloth and images of gods. The spread of Christianity has weakened the influence of feudal superstition.

2. It is said that Christians, on several occasions, returned money on their own initiative when shop clerks gave them too much change. They said, "We believe in our Lord and must not profit at the expense of others. If I hadn't returned the money I would have committed a sin." Numerous Christians have given up smoking and drinking.

3. The greatest influence of Christianity is on family relations. Many sons and their wives who had ill-treated their parents have behaved well after their conversion. A man nicknamed "Second Crazy Fellow" had struck and abused his parents many times but has become filial since his conversion. Relationships greatly improved after the conversion of a young woman who, for a long time, had paid no attention to her mother-in-law.

Two sisters-in-law had not provided food for their parents-in-law. When the elderly couple came to ask for food, they not only refused to feed them, but verbally abused them. Since their religious conversion they have completely changed, showing full courtesy to their in-laws, and always serving them first when the meals are prepared. Now the old couple always tell others, "Our daughters-in-law have changed for the good."

I saw with my own eyes a woman, about to strike her daughter, who drew back her hand when other Christians admonished her, saying that would be a sin. After first defending herself with an excuse, she then confessed her sin.

People from all walks of life, including numerous cadres (despite the fact that they are nonbelievers), all speak well of these people. On the other hand, I have also heard of an incident where a certain house caught fire. The husband was out and the woman, a Christian, knelt and prayed for God's protection and blessing instead of putting out the fire. The fire, of course, became even worse. This is an example where religious conversion made a person act foolishly.

A cadre in a certain brigade who was addicted to smoking and drinking fell ill with apoplexy. He spent a great deal of money for prolonged treatments without result. After conversion to Christianity he confessed his sins before God, such as embezzling relief funds, attacking others, and taking revenge. He was ridiculed near and far. Of course we have to be alert, for the current style of Christianity can easily be used by evildoers, but I have not heard of such things.

Questions on Faith Healing

Contemporary Christianity does not now advocate using religion to heal illness without medical treatment. Christians believe that doctors are needed to heal illness, and those who should go to hospitals should be taken there. Christianity teaches simply that one can be blessed and protected by the Lord if he is free from sin and has a sincere heart. However, many recent converts came to believe in religion because they themselves or their family members had fallen ill and failed to recover.

A woman who had undergone surgery for ectopian pregnancy had pains all over after the operation. She spent several hundred yuan seeking medical help and praying to the gods. Her husband was a laborer who arose before dawn each day to kowtow a hundred times, but still she suffered pains. But, after attending services and offering prayers, beginning with the latter period of the "Cultural Revolution," she eventually recovered. They say that she can now do housework and light physical labor. She often entertains fellow Christians, preaches Christian teachings, and arranges seating for the congregation. (When the number reaches one or two hundred it is not an easy matter to move the planks around.)

Two brothers whose mother, a long-time invalid, recovered her health after converting to Christianity are now key volunteers for Christianity, and their home in the county seat has become a small chapel.

Another young man who came down with bronchial asthma in childhood had undergone lengthy medical treatment, including surgery and acupuncture. After marrying, his condition worsened, and he was cheated by a sorcerer, losing one hundred yuan. It is said that his mother converted, and the whole family became Christians, with the result that the young man's condition has greatly improved.

Christians thoroughly believe in cases like these, never doubting them. After careful analysis we find that most of these examples supplied by the Christians are mental illness, or pathological changes of organic functions closely connected with the nervous system, such as schizophrenia, psychosis, arthritis, and functional disorders of the stomach and intestines. Some sick people, especially those with protracted illnesses, are filled with fear and anxiety, which puts pressure on the spirit, making it even more difficult to recover. Other illnesses are themselves the direct result of mental troubles. As long as these diseases have not yet caused serious qualitative change, it is possible for patients to get better or recover completely when, after religious conversion, they shed their spiritual burden, believing that they are now under the watch and care of God. There is nothing strange about this. With other health problems, such as a severed finger, no matter how sincere one's faith in God, He cannot help one grow a new finger. Christians themselves think this way, too.

Causes for the Rapid Growth of Christianity

The fact that Christianity is growing in a number of areas shows that in our country and society, particularly in the vast countryside, there is soil on which religion can grow.

For a long time after Liberation, religious activities had "disappeared" in these areas. To most people religion is a brand-new thing, despite its long history, and people are always curious about new things. Comrade Mao Zedong said that Marxism-Leninism is sure to develop, but if it remains the same old stuff it will be ineffective. Due to the interference and sabotage of the Lin Biao–Jiang Qing counterrevolutionary clique, the prestige of our party and of socialism has declined. Not only did they bring the social economy of our country to the edge of bankruptcy, they also caused a vacuum to form in the minds of many people, giving an opportunity for religion, which takes advantage of this weak point. This tells us how important it is to educate people to hold firmly to the four basic principles, to enforce ideological work, and to establish a socialist spiritual civilization.

Statistical data show that most new Christians came to this faith to ask God for protection of health or for healing of an illness, either their own or someone else's in their family. Health problems are undoubtedly the most important inducement for conversion. This situation, that is, the hope that people can free themselves from suffering caused by ill health, poses a serious challenge to our medical and health work and the level of medical treatment offered. Religion seems to have succeeded in freeing them from their suffering, where society has failed. Hospitals did not cure their illnesses, while God seems to have done so. How could they possibly be led to give up their belief in religion and their worship of God!

Statistics also show that among the Christians there are more elderly people than young, more female than male, more illiterate than literate, and more with low culture [little education] than high culture. All the statistics show that the number of Christians in different categories is in inverse proportion to the amount of cultural and scientific knowledge they have, and in direct proportion to their degree of backwardness, ignorance, and benightedness.

This shows that it is easiest for religion to form firm ties with people who possess no knowledge and know nothing of science. Religion is silently competing with our work in education, culture, and universal science for the masses of our people.

Apart from freeing themselves from the physical suffering of this world, people also need spiritual comfort, encouragement, strength, hope, and ideals. Religion satisfies their curiosity, broadens their social relationships, and, what is more important, fills in their spiritual vacuum. Christ has not asked them for a cent, but freed them from misfortune and calamity, giving them well-being in this world, while promising them happiness in the next.

All people are pragmatic, and peasants are even more so. Religion is also pragmatic. Peasants can begin to leave religion only when the pace of socialist modernization has greatly quickened, when their material and cultural life has risen to a sufficient level, when the knowledge of science has become universal, and when they can quickly free themselves from the ills and pains of their real life. Only when their spirit is fulfilled can they consciously place their hope in socialism. Therefore, the basic measures needed to free them from suffering and the fetters of religion are to promote diligently socialist modernization, to increase the speed of social productive forces, and actively to raise the level of their material and cultural life. Another important means to liberate them is rapidly to improve the level of medical and health work. Finally, an even better way to open up a direct route for their liberation is to develop education and culture and to popularize scientific knowledge.

Zheng Kaitang

Afterword

IN *Religion under Socialism in China*, the Institute for Research on Religion of the Shanghai Academy of Social Sciences has undertaken to respond to the designation of religion as a key topic for study in the fields of philosophy and sociology in the national Sixth Five-Year Plan. This monograph is the result of research on this topic.

Our basic methods for pursuing this research were to study and use Marxism, combine theory with practice, take reality as our starting point, and seek truth from facts. For three years, in numerous cities and villages, we carried on broad-scale field research, with guidance and support from party and government units in each locality (especially United Front and Religious Affairs work units), and received concern and help from each of the patriotic religious organizations. After the first draft of this book was written, we sought ideas from units doing theoretical research and practical work on religion, receiving advice from scholars, cadres, and friends in religious circles. The Religious Studies Society of Shanghai joined with us in carrying out this research. We offer our sincere thanks to all units and comrades who gave assistance.

Persons who participated in the field studies, research, writing and editing of this volume were as follows (names listed by stroke order): Fan Xing, Ye Luhua, Liu Jian (specially invited), Ruan Renzi, Zhang Siu, Shen Yifan, Xiao Zitian, Chen Yaoting, Luo Weihong, Yao Minquan, Gao Zhennong, Gu Yulu, Cao Shengjie, Chang Xiaqing, and Qu Mingming. After this book was written and edited, Su Zhishi and Chen Yaoting did the final proofreading. Others in our research institute took part in discussion and helped in working on the drafts.

The field survey reports in the appendix, aside from those by comrades He Yanji and Zheng Kaitang, were written by comrades chosen from the Religious Research Institute.

Religious questions under socialism is a new research topic, and this book is only an initial exploration. It is difficult to avoid making errors, and we hope that our readers will offer criticism and suggestions so as to promote deeper research into this topic.

Index

agriculture: Buddhist, 65–66, 80, 170–82; in Pi County, 160–62; religious contributions to, 27
Aleni, J., 28
Allah, Islamic belief in, 18–19, 81, 225, 229
All-True Daoism, 18
Alopen, 22
ancestor ceremonies, 164–65
Anglican church, 126
Anhui Province: Christianity in, xviii, 232–41; Daoism in, 87
Anti-Rightist Movement, 144, 147
Asian Conference on Religion and Peace, 127
astrology, 23
astronauts, 3
astronomy, 23, 25, 27, 28
Austin, Warren, 57–58

backwardness, as source of religion, 93–95
Bai Juyi, 25
Bao'an nationality, 20, 224
Baoding (Hebei Province), 52
Bao E'han, 72, 75
Baopuzi, 18
Beijing: Buddhist industries in, 65, 124; Muslim anti-Japanese action in, 50, 52; patriotic Catholics in, 49, 61
belief and nonbelief, 78–81
benevolence, 30–31
Bible: Chinese publication of, 140; Chinese translation of, 23; Korean, 207; new Chinese theology based on, 77, 80, 122; sent by foreigners into China, 100; two testaments of, 21

birth control, 129, 166
Bossardt, Alfred, 135
Boxer Uprising, 43, 47
Brahmanism, 16
Brother Andrew , 100
Buddhism, xvi; ancient buildings of, 25; antigovernment character of, 31–32; changes in theology of, 79–81; colleges and seminaries of, 140, 183; and Confucianism, 26, 32, 33; Cultural Revolution conversions to, ix, 99, 183; Daoism and, 18, 32, 33; democratic reform movement in, 64–68, 75, 141; on eve of Liberation, 35–36, 39–41, 75; imperial suppression of, 32; industries and agriculture of, 65–66, 80, 124–25, 170–82; influence on Chinese culture of, 25–26; international contacts of, 100, 126–27; literature and art of, 185–87; mountains and temples of, 86–87, 118; nationwide organizations of, 67–68, 139; negative aspects of, 128; origins and history of, 15–17, 24; propagation of faith by, 87–88, 91, 92, 94; publications of, 139–40; research on why young people enter, xx, 183–91; in Sino-Japanese War, 49–51; of Zhoushan fishermen, 36–37
"Buddhism in China" series, 139–40
Buddhist Association of China, 67
bureaucratism, 97

Cao Daosheng, 64

Donald E. MacInnis, for the past ten years coordinator for China Research at the Maryknoll Fathers and Brothers, is author of *Religion in China Today: Policy & Practice* (Orbis Books, 1989).

Zheng Xi'an is president of Anglo-Chinese College, Fuzhou, China.